The Bi-Centennial Celebration

# First Congregational Church of Preston, Connecticut 1698–1898

*Together with Statistics of the Church Taken from the Church Records*

*Rev. R. H. Gidman*

HERITAGE BOOKS
2011

# HERITAGE BOOKS
*AN IMPRINT OF HERITAGE BOOKS, INC.*

## Books, CDs, and more—Worldwide

For our listing of thousands of titles see our website
at
www.HeritageBooks.com

A Facsimile Reprint
Published 2011 by
HERITAGE BOOKS, INC.
Publishing Division
100 Railroad Ave. #104
Westminster, Maryland 21157

Index Copyright © 2000 Heritage Books, Inc.

Originally published 1900

*A copy of the program for the Centennial Exercises of the Preston Baptist Church has been included at the end of this book.*

— Publisher's Notice —
In reprints such as this, it is often not possible to remove blemishes from the original. We feel the contents of this book warrant its reissue despite these blemishes and hope you will agree and read it with pleasure.

International Standard Book Numbers
Paperbound: 978-0-7884-1586-9
Clothbound: 978-0-7884-8693-7

# PREFACE.

In arranging for the publication of a volume commemorative of the two-hundredth anniversary of the First Congregational Church of Preston the first intention included little more than the exercises of the day. On consideration, however, the Committee on Publication decided to enlarge the scope of the work by adding whatever of the church records might be judged desirable for preservation. This decision has greatly increased its value because of the full data now furnished upon questions of genealogy. This addition, together with that of other interesting matter which has been gathered since the anniversary, although it has made late the issue of the book, may be thought fully to justify the delay.

The writer would not fail to express earnest appreciation of all assistance in the work now accomplished, and especially would render thanks to the Rev. John Avery for valuable suggestions, and for his affectionate interest in all that related to the bi-centennial celebration; to Amos A. Browning, Esq., for his patient and diligent research in the preparation of his valuable paper on "The Original Members," and to Judge Samuel O. Prentice, without whose generous encouragement and hearty co-operation the enlargement of the book would not have been undertaken.

R. H. G.

PRESTON, CONN., January 13, 1900.

# CONTENTS.

|  | Page. |
|---|---|
| Addresses, etc., by | |
|   Rev. F. E. Allen, | 94 |
|   Rev. H. T. Arnold, | 111 |
|   Rev. John Avery, | 63 |
|   Amos A. Browning, Esq., | 49 |
|   Rev. George A. Bryan, | 122 |
|   Rev. C. L. Eldredge, | 96 |
|   Rev. R. H. Gidman, | 13 |
|   Rev. Andrew J. Hetrick, | 119 |
|   Prof. John H. Hewitt, LL.D., | 3, 5, 9, 13, 49, 63, 75, 91, 94, 96, 101, 111, 114, 119, 122 |
|   Rev. C. A. Northrop, | 91 |
|   Hon. Samuel O. Prentice, | 101 |
|   Dea. H. L. Reade, | 114 |
| Allen, Rev. F. E., Response by | 94 |
| Anniversary, General description of | 3 |
| Arnold, Rev. H. T., Response by | 111 |
| Avery, Rev. John, Sketches of Pastors by | 63 |
| Awakening, The Great | 26 |
| Bagley, William D., Chorister, | 5 |
| Baptist Church, The, Response for | 96 |
| Barnes, Mr. and Mrs. E. P., duet by | 4 |
| Biographical sketches of Pastors, | 63 |
|   Of original members, | 79 |
| Browning, Amos A., Esq. | |
|   Address by | 49 |
|   Sketches of original members by | 79 |
| Bryan, Rev. George A. | |
|   Prayer by | 4 |
|   Ministry of | 41 |
|   Biographical sketch of | 74 |
|   Response by | 122 |
| Buckingham, Miss Maude | |
|   Solo by | 4 |
|   Introduction of | 75 |
| Celebration, General Description of | 3 |

## CONTENTS.

|  | Page. |
|---|---|
| Church edifices, | 15, 25, 37 |
| Collins, Rev. Augustus B., Biographical sketch of | 71 |
| Committees upon Celebration, | 1 |
| Conference, Local, The, Response for | 111, 114 |
| Confession and Covenant, original | 200 |
| Covenant, The half-way | 26 |
| Daughter Church, The, Response for | 94 |
| Eldredge, Rev. C. L., Response by | 96 |
| Fobes, Caleb, Biographical sketch of | 84 |
| Fuller, Rev. Jonathan | |
|    Ministry of | 36 |
|    Biographical sketch of | 68 |
| Gidman, Rev. R. H. | |
|    Biographical sketch of | 74 |
|    Historical address by | 13 |
| Great Awakening, The | 26 |
| Greetings, | 89 |
| Half-way Covenant, The | 26 |
| Hetrick, Rev. Andrew J. | |
|    Invocation by | 4 |
|    Ministry of | 41 |
|    Biographical sketch of | 74 |
|    Response by | 119 |
| Hewitt, Prof. John H., LL.D. | |
|    Presiding officer | |
|    Introductory remarks by | 1 |
|    Address of welcome by | 3 |
|    Introductory addresses by | 9 |
| | 5, 13, 49, 63, 75, 91, 94, 96, |
| Historical address, | 101, 111, 114, 119, 122 |
| Hunt, Rev. Nathan S. | 13 |
|    Ministry of | 40 |
|    Biographical sketch of | 72 |
| Hyde, Rev. John | |
|    Ministry of | 38 |
|    Biographical sketch of | 70 |
| Invitation, Letter of | 2 |
| Laity, The, Response for | 114 |
| Leonard, Samuel, Biographical sketch of | 83 |
| Members, | |
|    List of original | 19, 129 |
|    Sketches of original | 79 |

## CONTENTS.

|  | Page. |
|---|---|
| Ministry, The, Response for | 111 |
| Morgan, Joseph, Biographical sketch of | 85 |
| Morrow, Rev. H. E., Prayer by | 4 |
| Mother Church, The, Response for | 91 |
| Mott, Gen. Samuel A., Manuscript of | 42 |
| Musical Program, | 5 |
| Northrop, Rev. C. A., Response by | 91 |
| North Society formed, | 22, 44 |
| Order of Exercises, | 4 |
| Original Members, | |
|     List of | 19, 129 |
|     Biographical sketches of | 79 |
| Palmer, Rev. Frank, Scripture Reading by | 4 |
| Park, Capt. John, Biographical sketch of | 84 |
| Park, Robert, Biographical sketch of | 83 |
| Parks, Thomas, Biographical sketch of | 79 |
| Pastors, | |
|     List of | 63 |
|     Responses by former | 119, 122 |
|     Biographical sketches of former | 63 |
| Prentice, Hon. Samuel O., Response by | 101 |
| Preparations for Celebration, | 1 |
| Program for Celebration, | 4 |
| Reade, Dea. H. L., Response by | 114 |
| Records of the Church, | 129 |
| Revolutionary Period, The | 31, 34 |
| Richards, John, Biographical sketch of | 81 |
| Rosseter, Rev. Asher | |
|     Ministry of | 29 |
|     Biographical sketch of | 66 |
| Separate Church in Preston, Address, | 49 |
| Separate Movement, | 27 |
| Sketches of Pastors, | 63 |
| Sketches of Original Members, | 79 |
| Statistics of the Church, | 129 |
| Sunday-school, Institution of | 38 |
| "Those who have Gone Forth from the Church," Address, | 101 |
| Tracy, Mrs. Cora, Solo by | 4 |
| Tracy, Jonathan, Biographical sketch of | 82 |
| Tracy, Thomas, Biographical sketch of | 80 |

## CONTENTS.

|  | Page. |
|---|---|
| Treat, Rev. Salmon | |
|    Call of | 16 |
|    Acceptance of | 17 |
|    Ministry of | 19 |
|    Biographical sketch of | 64 |
| Tucker, Rev. Elijah W. | |
|    Ministry of | 40 |
|    Biographical sketch of | 73 |
| Tyler, Hopestill, Biographical sketch of | 81 |
| Tyler, Rev. Lemuel | |
|    Ministry of | 37 |
|    Biographical sketch of | 69 |
| Welch, John, Biographical sketch of | 86 |
| Welcome, Address of | 9 |
| Wilcox, Rev. Asher H. | |
|    Ministry of | 40 |
|    Biographical sketch of | 74 |
| Witter, Ebenezer, Biographical sketch of | 85 |
| Woman's Missionary Society Organized, | 38 |

# PREPARATIONS.

At a meeting of the First Congregational Church of Preston, held September 29, 1897, it was unanimously voted to observe, with suitable exercises, the two-hundredth anniversary of the organization of the church, to occur on November 16, 1898, and the following persons were appointed a Committee of Arrangements: Rev. R. H. Gidman, Dea. H. H. Palmer, Chas. K. Crary, Mrs. R. H. Gidman, Mrs. H. H. Palmer, Mrs. Chas. K. Crary. This committee were authorized to appoint other committees, and to make any arrangements desirable for the commemoration, at their discretion. Subsequently Miss Mary E. Morse was elected Corresponding Secretary; also the following special committees were chosen:

*On Entertainment:* Dea. G. V. Shedd, Miss Addie Burdick, Miss Carrie Morgan, Mr. and Mrs. John Wilson, Mr. and Mrs. Henry Latham, Miss Emma Geisthardt, Miss Mary Woodmansee, Mr. and Mrs. William Crary, Miss Sophia Chesebro, Mr. and Mrs. James Crary.

*On Music:* William D. Bagley, J. Kellogg Hall, Miss Thusa L. Gidman.

*On Finance:* Henry Hopkins, James Burdick, Andrew Avery.

In response to the invitation of the Committee of Arrangements the following persons signified their acceptance of the parts requested of them in the commemorative exercises: Prof. John H. Hewitt, LL.D., as Chairman; Rev. R. H. Gidman, the Historical Address; Amos A. Browning, Esq., an address upon "The Preston Separate Church"; Rev. John Avery, "Sketches of Pastors"; Judge Samuel O. Prentice, an address upon "Those who have gone forth from the Church." The former surviving pastors of the church, also the First Congregational Church in Norwich Town, the First Congregational Church in Griswold, the

Baptist Church in Preston City, and the churches included in the "Local Conference"—Plainfield, Lisbon, Hanover, Jewett City—were specially invited to be present and participate in the proceedings. Also a circular letter of invitation, prepared and printed under direction of the committee, was sent to many outside the parish who might be interested in the anniversary. The letter was as follows:

PRESTON, CONN., September, 1898.

DEAR FRIEND:— Preparation is being made for a fitting commemoration of the two-hundredth anniversary of the First Congregational Church in Preston, to occur on November the sixteenth of this year.

The occasion, naturally, must be of unusual interest not only to those now directly connected with the church, but also to those who, although not living with us, have associations here which are cherished. We, therefore, hope that very many friends of the church may meet to participate in the commemoration and fellowship with which we would mark the day.

Permit us, in behalf of the Committee of Arrangements, to extend to you an earnest invitation to be present.

With fraternal greetings and good will,

Cordially yours,<br>
R. H. GIDMAN,<br>
*Chairman.*<br>
MARY E. MORSE,<br>
*Corresponding Secretary.*

*Committee of Arrangements:* Rev. R. H. Gidman, Dea. H. H. Palmer, Mr. Chas. K. Crary, Mrs. R. H. Gidman, Mrs. H. H. Palmer, Mrs. Chas. K. Crary.

The letter had numerous responses expressive of congratulation and desire to be present. The hearty interest and zeal manifested at home and abroad in anticipating and preparing for the event gave promise of a worthy celebration.

# THE ANNIVERSARY.

The middle of November is not a time to expect such a day as one would have for an important anniversary; but good fortune or, better, Providence made a welcome exception for the bi-centennial commemoration of the Preston Congregational Church. With the sixteenth of November, one might easily have supposed himself to be in a balmy, genial day of October. Earth, air, and sky conspired to make it good for the rare occasion.

Before the appointed hour, people of neighboring towns, as well as residents of Preston, came in large numbers, and throughout the day the church was filled to overflowing with interested hearers. The parts of the audience room about the pulpit were profusely and beautifully decorated with plants and flowers. On the wall in the rear of the pulpit, and conspicuously inscribed, were the names of the twelve pastors of the Church, and the dates of their ministry. In the transept on the right, hung an outline map of the town of Preston as it was in 1698.

At ten o'clock the pastor, Rev. R. H. Gidman, in behalf of the Committee of Arrangements, introduced Prof. John H. Hewitt, LL.D., of Williams College, as the chairman of the day, to whose conduct of the exercises, as it proved, the happy impressions of the commemoration in no small measure were due. In response to the word of introduction, Prof. Hewitt said:

"BRETHREN: It is one of the merits of the presiding officer, I believe, that he make his own remarks as brief as possible, as it is one of his privileges to allow others to do the speaking. I cannot, however, refrain from taking a single sentence, at the outset, in which to express to the Committee of Arrangements my high appreciation of the honor they have shown me in calling me to preside on this occasion, and to express to the pastor of the Church my sincere thanks for his kind words of introduction.

"Our first service in these interesting exercises will be to invoke the presence and blessing of Almighty God, whose kind providence and favor have been over this Church during all its past history."

## ORDER OF EXERCISES.

### 10.00 A. M.

| | |
|---|---|
| INVOCATION AND LORD'S PRAYER, | Rev. A. J. Hetrick. |
| HYMN, "Now thank we all our God." | |
| ADDRESS OF WELCOME, | Prof. John H. Hewitt. |
| READING OF SCRIPTURE, | Rev. Frank Palmer. |
| PRAYER, | Rev. Geo. A. Bryan. |
| HYMN, "A mighty fortress is our God." | |
| HISTORICAL ADDRESS, | Rev. R. H. Gidman. |
| ANTHEM, Gloria ("Twelfth Mass," by Mozart). | |
| THE SEPARATE CHURCH, | Amos A. Browning, Esq. |
| SOLO, "The Golden Threshold," | Mrs. Cora Tracy. |
| SKETCHES OF PASTORS, | Rev. John Avery. |
| HYMN. | |

### INTERMISSION.

### 2.00 P. M.

| | |
|---|---|
| SERVICE OF SONG. | |
| PRAYER, | Rev. H. E. Morrow. |
| GREETINGS, The Mother Church, | Rev. C. A. Northrop. |
| The Daughter Church, | Rev. F. E. Allen. |
| The Baptist Church, | Rev. C. L. Eldredge. |
| SOLO, "Holy City," | Miss Maude Buckingham. |
| ADDRESS, "Those who have gone forth from the church," | Judge Samuel O. Prentice. |
| QUARTETTE, "The King of Love my Shepherd is." | |
| "LOCAL CONFERENCE" GREETINGS. | |
| The Ministry, | Rev. H. T. Arnold. |
| The Laity, | Dea. H. L. Reade. |
| DUET, "Peace to this Sacred Dwelling," | Mr. and Mrs. E. P. Barnes. |
| ADDRESSES BY FORMER PASTORS. | |
| HYMN, "We are watching, we are waiting." | |
| BENEDICTION. | |

One of the very enjoyable hours of the day was the intermission. The rich and bountiful collation provided by the ladies of the church and served in the vestry brought friends, old and new, together in greetings and social converse pleasant to see and to share.

The musical parts of the exercises, conducted by the chorister, Mr. William D. Bagley, were entirely worthy of the occasion. A feature of special interest, and which gave a very pleasant diversity to the exercises, was the service of song at the opening of the afternoon session, introduced by the chairman, as follows:

"All appreciate, I am sure, how important and interesting a part of our exercises is that provided by our musicians. It was, at one time, the purpose of the committee of arrangements to provide for an evening session at which should be presented a program of sacred music under the direction of Mr. William Bagley, the leader of the choir of the church. As that plan, in view of the possible length of the day sessions, was deemed impracticable, it was decided to devote a portion of the afternoon to a service of song. The selection of pieces arranged by Mr. Bagley for this purpose will be presented now, and it is expected that some of the tunes will remind us of 'ye olden time.'"

The program of this service included:

"Strike the Cymbal"—Choir.
Bass Solo, "Zion"—Mr. Byron Mathieu.
Hymn of Sixteenth Century—Quartette.
Tenor Solo, "The Heavenly Song"—Mr. Louis H. Wheeler.
Hymn, "Come, All Ye Faithful"—Choir.

The general and hearty expressions of approval and of pleasure in the commemoration testified to its fitness and success.

The addresses delivered on the occasion, and giving it permanent value, are to be found in the following pages.

# I

## ADDRESS OF WELCOME

# ADDRESS OF WELCOME.

### By Prof. John H. Hewitt, LL.D.

*Sons and Daughters of Preston:* We have assembled to-day to celebrate the completion of the 200th anniversary of the establishing of the first church in Preston. In behalf of the committee of arrangements, of the pastor of the church, and of the parish, I give you hearty greetings and extend to you, one and all, a most cordial welcome to these scenes and these exercises. The occasion is unique and one of rare interest. When, in the summer of 17 B. C., the Roman Emperor Augustus instituted the so-called secular games, it was pronounced a remarkable festival, one that, in the words of the herald who proclaimed the coming events, no living man had ever seen or ever would see again. To-day we celebrate an event of greater significance than that of the Roman emperor, while it is quite as remarkable in that this is the first 200th anniversary of this church, and one that no living man will ever see again. While in the old world many churches trace their foundation back to the centuries near the time of Christ, in America few institutions of any sort have attained to the age of 200 years. Of the more than 300 Congregational churches in this venerable commonwealth, only about 30 can claim so great an age as this church, while in this county only four, I think, are older than this one.

The occasion is, in one sense, a celebration of the town, for the foundation of the church is almost coeval with the settlement of the township, and the church was established by act of the town. In the town records we find these entries;—of date, Jan. 26, 1687, "Town takes first steps to secure a minister at £50 a year," and of date, June 21, 1693, "Town made tax to build meeting-house 35 feet long, 25 feet wide, 16 feet between joints." And we are to bear in mind to-day that the influence of this church has not been confined to those families whose names have been enrolled in its membership, but every one who has dwelt within sound of this church bell has, Sabbath by Sabbath, been reminded of his higher and better nature, been reminded, too, of that beneficent commandment given for the highest good of man — *Remember the Sabbath day to keep it holy.*

It is quiet scenes to which you come back to-day. Neither steam nor electric car has yet invaded the precincts of the town as it is now bounded. This church has ever been far removed from "the madding crowd," yet the sweet influences of many a home in other parts of this land may be traced back to this rural church. Here, amid scenery almost idyllic, the process of character building has been going noiselessly forward for 200 years, and other towns and other commonwealths are enjoying the rich fruitage. And I can fancy that as former residents return to-day, and in many distant homes as the thought of this celebration reaches them, the reflections will be something like those of the poet Wordsworth on revisiting the banks of the Wye:

> Though absent long,
> These forms of beauty have not been to me
> As is a landscape to a blind man's eye:
> But oft, in lonely rooms, and 'mid the din
> Of towns and cities, I have owed to them,
> In hours of weariness, sensations sweet,
> Felt in the blood, and felt along the heart,
> And passing even into my purer mind
> With tranquil restoration :— feelings, too,
> Of unremembered pleasure : such, perhaps,
> As may have had no trivial influence
> On that best portion of a good man's life,
> His little, nameless, unremembered acts
> Of kindness and of love.

II

THE FIRST CHURCH IN PRESTON
AN HISTORICAL SURVEY

# AN HISTORICAL SURVEY.

THE CHAIRMAN: As you have learned from the program, we are this morning to listen to some of the more formal addresses of the occasion. It is with great appropriateness that the one appointed to deliver the historical address is one who, by careful research, has made himself so familiar with the past of this church and town, who has zealously devoted much of thought and time to the preparation for this anniversary, and who has been for the past fourteen years the faithful and beloved pastor of this people. I invite your attention to the Rev. R. H. Gidman, who does not need to be introduced to you.

### ADDRESS BY REV. R. H. GIDMAN.

The history of a New England church two hundred years old involves, especially in its early life, more or less of the history of the town where it has had a place. The intimate, inseparable relation of the two appears from the fact that, in the period in which the present history opens, the chief object in the making of the town, in the organization of society, was a religious object. The founding of this church takes us back within reach of the landing of the Pilgrims. Some of the *Mayflower's* little company possibly were yet living. The spirit of the Pilgrims was still prevalent and gave character to the life of the colony: the spirit expressed in their compact, "for the glory of God and advancement of the Christian faith"; and in their avowal that "the propagating of the Gospel is a thing we do profess above all to be our aim in settling this plantation." "Freedom to worship God" is the familiar phrase telling the constraining and moulding influence of the early years in our New England history.

This preliminary word is natural and proper in view of what seems to me to be the fact, that in our own town of

Preston, at least in its beginnings, we have an interesting, if it may not be said conspicuous, example of the Pilgrim spirit and purpose. This fact is recognized in, and to a degree directs, the course of the present address.

The earliest record relating to this town is concerning land to the amount of 450 acres deeded by Uncas to one Jonathan Brewster, his "trusted friend and adviser," to induce him to establish a trading post, which he did, on the river Thames, at the mouth of the Poquetanuck creek. This was in the spring of the year 1650, or more than thirty years before the organization of the town, and ten years before Norwich was settled by the colony from Saybrook. We may presume it was from this point, now known as Brewster's Neck, that the earliest settlements were gradually made, to be increased later by settlers from Norwich, and, at length, to gain sufficiently in number to justify application to the General Court for liberty "to make a plantation." Particular mention is made of this Jonathan Brewster, not only because he was a pioneer and probably the first settler in territory to be included in the town of Preston, but also because of his noteworthy antecedents, he being the oldest son of Elder William Brewster, the recognized spiritual leader of Plymouth colony. Jonathan, then a young man, did not, as it appears, come over with his father in the *Mayflower*. He, however, followed the next year in the ship *Fortune*. In course of time he came to New London and was clerk of that town; later, with his family, established himself at his trading-post on the Thames, where he remained several years; then, with his wife, returned to New London, and died there in 1660. His sons, Daniel and Benjamin, stayed here. Daniel, if not Benjamin also, was prominent in the effort to secure organization as a town, and signed the petition made to the court. It was not until October, 1686, that a petition was made. Up to this time land-owners and other inhabitants settled here under the authority of Norwich. The sole matter urged as a reason, in the application, it is interesting to note, was inconvenience in religious worship. "The petitioners state that, by the settlement of Norwich and New London bounds, they are left without either township, remote from any

place of public worship, that they are distant from New London fourteen miles and six or seven from Norwich, the way to either place being dangerous in winter by reason of the river." The petition was favorably considered:
"This Court doe see great reason to incourage them by a favorable answer to their desires, but being unacquainted with the country and what may be sufficient for them for bounds doe order that Capt. John Allyn, Capt. James Fitch, Capt. James Mason, Capt. James Avery, or any three of them doe forthwith view what may be convenient for a plantation and if seven miles square or the quantity of it will be a sufficiency they may lay it out to them and make return to the Governor who may grant them a pattent for the same and this Court will be ready to grant them the priviledg of a plantation when they shall be arrived at such a capacity as to mayntayne a minister."

Returns were made, and, on the 26th of the following January, liberty was granted; and on the same day the first steps were taken to secure a minister at £50 per year. It is interesting to observe here that ten years and more before the organization of a church, or even of an ecclesiastical society, religious services were held and maintained from year to year under the direction of the town. During this period "proposalls" were made to several persons to accept the pastorate. One of these was a Mr. Hale, who, although he did not engage to serve permanently, supplied, at intervals, for several years. Besides that of Mr. Hale, the names of Welds, Bogle, Evelle, Woodbridge, and Flint occur among those (ten or eleven, in all) who were considered and invited to act as ministers for the town.

Where religious worship was held during this earliest period of our history does not appear, but we learn from the town records that as early as June, 1693, a tax was made "to build a meeting-house to be 35 feet long, 25 feet wide, and 16 feet between joints." For some reason the work of building was delayed, but the house, evidently, was sufficiently near completion to be used sometime before the settlement of a pastor, for, on Sept. 8, 1698, " at a town meeting legally warned, it was voted that Hopestill Tyler, Josiah Haines, Peter Davison, and Joseph Stanton shall have liberty to build the fore gallery, and they and their wives to have the privilege of the fore seats for them and their wives, and they are to take a fifth person with them, that is to say, provided that those that are already seated shall relinquish the seat where they are now seated, and they are to put in joists and lay the floor home to one side and make a door and stairs at their own charge before the ordination." The ordination referred to was that of Mr. Salmon Treat, who was destined to have a large place in the history of town and church.

For two years or more before this Mr. Treat had served at intervals as minister for the town and plainly to the cordial acceptance of the people as shown by action of the town in December, 1697, making generous propositions to him, looking to a permanent relation. The entries of the town records, giving this and subsequent action together with Mr. Treat's responses, are of interest.

"Proposalls made to the revearant Mr. Sallmon Trate in order to his settlement in the work of the minist$^r$y among us and for his in corigment in the said ministariall work first we do reseave him as a lawfull inhabitant into the town and give him an aquall sheare with the purchesers in the Commons that Lies undivided in our town: 2 we doe ingage to give him forty six pounds in money a yere anually for a yerely salary so long as the sd m$^r$ Treat continues with us in the worke ministry and to add to it after the yere 1698 two pounds a yere untill it comes to fifty pounds and so to continue to be payed yerly untill his charg shall incrace so as to xcede more and the towns abilitie is such as to alow him more. 3 we give him present improvement of the house that we bulte for the minister and the land belonging to it which formerly belonged to Sargt Thomas Tracy and Jonathan Tracy being by estimation seventy acres more or less as it is bounded and if the sd m$^r$ Treat continue with us in the worke of the an be called to ofice then we doe ingage to give him a firme deed to him and his heirs for ever of the afore sd house and land only exsepting the priviledg of cutting of fire wood for his use and we doe allso ingage that he shall have the use of the hundred acres of land, which was Bought of M$^r$ Ephrem and joseph Minor during his continuance with us in the ministariall work only reserving a privilidg of cutting of wood for his use. 4 wee doe ingage to cute and carte thirty loads of fire wood yerely for him and also to cute ten cords of wood to be performed yerly for him."

"December: 15: 1697, at a town meeting these propositions ware votted."

About a month later. Jan. 13, 1698, further action was taken renewing the call and expressing in particular the desire of the people for the organization of a church, to which they now had obtained "the consent and incouragment of the honred Generall Court."

"We doe hereby desire of the Reverend m$^r$ Salmon Treat to take upon him the pastorall care and charge in this place and to procede in all needfull due methods according to Gospell rule to gather and embody a gospel Church here untill the work with the help of other churches be accomplished and more particularly to take the names of such as are church members in full communion or any other that shall give them in that out of them may be taken such as are found most meet and able to begin and Lay the foundation of a church and we are free to joyn with M$^r$ Treat so he doe not differ in his discipline with the body of the now Gospell churches in this Countrey and we desire good man Tobes and good man Branch to signifie this our request unto the Revd. m$^r$ Salmon Treat and make the return unto the town."

The unanimity and earnestness of the people in the call and the purpose above expressed is evident from the following additional entry:

"The same day Jan 13 : 1698 by a vote the whole town manifested theire willingness to contribute to the charge at the ordination and by a free and full voate chose a Comitte, Serg't Tracy, Ensigne Parke, Hopestill Tyler, Thomas Stanton, and joseph Morgan."

Mr. Treat's answer, deferred, in order, as we may judge, to carefully consider the matter, came at length in acceptance of the call and was in word and spirit of such a character as to win interest and regard here and now for Preston's first pastor.

"Sept 7 : 1698 to the inhabitants of Preston in answer to the above writt'n proposalls for as much as the holy and Soverain Providence of God has cast my lot among you and has seemed to take all considerable obstacles out of the way of my continuance among you, and for as much as the father of spirits has brought you to such a good measure of unanimity and agreement and hath led my spirit for aught that appears to a willingness to comply with your Desires this may signifie unto you that it is my intention to yeld up myselfe in the feare of God to be a minister of Christ in his works among you Desiring to trust in him for abilities for his great work hoping to have your good disposition and affections continue towards me and j hope j shall allwayes enjoy your prayers So that I may performe his work in the power and Demonstration of the Spirit.

"As to disciplining of Church when it is gathered j hope j shall endeauor to agree with neighbour Elders but aboue all j hope j shall be willing and endeauor to conform to the Rules of Christ as near as j can wishing grace mercy and peace may be multiplied j subscribe myself yours in any gospell service that j am able

Salmon Treat"

Let us recall that up to this time, September, 1698, all action that concerned the religious interests of the people had been by vote of the town. It was evidently in prospect of a permanent pastorate and with a desire to conform to the more regular and specific way of maintaining religious worship and carrying forward religious work that a petition was now presented to the General Court in Hartford for the privilege of church organization, and on October 13, 1698, answer was given to this effect:

"This Court grants free libertie to the inhabitants of Preston to embody themselves in church estate with the consent of neighbor churches and to call and settle an orthodox minister to dispence all the ordinances of God to them."

It was at the same term of the Court that Mr. Samuel Fitch petitioned "in behhalfe of some farmers in Norwich bownds that they might have libertie to joyn with the assembly in Preston and to pay to the ministrie there and be released from paying to the ministrie in Norwich," with answer from the Court that "being sensible of the difficulties that may attend them this Court doe recomend it to the serious and charitable consideration of the town of Norwich exacting their charitable and Christian compliance with the interest of their neighbors." The "difficulties that may attend," without doubt, refer especially to the hardness and danger of the journey from any point on the east side of the Shetucket river to the Meeting-house in Norwich Town. A descriptive passage from the "History of Norwich" by Miss Caulkins gives an idea of the way to church.

"For the space of 70 years after the settlement the greater part of Chelsea was technically a sheep-walk belonging to the inhabitants of the east end of the town and used by them for the pasturage of

## BI-CENTENNIAL CELEBRATION. 19

cattle. . . . A cartway through it was allowed, and in 1680 "a pair of bars" connected with this cartway was maintained by the town near the Shetucket and another pair below the house of John Reynolds. The whole space between Yantic Cove and the Shetucket was a wilderness of rocks, woods, and swamps, with only here or there a cow-path or a sheep-track around the hills where the trunk of a fallen tree thrown over a brook or chasm served in lieu of a bridge. Not only in the spring floods, but in common heavy rains, a great part of East Chelsea and all the lower on Water Street up to the ledge of rocks upon which the buildings on the north side of that street are based were overflowed, and even in the dry season these parts of the town were little better than swamps. What are now only moist places and slender rills were then ponds and broad infectious brooks."

These difficulties, not only of the inhabitants of Preston, but also of those living in the eastern part of Norwich, whose boundary line then was not more than two miles west of this house of worship, may account very well for the petitions, and for the interest manifested in religious worship here.

With liberty granted by the Court and a permanent minister secured there was no delay in the organization of the church and the ordination of the pastor. A brief account of the event constitutes the first entry in the records of the First Congregational Church in Preston. It is as follows:

"A church was embodied in Preston Nov.$^r$ 16, A.D. 1698. The Elders who embodied the church and performed ordination were the Rev. James Noyes, Pastor of Stonington; the Rev. Morse Noyes, Pastor of Lyme, and the Rev. Gurdon Saltonstall, Pastor of New London. The messengers from neighboring churches: Deacon Gershom Palmer of Stonington; Deacon Peck of Lyme; Daniel Witherell Esq$^r$ and Deacon Douglass of New London; and Deacon Simeon Huntington of Norwich.

"They who offered themselves as matter for a church, having been members of other churches in full communion were brought into order by giving their consent to articles of faith and renewal of the covenant. The persons were Thomas Park, Thomas Tracy, John Richards, Hopestill Tyler, Jonathan Tracy, Samuel Leonardson, Robert Park, John Park, Caleb Fobes, Joseph Morgan, Ebenezer Witter, and John Welch, 12 persons."

We also have preserved for us the articles of faith accepted and the covenant into which the church entered. The covenant, in part, was this:

"God having graciously received us into the Covenant of his grace which he hath sealed to us in baptism; we acknowledge ourselves indispensably bound to hold fast the doctrine of faith and good manners contained in the Scriptures of truth and to attend all those duties therein prescribed for the increase of our faith, growth in holiness and maintaining a good conscience. . . . We whose hearts God hath moved in this place to join together in the worship of God and partake of the Lords table and therein desire to have the prayers and approbation of the churches of Christ who may take knowledge of us, we, for the satisfaction of all men, declare as followeth: — That we unfeignedly resign ourselves and our seed unto the Lord, receiving Jesus Christ the son of the living God, very God and very Man as our Lord and Saviour, relying upon the free grace of God for salvation and blessedness and heartily submitting ourselves to be ruled by his word and spirit . . . and to teach all under our care, as far as in us lies, to know and fear the Lord."

We may imagine the scenes of the day: the call of bell or of drum-beat to church; the gathering of the people to this hill where we are now come; the simple but impressive service; the earnest attention; the hearty congratulations. We can in spirit almost be with them as we think that it was verily here where they were met for it all.

So it was this church entered upon its career. Before the first communion in the month of January near at hand, thirteen others "joined to communicate," making in all twenty-five members. Among them were Dorothy, the wife of Salmon Treat, whom he had recently married, the wives of Thomas and Jonathan Tracy, Mrs. Brewster, the wife of Daniel Brewster, to whom reference has already been made; also "Mrs. Standish" and "Mrs. Standish, the wife of Josiah Standish," at whose names we may stay, for at least a passing word. The first Mrs. Standish we may suppose to be the wife of Capt. Josiah Standish, deceased, and the other Mrs. Standish a daughter-in-law, the wife of a son by the name of Josiah. Capt. Josiah Standish was none other than the eldest son of Capt. Miles Standish of earliest New England fame, of whom Longfellow sings:

"In the Old Colony days in Plymouth the land of the Pilgrim,
  To and fro in a room of his simple and primitive dwelling,
  Clad in doublet and hose and boots of Cordovan leather,
  Strode, with a martial air, Miles Standish, the Puritan Captain."

So it is, that Preston township and its first church have the honorable distinction of numbering the one among its citizens, the other among its members, immediate descendants of both the spiritual and the military leader of Plymouth Colony. It is interesting to read in the church records these entries:

"Josiah Standish was admitted into full communion, Dec. 25, 1700."

"Daniel Brewster, received into full communion, April 5, 1702."

"Israel Standish and Elizabeth his wife, were received into full communion, Nov. 15, 1704."

"Miles Standish was admitted to the Lord's table, April 1, 1705."

The organization of the church and the induction of its pastor into his office was an event of great interest to the town, and also as considered in a broader relation. In 1698 there were, besides this, only five or six churches in the State (or colony as it then was), east of the Connecticut River. The most recent addition was the church in Old Lyme, five years, and in this immediate region, the church of Stonington, twenty-four years before. This church became one of a little fraternity of churches, sharing in the hopes and inspirations of a colony having before it the work of exploring, opening up, and occupying a country whose settlement had then only fairly begun. Each advance of the Gospel was, we may believe, matter for earnest congratulation.

The church thus auspiciously organized appears to have prospered steadily during nearly all of Mr. Treat's pastorate of forty-six years. As illustrated in some period of their career by many other churches of considerable age, as, for instance, in Bethlehem in western Connecticut, under Dr. Bellamy, and in Franklin, in the eastern part of the State, under Dr. Nott, this church in its beginning was favored with the leadership of a man of such scholarship and energy, integrity, and strength of character, and devotion to his calling, as to win the confidence and honor of his people. Preston's first pastor made an impress upon church and town not soon to be effaced. Who shall say that it has wholly gone even at this day?

From the time of its organization onward throughout this ministry there was a gain year by year in the membership of the church, and mostly on confession of faith. As appears from the church records, it is interesting to observe how large a territory at the first was virtually included in this parish, extending as it did beyond the bounds of the town or society, which then were coterminous, into other towns, as indicated by such entries in those earliest years, as these:

"Received into full communion John Hill. in Stonington bounds." "The wife of Benj. Fitch, in Norwich bounds." "Abigail Knite, a maid living in Plainfield."

We may note also the wide circle from which additions came by letter — Windham, Enfield, Ipswich, Haverhill, Beverly, Cambridge — showing whence came material for growth in both church and town.

For seventeen years the church continued in the capacity and in the field of work which it had when constituted.

In the year 1716, by vote of the town, and by grant of the Assembly, upon application from the north part of the township, Preston was divided into two ecclesiastical societies, to be called "North" and "South" society.* Probably the chief, if not the only, reason for this division, was the matter of convenience in attending religious worship. By this time the population of the town had very substantially increased, and, as it would seem, gave assurance of ability to maintain a second church organization. The event made good the promise. The project of maintaining separate religious worship and at length of formal organization was successfully carried out. Formed as that society and church were, from our own, a little taken from their records is not without appropriateness in the present history.

The first record bears the date, "Nov. 21, 1716." "At a meeting legally warned in the No. Society in Preston Isaac Averill was chosen clarke of the above said Societie and sworn to a faithful discharge of that offis before me John Brown one of his magistes justices of the peace." At the same meeting "John Brⁿ and joseph Geer and Thomas Davison were a Committe chosen for to cause Soc. meetings that may be lawfull . . and it was voted that they shall set

---

* For particulars in regard to action of town see Note B, in Appendix hereto.

up warnings at each gristmill to caulle such Societie meetings for time to come."—" Nov. 29, 1716. At a meeting legally warned a Com. was chosen to caulle a minister for our North Societie when we have Ocasion for one "— " Dec. 17 1716, Committe chosen to acte about Building of a meeting house as the Societie shall order them." Preparation for building appears from the records to have gone forward during the next year and to have progressed sufficiently to warrant beginning the work in the spring of the year following, as is shown from a vote taken April 21, 1718, which gives incidentally a little glimpse of the customs of the times: "Voted that there shall be 41 shillings of the Societies money laid out for one hundred wait of Chease for the raising of our meeting house." The edifice was completed the next Fall. But the most important record bearing upon our history is one showing that the movement which resulted in the organization of the second church in Preston in the year 1720 was not from strife or from any lack of fraternal feeling, but for reasons that both societies honored. It is in the form of a communication to this church, and is as follows:

"Gentlemen of the South Society, we render to you hearty thanks for all the tokens of favor that we have Received from your Bountifull hand and doe beg leave to tel you, that we have Considered the proposals which you sent to us and have imbraced ye first of them namely to draw of and provide for ourselves — As soon as possible may be with convenience and to that end have chosen two men to get a minister forthwith, Nov ye[8th] 1717."

"At a meeting legally warned of the North Societie in preston the above writen was voted to be sent to the gentlemen of the Committe in the South Societie to be communicated to the inhabitants of s'd Societie in Preston."

For a hundred years these two churches, mother and daughter, lived together in the same township. The younger church as well as the elder making for herself then and since a record of usefulness not only in the service rendered by her sons at home, but by those who have gone forth to live and labor elsewhere, as witnessed by the names of Burton and Haskell and Staunton and Cleft and Averill and Johnson and Tucker, with others who have been raised to enter and honor the Christian ministry.

It might naturally be inferred that by this division into two societies the first church would be greatly weakened financially and spiritually. There appears, however, to have been no serious break in its prosperity. Mr. Treat's salary of £62 was continued, and in later years increased to £100; the church edifice was repaired and somewhat remodeled; and examination of the record of admissions to membership shows what is remarkable, that in the decade following the division the additions to this church were larger than in the ten years preceding. As has been the case more than once, where there has been good reason for two churches instead of one in a given territory, the increase of energy and devotion given to the work more than met the loss.

The course of remark thus far has been in reference to the strictly religious aspect of the church's work. There is, however, another which should be considered, namely, the educational. Miss Caulkins, in speaking upon the subject of education in the early part of New England's history, says: "It may not be true of all New England, but in some portions of it for a considerable period after the first generation had passed away education was neglected. The schools were of an inferior grade and very grudgingly and irregularly sustained. . . . The consequence was that the grandchildren of the first settlers were more illiterate than either the generation before or after them." This remark could not, I think, be applied to Preston; not so much because of what the town did as a town, but because of what the church did. During a large part, if not the whole, of its first century, the church evidently had under its charge the general instruction of the youth of the community, and appears to have undertaken and carried on the work of education as if it were as truly a part of its business as the maintenance of religious worship. The records of the ecclesiastical society are numerous and varied in regard to its action covering such particulars as the division of the society into school districts (or "societies"), the changing of their boundary lines, the laying of taxes, the making of appropriations from its treasury. The earnest and continuous attention given by the church to education in the early, and well on towards the latter part of the first hundred years, attributable largely, as we may assume, to the advice, direction, and inspiration of a thoroughly educated ministry, forms a creditable and noteworthy part of our history.

Among the events that occurred in the closing years of Mr. Treat's ministry was the building of a new church edifice which was completed and occupied near the close of 1739 or the beginning of 1740, as shown by action of society's meeting in February of that year, in which it was voted to accept "of ye new meeting house and that the sd house was finished and dun workmanlike" — "at ye same meeting Cap$^t$. John Brewster and Lieut. John Avery was chosen committey in addition to a committey that was chosen to seat the meeting house."

Reference is here made to a committee appointed in the previous December, with the direction that "each person be seated according to Thair age and Thair Meeting house Rates," a method or rule much less likely to excite unamiable feelings and behavior than that — quite general in those times — of seating according to social standing. The new house of worship was forty-eight feet in length, thirty-eight feet in width, and twenty-two feet in length of posts. This made it of more than twice the seating capacity of the old house. It was built on the same site and a vote was passed that "a small piece of ye land in sd society called ministry Land where sd meeting house now stands shall be and remain for a meeting house Lot for ye use of this Society forever."

The survey of the period which has thus far been specially in mind must give the impression of an enterprising, active, successful church, and this impression may be deepened when, merely as a matter of statistics, it is added that during the pastorate of Mr. Treat nearly 400 members were received. We must not infer, however, that there was nothing in this period that pastor or people would have had otherwise. On the contrary, there were, for one thing, cases for discipline with which the church needed to deal, and did, in severity. Of the particulars, excepting in two or three instances, we have no knowledge, but sufficient appears to make plain not only its charitable consideration and its carefulness to proceed according to the rule of Christ, but also its fidelity, firmness, and impartiality in the treatment of such matters. And this, let it be observed, appears to have been characteristic throughout the church's history. When from impurity or dishonesty or intemperance or slander there has been judged to be cause for disciplinary dealing the church has gone forward with a sense of the significance of the action, regardful of Christ's law, but if needful to assert its regard for righteousness, not withholding "the dreadful sentence" or (as a later phrase expresses it) "to raise the hand of excommunication."

We may also conclude from the trying experiences through which it was called to pass, beginning near the close of the first ministry and continuing for very many years, that the church did not wholly escape the spirit of worldliness and of formality in religion, which was so prevalent in New England in the early part of the eighteenth century. The low spiritual state of the times plainly was due to the looseness in conditions of reception to church membership. Without doubt the "half-way Covenant," as it has been termed, allowing baptism and other privileges but not full communion by partaking of the Lord's Supper, admitting candidates on the ground of good moral character without assurance of any experience of vital religion, very seriously affected the piety and zeal of the churches. "Owned the Covenant" was a phrase used to signify such admissions. In the early records of this church the phrase occurs in but very few cases (scarcely more than a dozen in the course of Mr. Treat's pastorate), but the low standard of religion in general which marked the period exerted a depressing, deteriorating influence. Even though the sanitary regulations of one's own house be pretty good, if the atmosphere about is bad, one's health is sure to suffer harm. A writer, referring to the spiritual condition of the period, says: "All New England seemed sunk into worldliness and formality, exhibiting no spiritual growth, and little, if any, fervent religious emotion." But this was not to continue indefinitely. "In the midst of this," he adds, "a wonderful manifestation of spiritual activity was suddenly developed." This was what has passed into history as the "Great

Awakening," recognized as one of the most remarkable experiences of the modern church. The chief human factors in the event were George Whitfield, whose impassioned eloquence moved with an almost unmatched power all classes of society, and Jonathan Edwards of Northampton, a man not only eminent, but pre-eminent in intellect and piety, by whose influence it has been said that "the religious thought and life of New England has been determined more than by that of any other man." Hundreds of communities were intensely affected by the revival attending the efforts of these men and of others who caught the inspiration of the time. Many of the churches of Connecticut, including most of those in this part of the state, had large accessions of converts. In so far as the irreligious were concerned, Preston seems to have been little affected, but the church was greatly stirred, and the results (some might say for evil, but let us not be quite sure of that), were manifest for two generations.

We are brought now to what is called the Separate Movement, which began near the close of Mr. Treat's service, continued through the long pastorate of Mr. Rosseter, on through the ministry of Mr. Fuller, and still affected the church more or less during the twenty years' pastorate of Mr. Tyler at the close of the last and the beginning of the present century. The serious depletion in church membership it occasioned is told by a comparative statement of figures at the opening and at the close of Mr. Rosseter's term of service. At the beginning, males, 42; females, 64 — 106. At the end, males, 4; females, 13 — 17. The fact that Preston (largely on account of the ability and devotion of its leader here) was a center of influence for the new denomination, makes it all the more important that the movement have consideration in a historical review of our two hundred years. So it is that the distinct treatment of the subject, which is to follow the present address, and which permits passing it now without detailed reference, may be awaited with interest.

Two or three remarks of a general character relating to the schism may be offered. One, regarding those who went out of the church, is to express the conviction — despite a zeal that, in some cases, rose to fanaticism — of their conscientiousness. Men and women committed themselves to the Separate movement, whose intelligence must be allowed, and whose sincerity and purity of motive cannot be questioned. On the other hand, no one can fail to honor those who, in the long years of trial, and of calls to unwonted self-denial in support of the church of the fathers, stood firmly by it, and through their devotion kept alive that which appeared ready to die. In this connection it seems to me but a just thing to mention the noble support given by the Ecclesiastical Society in the financial straits into which this church was brought. As a sufficient illustration and proof of this, let us notice the record in the society's book, headed "Subscription for permanent fund," and, under date of "Aug. 12, 1784," the opening sentences of which are as follows:

"We, the subscribers, inhabitants of the first Society in Preston in the County of New London and State of Connecticut (and others joining with us) taking into consideration the difficulties that attend supporting the ministers of the Gospel in the method the law hath prescribed by taxing the whole of the inhabitants of the Society, are inclined and disposed to raise and establish a fund of twelve hundred and fifty pounds and upwards in lawful money or public securities (for hard money) Issued by authority of the State of Connecticut, and on Interest at six per cent. per annum, the Interest arising on Said Sum to be improved for the support of a regular orthodox Minister of the Gospel in S$^d$ Society and to no other purpose, and in such manner and form as is hereafter mentioned, etc."

At the close is a list of subscriptions amounting to £1,279 9s. 0p.

In regard to the effect on the church, spiritually, of the secession of the Separatists (or "New Lights," as they were sometimes called), what can be gathered from our own history confirms the judgment of church historians, in reference to the general influence of the movement, that it was to reduce formality in worship and to increase carefulness in the admission of members into the church. Two interesting acts of this church — one near the beginning of Mr. Rosseter's ministry and the other just before the ordination of Mr. Fuller, his immediate successor — are an indication of the truth of such judgment: "Preston, Feb. 14, 1745. It was proposed to the brethren of the church whether they would begin and uphold conference meetings by mutual prayer and reading the word of God, or any orthodox book. The brethren readily consented." Mr. Fuller's ordination was on Dec. 8, 1784. " Previous to it," as the record states, "the church of the first Society in Preston met and came to the following resolutions:

1. To admit no persons according to the half-way practice.
2. To baptize the children of persons already in such standing.
3. In so far as Christian judgment will extend, to consider grace as a term of communion."

A relieving feature, a bright spot in the long and trying experience caused by the schism of which we have been speaking, is the earnest and fraternal action of the Ecclesiastical Society looking to a reunion of the two churches, as shown by entries in its book, one of which I will read. "27 March, 1782. Voted, that we make an attempt to unite with the congregation of Mr. Paul Parke. Voted, that Col. Sam. Mott, Messrs. John Safford, and Amos Brown be a committee to confer with Mr. Paul Parke and his congregation to obtain and make agreement for them to unite on Sabbath days in the meeting-house where the Rev. Asher Rosseter used to preach, and for the said Mr. Parke to preach there to the hole society, and become one meeting untill further ordered." Such approaches could not well have failed to bring the two into greater peace and more charitable consideration of each other; they could but have had a softening, gracious influence, even though the full result hoped was not immediately gained.

From what has been said we have disclosed to us much of the character of Mr. Rosseter's pastorate of thirty-seven years. It was evidently a struggle against odds, that at times may have seemed too great to keep even a remnant of the church that had been. Nevertheless, that was done; and we may infer, not only from the noteworthy length of his service, but from the little that is recorded, bearing upon the mutual relations between him and his people, that he had their confidence and affectionate regard. Not only was his salary kept in its full measure, but more than once his people in their generous consideration went beyond this, as instanced in the action of the society in a meeting on Christmas day, 1760. "Voted, to give Mr. Rosseter 12 pounds, in consideration of ye extraordinary price of provisions in the year 1759, and, also, 8 pounds in consideration of ye extraordinary price of provisions in ye year 1760."

Among the losses in membership in the period now in mind, and toward the close of Mr. Rosseter's pastorate, was one by death, which may have a word in particular. It was that of Deacon Jedediah Tracy, in the eighty-seventh year of his age, caused by a fall from his horse as he was going to mill. He left, it is said, 137 descendants. He was a grandson of Lieut. Thomas Tracy, a first settler in Norwich; had been honored by the town with the office of justice of the peace, and in being called at least four times to serve as its representative. He had been a deacon of the church for fifty years, being called to the office not long after his uniting with the church in 1725.

His name and these particulars are mentioned as naturally bringing to mind the important place held, not simply by the ministry, but also by the laity, in the history of our churches. One of the moving spirits, if not the chief, in the religious affairs of this town in its beginning, and in the organization of this church, was a layman. It was Dea. Thomas Parke, the first deacon of the church, who came here from New London, and was among the earliest settlers on Preston territory, and who died in the year 1709. And these two are but instances of the way in which the life of the church has been perpetuated, its work undertaken and performed, its history largely made. The names of Avery, Brewster, Branch, Downer, Freeman, Fobes, Kimball, Loring, Morgan, Richards, Witter, and of many others perchance not less worthy, are of those who year by year, generation by generation, wrought and sympathized with the ministry in such wise that they might well say as Paul did of his brethren, "For now we live, if ye stand fast in the Lord."

With this reference to the lay members of the church in

respect to their vital relation to its mission and work, we may naturally call to mind their important, and, at times, determining influence in affairs of public concern in inaugurating, undertaking, and carrying forward to results what, but for them, might not or would not be attempted. Not only the religious but the civil and social well-being of the community depends largely upon this Christian element within it. Mention has already been made in regard to the activity of the church in the interest of education in which the minister appears to have been the leader. There is another matter of our history, and one of serious and great interest, in which this church had an earnest and noteworthy part, in which not the minister, but the laymen, were the prominent actors. I refer to events occurring in the latter years of Mr. Rosseter's ministry, the events of the American Revolution. In calling particular attention to these events, let us not think that we are departing from the legitimate course of our address.

In the judgment of the historian the question of political freedom for the American colonies involved that of religious freedom if, indeed, the question of liberty of conscience and of religious action may not be affirmed to have been the underlying ground of protest and of conflict. Dr. Dunning, in his "Congregationalists in America," says: "A candid study of the early history of New England can lead to no other conclusion than this, that the most powerful motive in originating the War of Independence was a religious motive. It was the same as that which first brought the Pilgrims to this country, that they might worship God unmolested in the way they believed most pleasing to Him; that they might plant churches of the Congregational order and a civil government in harmony with the principles of such churches."

The prominence and efficiency of members of this church and society in the events of that period deserve more than a passing notice.

In looking over Miss Caulkins' History of Norwich, I fell upon this word touching our own town:

"Preston was so near to Norwich, and its military companies were so often united with those of the latter, that the names of its prominent officers slide easily into our history. Colonels John Tyler and Samuel Mott; Majors Nathan Peters, Jeremiah Halsey, and Edward Mott, Capt. Samuel Capron and Jacob Meech were some of the patriots and soldiers from that town who breasted the first waters of the Revolution, and were often afterwards in the field during the war."

On turning to the records of this society, it was interesting to find in or about this Revolutionary period, one, two, and, in one case, as many as four of these officers appointed on society's committees; that is to say, these men recognized as leaders of public sentiment, as well as honored actors in the events of the war, were men intimately connected with this church — expressing its mind and carrying out its will. We may certainly look upon this church and society as deserving an honorable place in the history of the town as it relates to the War of Independence, and that history is one of exceptional interest and importance. A gentleman who, some time ago, at the Government's request, made a special examination of our town records in order to find what might bear upon the Revolutionary War, expresses to me the opinion that Preston was one of the first and most earnest and most thorough in its action, and one of the most devoted in its contribution of men and money to sustain the colonies in their protest and resistance against the measures of the British government. It is of interest to add that this gentleman, in fulfilling his commission from the Government, copied from the records forty thousand words,— enough to make a volume of considerable size, a fact that is a sign of the deep and absorbing interest of this community in the serious questions of the times.

It is possible to do scarcely more than touch upon the subject. Two or three brief passages from the records may give a little impression of the spirit of the people. One, giving the action of the town at a meeting held Aug. 27, 1770, or six years before the Declaration of Independence, is as follows:

"Taking into consideration the difficulties which this town, together with all America, labors under at this time, and as it is the duty of every man to lend a hand to save his country; so, notwithstanding the smallness of this town in its situation, extent, and number, yet, as they Consider themselves as a Member of the Whole Body and Interested in the Event of the Common cause, therefore, Voted as the oppinion of this Town that the Resolutions of Parliment Claiming a Rite of Taxation over the Colonys is Grievous Burdensome and against our Constitutional Rights, Voted . . . that we have a right to take all Lawfull and Proper Measures to avoid Submition to such Influence though at the same time we acknowledge our Selves Dutifull and Loyal Subjects of our Sovreign King George the 3$^d$."

Another passage is from record of a meeting held July 11, 1774, and is of particular interest as showing the reverential or religious spirit that dictated the action:

"Voted as the Oppinion of this Town that we as well as all other Corporations in America are bound in Duty to God to our Country and to our Children to Discuss Declair and Record our Sentiments that future Generations May Know the oppinion of us there forefathers Concerning the Public transactions of this Moste Melancholy Period of time, Voted, that we the Present Generation have Great Reason to Humble our Selves before Almighty God for all our many Loud Defileing Sins which have provoked Him to permit our land to mourn because of the Opression of those that Seek our Ruin."

The action of the town, it should be observed, was by no means confined to earnest discussions and resolutions in town meetings. Conferences were held with other towns, and with bodies of citizens met in convention, as at New Haven and Hartford, where Preston delegates took a prominent and influential part in the proceedings. As an indication and illustration of the public spirit and sympathy felt in co-operating with others, the following correspondence, contained in the Massachusetts Historical Collections, and given in the History of New London County, may be noted. In July, 1774, the town passed resolutions of sympathy with Boston, and the passage that I will now read is from a letter from the Preston Committee of Observation and Correspondence, as it was called, addressed to the Committee of Correspondence in Boston. After referring to the condition of public affairs, it says:

"Capt. Belcher who is one of our Committee and a zealous friend of the liberties of this country waits on you with this and will acquaint you with the spirit of our people and give you a copy of the doings of our town on the 11. of July last. He will also bring you a

small sum of Money towards the relief of your poor. For these, our subscriptions are still out and we expect to make up in all about fifty pounds lawful money. (Signed) SAM'L MOTT,
per order of Committee."

To this, answer was given Aug. 24, 1774:

"We have received by Capt. B. your letter of the 20. and the sum of money you were kind enough to send for the support of our poor and it gives us pleasure amidst our sufferings to find our brethren determined to aid and support us while we are struggling for American freedom. (Signed) JOSEPH WARREN,
per order of Committee."

When the war actually began, Preston was ready to contribute not only money, but men. On hearing of skirmishes at Lexington and Concord, three companies of militia were enrolled, commanded by Captains Ebenezer Witter, William Belcher, and Roger Billings. (Capt. Witter, by the way, was one of the members of this church who were faithful to it in all its years of decline.) These companies were held in readiness for the relief of Boston, should their service be needed; and, after the battle of Bunker Hill, in June of the next year, were placed in active service.

A letter which I will read is of interest in this connection.

NORWICH, October 31, 1898.
REV. R. H. GIDMAN,

DEAR SIR:—I mentioned to you some days since that the town of Preston had taken an active part in the movements that preceded and led to the Revolution — a part not chronicled in history but worthy to be recalled as showing the spirit of the immediate descendants of the earliest settlers and of the inhabitants, and quite as spirited and patriotic as that taken by the larger and seaport towns.

I do not know that any recognition of the actions taken appear upon the records of your church, but the meetings of the town people were held in that section of Preston which is in the immediate neighborhood of the First Church of Preston—and were instigated and dominated by men who were members of and prominent in that church. The names that occur most frequently were those of the Averys, Belchers, Coils, Downers, Kinneys, Lesters, Morgans, Motts, Sterrys, Tylers, Witters, and others.

As early as August, 1770, meetings were held to protest against the action of Parliament and the King's Ministers, and to denounce by name all persons whose sentiments were opposed to any declaration of the rights of the people as opposed to what some considered to be the divine rights of kings.

The town continued its agitation, calling successive meetings and declaring the devotion of its inhabitants to the cause of liberty and its opposition to the principle of taxation without representation, or without the consent of the taxed.

When the news came of the battle of Lexington one hundred and eight persons volunteered to take up arms and defend their country. They were commanded by Capt. Ebenezer Witter. For thirteen years and until peace was declared, and the country was free and independent, the same spirit was manifested. Soldiers were enlisted, officers and privates went to the front, and the town undertook the care that the families of those who went to the war should not suffer. Very respectfully, S. CLEVELAND.

As evidence of the patriotic zeal and devotion which had moved and in years after the war closed continued to move church and people, permit me to read the page already referred to, giving account of what we may judge to have been one of the most noteworthy commemorative services in our history.

"Several of the inhabitants of the first Ecclesiastical Society in Preston being convened at Mr. John Crary's on wednesday 12th of Feb.y, 1800 To Consider the propriety of Noticing the 22nd Feb.'y instant being the Birth Day of his Excellency Gen. Geo. Washington, upon mature deliberation it was judg'd proper to pay some particular attention to Said Day and choose Messrs. John Crary, Sam$^l$ Mott, Thomas Meech, Calvin Barstow, Isaac Avery, Daniel Morgan and John Safford Jun$^r$ a committee to regulate the performances of the Day.

"By request the Rev. Lemuel Tyler delivered a sermon and Mr. Amasa Trowbridge an oration well adapted to the occasion.

"About 500 people being assembled at about 11 o'clock Form'd a procession from the revn$^d$ Lemuel Tyler's to the meeting house where Services began by singing the Psalm, Common Metre Prayer, then sung a hymn compos'd on acct of this Great Man's life & Death (viz)" Here follows the hymn, two or three stanzas of which are as follows —

>"What solemn sounds the ear invade!
>What wraps the land in sorrows shade?
>From Heaven the awful mandate flies —
>The Father of his Country dies.

"Where shall our country turn its Eye?
What help remains beneath the Sky?
Our Friend Protector Strength & Trust,
Lies low & mouldering in the Dust.

. . . . . .

"Hear, O Most high! our earnest prayer —
Our country take beneath thy care
When dangers press and foes draws near
May future Washingtons appear."

In thought of the period just reviewed it may well be matter for congratulation among us to-day that we have such a worthy and enduring recognition of the loyal and conspicuous service rendered in those years of conflict by one associated with this church, as is given in the stately and beautiful monument bearing on one of its faces this inscription:

THIS MONUMENT
MARKS THE DWELLING PLACE OF
GEN. SAMUEL MOTT
EMINENT CITIZEN
UPRIGHT MAGISTRATE
SOLDIER OF THE REVOLUTION
FRIEND OF WASHINGTON.*

In this noble memorial to him as a leader we may find commemorated the patriotic and heroic service which many of Preston's sons, together with him, gave to their country in the war of Independence.

The ministry of Mr. Fuller, whose name has already occurred, was very brief. It began about the first of September, 1784. His ordination was on December 8th of that year, and he died early in 1786, not then 23 years old. His youthfulness gives interest to his ministry. That he could be approved as he was for the pastorate when scarcely twenty-one years of age indicates gifts and character of unusual promise.

A period (or "Intermediate Season" as the record has it), of three years without a pastor followed Mr. Fuller's death. In the course of it Dr. Joshua Downer, whose name

---

* See Note A at close.

is still familiar and honored, was "admitted to full communion."

It was near the beginning of 1789 that Mr. Lemuel Tyler was "invited and called without a dissenting voice to settle in the gospel ministry with us" with offer of £100, also "twenty cords of wood annually delivered at his dwelling house," for his support.

As already remarked, Mr. Tyler's pastorate, particularly in its early part and more or less through it all, was affected by the troublous experiences coming from the division in the church. Notwithstanding this, however, there was a gain, the church with eighteen members at the opening of his ministry having twenty-eight at the close.

Shortly after his pastorate began, and before ordination, the Articles and Confession of Faith were revised and attention appears again to have been called to carefulness and thoroughness in the consideration of candidates for membership in the church as shown by its action in the vote "that all persons desiring admission into this church shall previous to their being propounded to full communion give the members opportunity to converse with them and examine them respecting their religious qualifications and motives."

The latter part of Mr. Tyler's pastorate was marked particularly by the building of a new meeting-house, the third erected upon the present site. It was completed, as we infer, some time in the year 1808, the following vote being passed at a Society's meeting on January 18th of that year:

"That Denison Palmer, Jesse Starkweather Jun, John Morgan and Elisha Kimball Jun. be a committee to circulate a subscription to finish the steeple of the meeting-house in P. Society."

Tradition speaks of Mr. Tyler as a preacher of more than ordinary gifts, and calls to service in connection with the meetings of New London Co. Association (which, by the way, as appears from the records of the Association, were, in the pastorate of Mr. Tyler as well as in that of Mr. Rosseter, frequently held in Preston), show that he was held in honor by his brethren in the ministry as well as by the people of his parish. Mr. Tyler's ministry was closed by his death in the year 1810.

The interval of about two years between Mr. Tyler's decease and a successor is wholly unrecorded, but from reference to it in the letter of his acceptance of a call from the church written by Mr. Hyde who followed him, we may conjecture that it was a period not encouraging to the interests of the parish. A few sentences from this letter may be read:

"The prospect of present usefulness, the apparent unanimity among the people after being so long a time in a broken state and one of anxiety and suspense, the uncertainty of union again among the people should they be left long destitute, together with the great and unwearied exertions made for my support, are all circumstances which have operated in my mind to convince me that the providence of God calls me to labor statedly in this part of his vineyard."

Mr. Hyde was installed July 1, 1812. The good promise with which his ministry began was fulfilled in an increase of members and a return, at least in large part, of the old-time prosperity. In the course of the fifteen years of his service, 67 were added by profession, 3 by letter; 18 of those on profession of faith joined in the year 1824. In the year 1813 (Nov. 5), a revised Confession of Faith was adopted on the ground that the old articles "were not sufficiently extensive to add a due degree of solemnity to the rite of admission to the Communion." In 1815, May 31, it may be said incidentally, the Consociation of the churches of New London County was organized here. The Sunday-school connected with this church was probably instituted in this period, destined to be for many in the years to come, a way of entrance into the church, as shown by the fact that very many, perhaps I may say the most, of its additions since have come from its members and, apparently, through the personal influence of its teachers. Another and interesting event in this pastorate and near its opening was the organization of a Woman's Missionary Society. A little quoted from a paper prepared by the late and beloved Mrs. Shedd, the recent secretary of our society, may well have place.

"This organization, as far as can be ascertained from a limited investigation, stands alone among the churches of this vicinity. The reason for this pioneer movement seems to lie in the fact that its first president, wife of the then pastor of this church, was a near relative of Mr. Nott, one of the first missionaries of the American board, and the loving, prayerful sympathy felt for her young relative assumed form and hardened into a definite purpose to 'do what she could,' and the outgrowth of this was the Ladies' Missionary Society. . . . The American Board was then in its infancy, a new, unfledged movement prayed into existence by those brave, devoted young students beside the consecrated haystack in Williamstown. They had been ordained and had gone on their mission so fraught with trials and dangers, only fourteen months before this April meeting of the ladies in the schoolhouse in South Preston. Let us look for a moment at its list of officers; imagine the faces of those women so earnest to do their work and stand in their place in the world, and listen to the voices hushed so many years in silence.

"Mrs. Lydia Barstow was chosen moderator and Miss Louisa Tyler scribe. Mrs. Susan Hyde offered prayer, and the constitution was read and adopted. A choice of officers then made gave to Mrs. Susan Hyde the position of president, to Mrs. Bridget Smith, Mrs. Elizabeth Fanning, and Mrs. Lucy Meech, that of vice-president. Miss Rebecca Tracy was chosen secretary with Mrs. Lydia Barstow to audit accounts.

"In Mrs. Hyde we can see a calm, dignified woman, with a gentle, pleasant manner and a share of executive ability long remembered by the people of this parish. It seems that to her faith and zeal and perseverance is this society largely indebted for its continuance and efficiency for many years. As nearly as can be ascertained, the meetings were still held with regularity, when, by Mr. Hyde's dismissal, the family left the town. . . . Mrs. Lucy Meech, wife of Mr. Stephen Meech, so loved and honored in this church, was one whose life of good deeds was like the course of the brook from an unfailing spring, leaving upon each bank freshness and verdure.

"Miss Rebecca and Miss Sabra Tracy, the secretary and treasurer, were evidently no butterflies, but very industrious and orthodox bees in this hive.

"Mrs. Cynthia Meech was one who not only strove herself to do and to give, but taught her young daughters self-denial for the missionary cause, as a receipt in my possession, bearing the date of July 25, 1818, gives abundant testimony, said receipt affirming that the little girl abstained from the use of sugar that she might contribute to the establishment of a missionary school and that she had sent to the Board fifty cents. . . .

"Miss Louisa Tyler, scribe for the day, is known and well remembered by most of us as Mrs. Dr. Downing, a sweet, gentle, lovely woman, a steadfast friend to this church and its interests both near and remote, showing a love and zeal which, through her long life, knew no faltering or shadow of change.

"We can imagine these with others who came to the schoolhouse on that eventful April day with minds fraught with a new purpose, returning home to their duties and cares, glad of having made so good a beginning. We fully believe 'they builded better than they knew,' for only the last great revealing will show to us what their persevering faith, prayers, and self-denial have wrought."

This glimpse of the women of the church serves to remind us of the large, though it may be unregarded, place they have had in its history. Without their devotion, their self-sacrifice, their gentle but persuasive influence, their fidelity, and withal their gift to inspire cheer and hope and courage, our church life must have had a very different and less worthy record. Like the apostle of old, every minister, surely, has cause not to forget those women who have labored with him in the Gospel.

In numbers, as we know, in all our churches they are the greater company, and let us be slow to say they are less in power.

The fruitful period of Mr. Hyde's pastorate, which closed in 1827, was followed by another period of nearly 20 years, under the ministry of Mr. Collins, marked by still further growth and also by a temperance movement resulting in a great reformation in the community in respect to its drinking habits, interesting reminiscences of which are recalled and told by our older inhabitants at this day. Among those received into the church (in 1841) is the name of Elizabeth Choat, " in the 91st yr. of her age."

Mr. Nathan Hunt, successor to Mr. Collins, was settled here for ten years. In each year there was an increase of members; in the last an addition of 31, the highest number received in any one year in our history. Of those who joined the church in this year of special religious interest, some have passed away, leaving behind them a record of fidelity and devotion such as gives evidence that the revival was not without genuine enduring spiritual power.

With the passing of Mr. Hunt's ministry we come into a time whose history is familiar or within easy reach, so all that need be said is a general word.

Rev. Elijah W. Tucker began his pastorate in January, 1859, and was dismissed in March, 1865.

Rev. Asher H. Wilcox was ordained June 29, 1865, and continued, with a short interval elsewhere, until 1872.

Rev. Andrew J. Hetrick began his service Nov. 3, 1872, and continued until the close of 1874 (Dec. 27th). Rev. George A. Bryan received a call to the church in April, and commenced his ministry in May, 1876, to remain eight years.

The year of largest accession in this period is the year 1871, when fifteen were admitted to membership.

Each one of these pastors, by his personal character, by his gifts, and by service rendered, has, I would fain believe, won for himself an enduring place in the esteem and love of his people.

Concerning the most recent years, I would speak of one thing, and that is the renewal — in the midst of a depletion by death and removal that has been serious — of that spirit so nobly shown in those who, a century ago, gave freely of their substance for the church's continued maintenance and usefulness. Examples of this spirit given in these last years occur to us as we meet here, and bring to remembrance those who, in their life and in their death, had generous thought for this church's needs and well-being. How assuredly these, with others who may have had just as true a devotion, would have been glad to be with us, gathered here and now in this interesting, praiseful commemoration and hopeful outlook. Perhaps they are.

This is but an imperfect review, but enough may have been said or signified to kindle gratitude within us for a past that we may believe has been for the betterment of this community, in which, for which, the life of this church has been lived. This town of Preston, which, in its beginning, so fostered and honored the truth and the worship of God, has been a better town because of the church that it organized here than it could have been without it. With it there came both restraints and inspirations that naught else could have given. Says Charles Kingsley: "Will anyone mention any civilization, past or present, whose center has not been (as long as it has been living and progressive) a church?" The civilization of New England, of any town within its bounds, is a civilization that, more than aught else, or all else, the church has brought. And this because it teaches good morals, cherishes education, honors and inspires patriotism, works for brotherhood.

And, amid all changes that are going on, generation by generation, century by century, I see not why it is not so to be. "To the world's end," again says Kingsley, "a *church* . . . will be the center and symbol of every civilization that is worthy of the name."

And this will be because it takes for its guide and inspiration and holds forth to others the Word of God. Not two hundred, but two thousand years ago, the Psalmist said, "Thy word is a lamp unto my feet, a light unto my path." A greater than the Psalmist said, "Sanctify them by *thy truth;* thy word is truth."

The church has been, is, and will be, a chief beneficent power because the source of its influence is the Bible, whose truth remains, endures. "Heaven and earth shall pass away, but my words shall not pass away." "The grass withereth, the flower thereof falleth away, but the word of the Lord endureth forever." "And this is the word which by the gospel is preached unto you."

## NOTE A.

An extant manuscript of Gen. Mott, written in an even and clear hand, and still very well preserved, deserves mention, particularly in that it contains an unreserved account of certain of his *religious* experiences as indicated by the following words upon the title page:

"Meditations on various Religious Subjects Both in prose and in Verse

"In the front of which is Related some of the Discoverys and Experiences of the Author in what He has reason to hope, was the work of the Divine and Holy Spirit Carried on by the Mighty Power of God to the Conviction and He hopes Conversion of His Soul whereby tho with The Deepest Humility and Self abasement admiring At the free and Abundant Grace of God in Christ Jesus He hopes he is Raised from Death unto Life by the Power of the Resurrection of Jesus Christ our Lord From the Dead.

"Not of works lest any man should boast. Paul"

The account opens with the words: "Tis no Doubt the most Delightsome and Satisfactory meditation to Call Over in our minds the Mysterious and all mercifull workings of the Spirit of God in our Effectual Calling. But when we are about to give to our fellow men an account of That Blessed work it ought be Done with Deep Humiliation and the Greatest Care and Caution Lest we should Through our Shortsightedness or otherwise add to our Real Experience or Relate such things as being wrought by the Spirit of God which he was not the author of."

What follows relates in great part to his conversion, which occurred while he was yet a youth:

"The first Dawning of a Concern in me for a future State was if I Remember Right when I was between Sixteen and Seventeen years of age. Tho I had before a sort of a Watch over myself Concerning Prophane Language to which I had before obtained a kind of Traditional Aversion but now I began to take some particular Notice of some particular passages of Scripture which Contained any alarming Threatenings of God to the Wicked." Other things deepened his conviction and brought him at length into great distress of mind. Among these he mentions the prayer of a certain man, under awakening like himself, offered one evening "in the open field with an affecting and somewhat loud voice when he supposed himself out of the hearing of anybody."

This spiritual anxiety, at times intense, was protracted. "Thus I continued if I Remember right some months and could find no Comforting or Refreshing Cordials in any book that I read or any Sermon that I heard." The means of his enlightenment and relief came at length in a discourse in a book of sermons of Mr. George Whitfield, upon which he "lit" in his search "for something to help." The text of the sermon was Matt. 22:42 — "What think ye of Christ." "The discourse seemed," he says, "to open to me an Intire new field of Contemplation." The great change effected may better be told in his own words. "I went about the Business of the Day, But my mind was vastly more Exercised with the concerns of a Future State than with the concerns of any present Comfort or Existence, all worldly concerns seem'd wholly to vanish and be of no moment with me. Futurity and the things of futurity took the ascendancy and Wrought vehemently on all my mental faculties When all as in A moment the Eyes of my understanding were opened and I trust that God in his Infinite Mercy and Condecention, being moved in himself according to his Eternal purpose, was pleased to Reveal himself through Jesus Christ to my soul the Sensation I now had I however can find no words to express and I think before the Great Omniscient and Omnipotent Jehovah I can Honestly say I really did not know for some space of time whether I was in the body or out. It seem'd as if I had been Drawn or Caught up, not bodily but spiritually (and in a manner altogether unknown to me before) where I seem'd to behold the Transcendant Glory of the Omnipotent God and Jesus the Mediator of the New Covenant at his right hand."

The remaining pages of the narrative are devoted mostly to further account of remarkable spiritual experiences in the beginning of his Christian life. It closes with a word of sorrow that he had not lived so as to make them abiding, but also with expression of comfort and joy in them as ground for faith and hope. "May the God of all grace who was pleased to reveal to me some glimpse of his ineffable glory, keep that which I have committed to him untill the time when I shall with the rest of his unworthy flock be received into those blessed mansions before the throne of his glory."

The narrative was written, probably, about the year 1773. It is, therefore, of somewhat peculiar interest in that it is a disclosure of a deep undercurrent of thought and feeling upon religious subjects in one who was actively engaged, and, doubtless, apparently absorbed, in civil and military affairs.

In the manuscript or manuscripts (there are two) besides this story of religious experience, there are several poems : " The Creation of Man," " Ode to the Memory of Rev. M$^r$ George Whitfield," " Soliloquy upon Human Existence, Frailty & Mortality," etc. Also, " A Short Treatise on the Duty and Necessity of Universal Christian Fellowship and Absurdity and Wickedness of Christians Refusing Fellowship with those of other Denominations." This is quite an elaborate argument covering nearly sixty closely-written pages.— *Ed.*

NOTE B.

The following is of interest in regard to action of town on the question of division. — *Ed.*

PRESTON RECORDS.

Town meeting Book pages 158 & 159 —

" At a Town Meting Legally warned on y$^e$ 19$^{th}$ of January 17$\frac{18}{19}$ it was Voted that there Shall be two Sosieties in this Town by a fair Division and It was Also Voted at y$^e$ Same Meting that J$^n$J$^n$ Billings John Brown Joseph Gears Cap$^{tt}$ Parke John Ames and Caleb Ffobes Shall be a Com$^{tt}$ to Make a fair Division of this Town to be two Sosieties and to Make their Return to y$^e$ Town att y$^e$ Next town Meting."

" We whose Names are under written being a Committy appointed and Chosen by y$^e$ town to Devide y$^e$ town for two Sosieties we met togather for y$^t$ work on February y$^e$ 9$^{th}$ Day 17$\frac{18}{19}$ and we Did agree to Devide y$^e$ town as followeth, beginning att Norwich Line thence y$^e$ Devideing line to Run half way betwixt y$^e$ hous of Jonathan Gears and y$^e$ Now Dwelling hous of John Richards and from thence a Straight line twenty Rods East from y$^e$ Now Dwelling hous of Sam$^{ll}$ Sterry and So y$^e$ Same Line tell it Coms to Stoningtoun bounds we also Do agree that y$^e$ North Sosiety Shall hold one half of y$^e$ ministry Land or to haue two hundred and fifty acres of Land out of y$^e$ Common Land

      John parke
      Will$^m$ billing$^s$
      Jno Brown
      Joh$^n$ Ames
      Caleb ffobes "

" The aboue written was Excepted att a town Meting Legally

warned on y*e* 9*th* of February 17$\frac{6}{18}$ by a legal vote and Delieured to me to be Entred

"Test Sam*ll* Sterry T*n* Cleark

"M*r* John Stanton Joseph prentes Sam*ll* Lenardson Sam*ll* Guile and Benaiman Guile protest against y*e* aboue written at y*e* Same meting aboue Sd

"And it was Allso voted att y*e* Same Meting that when y*e* North Sosietie See Caus to Draw of they Shall be a Destinct Sosietie of them Selves and Enuested with all Town priueledges and to be freed from all Town Rates and Charges from y*e* Antient part of y*e* town"

"At a Town Meting Legally warned on ye 6*th* Day of Desemb*r* It was voted that y*e* town of Preston Shall pay y*e* Rate that is now Dew to M*r* Treat as they use to Doe formerly and that ye preasent towns Men Shall make y*e* Rate as they were formerly use to Doe and that y*e* North Society Shall haue free Liberty to attend upon ye publick worship of God tell y*e* next June Inseuing y*e* Date hearof att y*e* Meting hous And att y*e* Same Meting it was voted y*t* Each of y*e* Societies in this town of preston Shall for y*e* time to Come haue power in and of themselves to leavie taxes and Rates to Rais Money when and as often as need Shall Require for y*e* promoting procuring and maintaining of y*e* publick worship of God in Each of y*e*.aforesd Sosieties. And itt was allso voted att y*e* Same Meting that y*e* Nort Sosiety Shall hold one half of y*e* ministry Land and that y*e* South Sosiety Shall haue and hold y*e* other half of ye Ministry Land which Sd land is to be Equally Deuided both for quantity and quality by a Com*tt* Chosen by y*e* town for that work And itt was voted that Cap*tt* Billings Injn ffreeman Sergn*t* Geers and Caleb fobes Shall be a Com*tt* to make a fair and Equill Division of y*e* abouesd Land and if they Cannot agree they are to Call in one inDefirant person belongin to one of y*e* nearest towns to asist in makeing y*e* aforesd Diuision" —

# III

## THE PRESTON SEPARATE CHURCH

# THE PRESTON SEPARATE CHURCH.

THE CHAIRMAN: About the middle of the last century there rolled over parts of New England a wave of religious enthusiasm,— started, in part, perhaps, by the fervent preaching of the Rev. George Whitefield. Some of the results of that revival threatened great harm to the churches, but out of that movement have sprung, under the providence of God, some of the most valued principles of religious liberty. I refer to the Separatist movement. The Separatists were sometimes called "New Lights." I suspect the full significance of that movement is not generally and fully understood, and I am going to call upon a lawyer to unravel for us some of the knotty points and throw some "*new light*" upon the subject,— a gentleman whose father was for many years an honored officer in this church, — one, too, who represents the sort of contribution which this church, from time to time, makes to the city of Norwich — Amos A. Browning, Esq.

ADDRESS BY AMOS A. BROWNING, ESQ.

This anniversary celebration more than memorializes a distant event. Before us passes in review the rich and varied history of this ancient church. We recall its spiritual life and influence, its several edifices, its inspired pastors, its long list of righteous men, its devout women not a few.

Every picture has its lights and shades. The history of no organization would be of value which recorded only its successes and advancements. In the brief time allotted to me I am to recall a dissension in the church which removed some of its most influential members and their families, and tell the story of the establishment, growth, and decline of the church of the seceders. Happily, to-day we can review contentions in which, perchance, our own great-grandfathers and great-grandmothers had a part — contentions which arrayed neighbor against neighbor, and even brother against brother — without animosity or kindling emotion. The actors have long since passed away. The controversies have ceased to cause heart-burnings and are well-nigh forgotten. But they are interesting matters of history and may afford us some simple lesson of faith or charity, though they seemed ill-fitted to make for righteousness either among those of that day or the generations that were to be.

It was on Tuesday, March 17, 1747, that a little company of six persons took the responsibility of organizing, outside the sanction of the law, the Separate Church of Preston. In language lofty and sublime, the Separate record declares that they entered into "solemn covenant with God and one another, under ye sweet and powerful agency of ye Holy Ghost." Their names were Hezekiah Park, John Avery, Thomas Woodward, Paul Park, Ephraim and Martha Jones. Probably all these persons had been members of this First Congregational church. Their number by no means represents the extent of the disaffection, however, for others soon afterwards transferred their connection from the old to the new church.

And what caused the separation? To answer this question we must take a wider view, for it was but part of a general movement especially pronounced in Eastern Connecticut. The extensive religious revival which began in 1733, under the preaching of Jonathan Edwards at Northampton, and was known as the Great Awakening, was followed, unfortunately, in many places, by dissension. A party called New Lights sprung up, who boastfully claimed special divine direction, and denounced the established churches and their ministers in unmeasured terms as anti-Christ and hypocritical. They demanded greater freedom in the matter of lay preaching, complained of the Presbyterian tendencies in the churches which had resulted in the establishment of the consociation, and had much to say against a paid ministry. They maintained that churches should be free from governmental control, their views in this respect doubtless receiving added coloring from the fact that they were the "outs." More than all were they grieved at the admission into the churches of persons not professing conversion, who became what was known as half-covenant members, having the privilege of baptizing their children, and, in some churches, of joining in the communion. Upon the other hand, the zeal of the Separatists led them into many extravagances of word and act, which caused the conservative party to denounce them as fanatical. Outcries, shoutings, and bodily writhings sometimes made their meetings disorderly. A fierce exhorter at Norwich expressed the delight it would give him to witness the everlasting destruction of certain persons named, and called upon God to witness that he was speaking under divine influence. At a meeting held by the evangelist, Rev. James Davenport, in New London, books and jewels were brought by his hearers, at his suggestion, and consigned to the flames, in order to cut off, as he said, the idolatrous affection of the people for worldly things. The conservative party insisted upon an educated, and, in consequence, a paid ministry, and viewed with disfavor the illiteracy and extravagance of the Separate preachers.

These grievances occasioned, at first, separate meetings. At length, however, the antagonistic feeling between the two parties had become so strong that reconciliation seemed impossible, and Separate churches began to be organized. Canterbury and Mansfield took the lead in the eastern part of the State by establishing Separate churches in 1745. The movement, once inaugurated, went rapidly forward. Twenty New Light bodies sprung up in Eastern Connecticut in half a dozen years. In nearly every town of New London and Windham counties, Separate meetings were held and congregations gathered, which, in most instances, were cemented by church covenants. The established churches viewed with astonishment the swift maturity of the dissenting movement. The very foundations of ecclesiastical order seemed to be breaking up.

Events in Preston kept pace with the movement in other places. Separate meetings were held during the pastorate of Rev. Salmon Treat, which terminated in 1744. In 1746, twenty-three persons were summoned before the church as offenders, because they refused to unite with the church in its ordinances and attended a separate assembly on the

Lord's day. Later these persons were all more or less prominently connected with the Separate Church.

Paul Park, then twenty-six years of age, was chosen pastor of the new church and was ordained July 15, 1747, the Separatists of Stonington, Norwich, Canterbury, and Plainfield being represented. In Trumbull's History of Connecticut, it is related, as illustrative of the extravagant pretensions of the Separatists to divine direction, that in the solemn charge given to the young pastor, he was enjoined by no means to study or premeditate what he should say in public, but to speak as the Spirit should give him utterance.

During its earlier years, the new church, small though it was, enjoyed a good degree of prosperity. By the end of the first year the membership had doubled. In 1748, ten new members were added; in 1749, nine; in 1751, nineteen. In the latter year the membership had grown to exceed fifty. Forty families and three hundred persons were represented. Ten years after its organization, it had received a total of eighty members. But internal dissensions about infant or household baptism had arisen before the end of the first decade, which at length resulted in secession from the seceders. Here again the history of the Preston Separate church synchronizes so closely with that of the Separatists elsewhere that we must recur to the wider survey.

At first Separatists and Baptists held a most friendly attitude. They agreed in manner of religious worship and in most matters of doctrine and discipline. Both likewise opposed the Connecticut church establishment and compulsory rate-paying. Their differences were in regard to baptism, especially as to proper subjects to receive that rite.

For a time this proved no bar to co-operation and fellowship. But soon the Baptists discovered that they were unwilling to commune with those they deemed unbaptized and the Separatists would not consent to re-baptize those sprinkled in infancy. A great council was held at Exeter, R. I., at which 27 churches were represented and a union effected. It was agreed that "if any baptized by sprinkling or in infancy, and belong to a Congregational church desire baptism by plunging and went to a Baptist elder and was immersed, or if a brother had his child baptized, neither should be censurable."

But how powerless are the resolves and decrees of councils to bind dissenting minds! In 1754 another great council was found necessary. It met in Stonington (probably in that part of the town which is now North Stonington), and 24 churches in Connecticut, 8 in Massachusetts, 7 in Rhode Island, and 1 on Long Island were represented. The Preston Separate Church sent its pastor, Deacons John Avery and Moses Morse, and Brothers Joseph Witter, Robert Park, and Gideon Safford. Like its predecessor, the council sat for three days. But the outcome was a permanent disagreement. Elder Solomon Paine of Canterbury, in keeping with his aggressive temperament, ascribed the result to "bad temper in the Baptists." His brother, Elder Elisha Paine, the Apostle of the Separates, as he has been styled, more gravely and discreetly declared that the difficulty sprung from opposite principles.

In the Preston Separate Church, differences about infant or household baptism appeared as early as 1752, and culminated in 1757. The local church was as unsuccessful as the great council had been in restoring harmony. Ten years after its founding nine members were dismissed by a testimonial letter, stating that the disaffected members held to " Baptist principles of baptism and we to infant or household baptism." The names of those dismissed were Daniel Whipple, Samuel Clark, Samuel Palmer, Jemimah Clark, Abigail Clark, Eunice Whipple, Freelove Pettis, Bridget Gates, and Anna Branch.

The Preston Separate Church continued, however, to stoutly uphold the principle of infant or household baptism. Its records show that at least 362 children were baptized under its auspices. Indeed, the last entry in the church chronicles is that of the baptism of Edwin, infant son of Benjamin F. Park,— a witness of the firm adherence of the church to the doctrine and practice to the end. This child was known to us in later years as Dr. Park of New Haven.

As to the form of baptism, the same strictness was not observed. While sprinkling probably was the only method practiced by Elder Park, after his time, there were several baptisms by immersion.

There is a tradition, by no means improbable, that some of the first meetings of the Preston Separatists were held in the open air. Strange as it seems, the records of the church make no reference to any edifice. We know, however, that a meeting-house was in existence as early as 1751, that is, within four years after the organization of the church. It was located two or three miles south of the village of Preston, a little north of the Jeremiah Halsey house,— a landmark in its day which later became the property of Warren Cook. A field on the Cook farm is still known as the meeting-house lot. The structure was built of pine brought from the Ledyard cedar swamp. A wide center aisle led from the double entrance doors to the pulpit, which was built small and high, according to the fashion of the times, with sounding board above it. The building may have been 45 to 50 feet long by 35 to 40 feet wide. On each side of the aisle were square box pews. There was neither vestibule, carpet, chimney, bell, or tower. Foot stoves in those times were an important article. It was before the age of light wagons and long before the age of Sunday-schools. A sermon less than an hour long was short of the ideal, and the prayers, like the English drum-beat which Webster immortalized, went quite around the globe. That interesting social adjunct of later times, the horse shed, was wanting. Those who came long distances on horseback tied their animals to the trees about the grounds.

The meeting-house is remembered by a few persons still living. After serving the purpose for which it was constructed, for perhaps three-quarters of a century, it was sold and the proceeds devoted to improvements at the Avery cemetery.*

One of the grievances with which the Separatists had to contend was their taxation for the support of the established churches. The Separatists were peculiarly unfortunate, for while the Baptists and Quakers were allowed the benefit of the English Toleration Acts, the Colonial Assembly had

---

* See note hereto.

decreed that only those should take the benefit of the Acts who had a "distinguishing character from Congregationalists or Presbyterians," an enactment aimed of course at the Separatists.

The Preston church united with the other Separatists in petitioning the Assembly, and later the crown, for relief. This church also petitioned the Assembly independently for its own exemption from taxpaying.

A duly attested copy of the memorial of 33 prominent members of the Preston Separate Church to the Colonial Assembly at New Haven, in October, 1751, is still in existence. The respondents summoned were the First and Second Ecclesiastical societies of Preston (the latter being now Pachaug), the Second Society of Groton (now Ledyard), the Fourth Society of Norwich (Long Society), and the Second Society of Stonington (now North Stonington). This interesting memorial set forth that some of the members of the Preston Separate church resided in each of the above-named societies; that all were within eight miles of their meeting-house; that they were law-abiding citizens and conscientious dissenters; that many of them had been imprisoned for refusal to pay church rates to the societies named; and asked that they be given the benefit of the Toleration Acts and discharged from rate paying to said societies.

But petition and remonstrance were for a long time of no avail. Among those who are known to have been imprisoned was the senior deacon, John Avery. He refused either to pay the tax or consent that it should be paid in his behalf. But the authorities were inexorable and it seemed that he was destined to life-long imprisonment for conscience's sake. At length, through the importunity of his wife, he was induced to pay the tax and was discharged.

Not before 1784 did the Separatists secure any adequate relief. In that year the Saybrook Platform was made no longer obligatory and all persons were made free to support such church as they preferred, provided they contributed to some form of worship.

The time of greatest prosperity of the Preston church seems to have been at the period of the Revolution. Even before this it had become evident that the Separate Church movement must fail. Indeed, no Separate church was formed in Eastern Connecticut after 1751, and soon after that date some of those existing showed signs of decay. The early and zealous leaders of the Separatists, Frothingham, Stevens, Solomon Paine, Willoughby, Denison, Fuller, soon passed away. Of those that remained, apparently the foremost was he whom his colleagues in the Separate ministry were wont to call "our beloved brother, Paul Park."

The end of the century found the Preston Separate Church rapidly declining. Its venerable pastor had become aged and infirm. He died in 1802, aged 81 years, and his place could not be filled. For nine years after 1801 the church records are silent, save an entry of two persons to membership in 1806, and of three in 1807. In 1815 an effort was made to revive the church, and twelve new members were added to the roll. In less than two years more the record ceased to be kept, and the church was extinct. The last entry is under date of July 27, 1817.

The most kindly feeling existed between the Separate churches of Preston and North Stonington. They together remained into this century, standing side by side like two weather-beaten oaks that had survived their companions. The year before the Preston Separate Church expired, that in North Stonington joined with the regular Congregational church at that place in erecting a meeting-house. It was occupied by both congregations for eleven years, when a union was effected, and the last of the Separate churches in this county, if not in the State, ceased to be.

But what shall we say of Elder Paul Park, the inspiration of the Preston Separate church? No doubt a man of superior natural endowments was this farmer preacher. He brought to his work neither education nor theological training. We can imagine that he possessed gifts of speech however, such that he could in large measure follow the injunction not to premeditate what he should utter in public.

For fifty years he held his flock about him, ministering to them as pastor, kept with his own hand the records of the church, maintained regular Sunday services, participated prominently in every council in which his church was represented, while at the same time supporting himself and family upon his farm, without ever receiving one dollar as salary or stated remuneration. He resided at what is still known as the Park homestead, in the southeastern part of the town of Preston. Ministers' rates were denounced by the Separatists. The only pecuniary assistance he received from his people, it is believed, was the aid his parishioners may have rendered him about his farming work. We can imagine for ourselves the sewing bees and the husking bees that may have been held annually upon the elder's plantation.

In 1797 Elder Park preached his half-century sermon, which is said to have taken several Sundays for its delivery. It is still preserved in his own handwriting. Large audiences gathered to hear him, few if any of whom had been participants in the early struggles of the church, and the story he told with emotion fell upon the ears of a new generation.

The visitor to the Avery Cemetery stops a moment to gaze at a stone which bears for its inscription the words of Paul the Apostle, "I have fought a good fight, I have finished my course, I have kept the faith." It marks the last resting place of Elder Paul Park.

Next to Elder Park in influence in the Preston Separate Church was John Avery, who was for forty years its deacon, and died in 1789. Other deacons were Moses Morse, Elisha Fitch, Joseph Tyler, Jonathan Brewster, Amos Avery, Jedediah Palmer, Walter Palmer, and Amasa Standish. The subsequent church relations of those who worshiped at the Separate Church, and their descendants, we cannot attempt to trace. Some returned to this church, some became Methodists, some Baptists, and some Universalists.

The book of records of the church, nearly all in the handwriting of Elder Park, is still in existence. A few years ago it passed from hand to hand as an interesting memento, but it is now carefully preserved in the archives of the New London County Historical Society.

The Separate Church movement was destined to failure, but some of the principles that it stood for have survived. The regulation of churches, their principles and practice, by law, has been done away, and the divorcement of church and State long ago became complete. The pernicious practice of receiving into church fellowship persons not professing conversion has been condemned, and forever discarded by Congregational and kindred churches. The movement pointed to the conclusion that the church must depend for its success upon the faith and devotion of its members, rather than upon temporal power and influence.

Alas, that greater toleration and liberty could not have been shown upon both sides. Alas, that their agreements should not have been magnified rather than their differences, and that they could not have dwelt together in harmony. The established churches needed something of the enthusiasm and Christian zeal of the Separatists. The latter needed the cultivating and conservative influence of the educated ministry at the head of the regular churches.

The lesson, so plain that he who runs may read, is that long ago written for all ages,

"Above all these things put on CHARITY, which is the bond of perfectness."

### NOTE.

The letter given below, taken from the *Norwich Record*, is of interest in connection with Mr. Browning's description of the Separate Church edifice. — Ed.

"Allow me through your columns to supplement the address of Lawyer Amos A. Browning, delivered at the bi-centennial of the Preston Church, to give a brief description of the old Separate Church edifice, which stood on my father's farm, which he purchased of Col. Jeremiah Halsey, grandfather of Jeremiah Halsey, late of Norwich.

"Nothing could be less imposing than the old Separate meeting-house. Like an old barn in appearance, and the field in which it stood was not decently smoothed. No gravel walks, no shade trees, no cheering flowers, nor any of the accessories of the modern church edifice. There was no bell, no belfry, no chimney. There was no gallery.

"Such, in brief, is a description of the old Separate Church or meeting-house, situated two miles south of Preston City, in Cooktown.

"One word about the congregation. Those hardy old pioneers attended church for the express purpose of worshiping God. They came on horseback (no wagons or carriages in those days) and on foot — some a distance of eight miles. They were all warmly clad in

## BI-CENTENNIAL CELEBRATION. 59

good woolen clothes manufactured and made up at home. No silks or satins, no ribbons or laces or feathers. The latter were left to the half-naked savage to adorn himself when on the warpath.

"When the old meeting-house was abandoned some of the congregation affiliated with the Methodists, who held services in the schoolhouse on Preston Plain; some with the churches of Preston City, Griswold, and Poquetanuck. Many generations have passed since meetings were held in this rude temple, which was purchased by my father, and demolished some time in the early thirties.

JAMES A. COOK."

Preston, Nov. 21, 1898.

# IV

## THE PASTORS OF THE CHURCH

# THE PASTORS OF THE CHURCH.

THE CHAIRMAN: The ancient pamphlet which I hold in my hand is the printed copy of a sermon preached one hundred and ten years ago next May by the Rev. Benjamin Trumbull of North Haven, at the ordination of the Rev. Lemuel Tyler as fourth pastor of this church. Besides this and two copies which are in the library of Yale College, I do not know that there are any other copies of this sermon extant. It may serve to help connect the present with the past if I state that this Rev. Lemuel Tyler was the great-great-grandfather of the children of the speaker. We are now to have an address giving sketches of some of the pastors of this church. The one who is to give this address is a member of a family whose name appears often, from the very earliest, and always in honorable connection, in the annals of the town and of the church,— one who went from this community to Yale College and to Yale Theological Seminary, and who returned from his studies to hold long and successful pastorates in his native county and near his native town. He has been a prophet not without honor in his own country. I ask your attention to the Rev. John Avery of Norwich.

## SKETCHES BY REV. JOHN AVERY.

I am to speak of the ministers who have lived in this place and been pastors or acting pastors of this church from the date of its organization down to the present time — a period of 200 years. The whole number of these ministers is twelve. Their names are as follows:

1. Salmon Treat,
2. Asher Rossiter,
3. Jonathan Fuller,
4. Lemuel Tyler,
5. John Hyde,
6. Augustus B. Collins,
7. Nathan S. Hunt,
8. Elijah W. Tucker,
9. Asher H. Wilcox,
10. Andrew J. Hetrick,
11. George A. Bryan,
12. Richard H. Gidman.

The first eight of these ministers are dead. The first four — Treat, Rossiter, Fuller, and Tyler — began and completed their ministerial lives here. Here they died, and here they were buried. The next four — Hyde, Collins, Hunt, and Tucker — had been settled in other places before they came here, and were settled elsewhere after they left this place.

The first pastor of the church was

### SALMON TREAT.

He was a native of Wethersfield, where he was born about 1672. He was a son of James Treat and a grandson of Richard Treat, who was one of the first settlers of the town of Wethersfield. His uncle, Robert Treat of Milford, was Governor of Connecticut from 1683 to 1687, and again, from 1689 to 1698 — thirteen years in all. His cousin, Samuel Treat, oldest son of the Governor, was pastor of the church in Eastham, Mass. Several of his ancestors were clergymen in England before the family came to America. The subject of this sketch was *not* "educated at Yale College," as is affirmed upon his tombstone in the cemetery, but was a graduate of Harvard University in 1694, eight years before Yale College sent out its first graduate. In 1702, the year in which the first class, consisting of a single individual, was graduated from Yale, Mr. Treat, who had now been four years in the ministry, received in common with three other young men — all of them graduates of Harvard — the *honorary degree* of A. M. from the newly-established Connecticut college. In 1695-'96-'97 he preached in Greenwich, Conn., and received a call to settle there, which he declined. As early as Dec. 15, 1697, arrangements began to be made with reference to his settlement in Preston. But it was nearly a year before the result was fully consummated in his ordination, which occurred on the 16th or 17th of Nov., 1698. On the council which met here at that time to organize the church and ordain the minister, all the churches that had been organized in Eastern Connecticut up to that date, except the church in Woodstock, were represented. But there were only four of them, viz., the church in New London, the church in Norwich Town, the church in Stonington, and the

## BI-CENTENNIAL CELEBRATION. 65

church in Lyme. The church in Norwich Town just at this time was without a pastor, and was represented only by Dea. Simon Huntington as a delegate. The three ministers who conducted the services were Rev. James Noyes of Stonington, Rev. Moses Noyes of Lyme, a brother of the Stonington minister, and Rev. Gurdon Saltonstall of New London, who afterward became Governor of Connecticut. As Mr. Treat's was the first, so it was the longest pastorate the church has ever enjoyed,—continuing, as it did, from 1698 to 1744—a period of forty-six years. At his own request it was terminated by action of council on the same day that his successor was inducted into office. Probably he did as much to give shape and character to the community as any man that ever lived in it. Many questions not necessarily connected with his ministerial work were referred to him and decided by him; *e. g.*, when there was a difference of opinion among the people as to the place where the meeting-house should stand, and the matter was referred to him to decide, he gave four acres of land for the purpose, and upon it designated the site which has from that day to this been occupied by the Congregational church edifice. So the location of the cemetery, as to which the people were not fully united, was fixed by him. In 1750—six years after his dismission—he gave to the church and society the sum of eighty-seven (87) pounds and ten (10) shillings, as the nucleus of a fund for the support of the gospel. One condition attached to the gift was that no professor of the Church of England, nor such Separatists as are among us, nor the Baptists, nor any other sect than the Presbyterian (*i. e.*, Congregational) society and church, that had formerly been under his pastoral care, should have the benefit of it. Another condition was that "the gift should profit his children, that they might dwell on his farm that his old and his new house stood on," and be exempted from paying for the maintenance of a minister and the service of God. This gift was accepted by the society. Mr. Treat, throughout his professional career, was an active participant in ecclesiastical affairs in Eastern Connecticut, being often called to sit on ecclesiastical councils convened for the organization of churches, the ordination and dismission of ministers, and the settlement of church difficulties. Mr. Treat's first wife was Miss Dorothy Noyes, daughter of Rev. James Noyes of Stonington. Her family, like that of her husband, had a great many ministers in it. Her father and her uncle were ministers in this county. Her grandfather, James Noyes, Sen., was pastor of the church in Newbury, Mass. Her great-grandfather, William Noyes, was rector of the diocese of Salisbury, England. On the side of her mother, Dorothy Stanton, she could also trace back her line through one or more ministers. The house of Mr. Treat stood on the north side of the road leading from the Baptist church to Norwich, not far from the site of the blacksmith shop of Mr. Robbins. The first wife of Mr. Treat was the mother of all of his nine children — two sons and seven daughters. She died at the age of 38, when her youngest child was only eight or ten days old. In about two years he was married to Mrs. Mary Park, widow of Capt. John Park, whose home was on the west side of Avery's Plains, the place now occupied by Mr. Charles Hewitt, Sen. Mr. Treat died Jan. 6, 1762, in the 90th year of his age. He has numerous descendants living in different parts of the country. Several of his great-great-grandchildren, with their children and their children's children, are here to-day.

The second pastor of the church was

### ASHER ROSSITER.

He was a son of Timothy and Abigail [Penfield] Rossiter of Durham, Conn., where he was born, Oct. 16, 1715. His ancestors came from England in 1630; settled first in Dorchester, Mass., afterward, in 1636, moved to Windsor, Conn., and later still, to Guilford. His grandfather, Josiah Rossiter of Guilford, occupied important positions in the colonial government of Connecticut. His grandmother, Sarah Sherman, belonged to the same family in which Gen. Wm. T. Sherman and Hon. John Sherman have appeared in our day. Rev. Asher Rossiter was graduated at Yale College in 1742. At that time the names of the students on the Yale catalogues were arranged, not in alphabetical order, but according to the social standing of the families to which they belonged. This fashion prevailed from the time the first catalogue was issued early in the last century, on to 1767. And in the triennial catalogues that are published in our own times the names of the students in all those early classes stand in the same order in which they were originally arranged. The sons of judges, I think, were placed first, then the sons of clergymen, then the sons of farmers, mechanics, laborers, etc. A story used to be told at Yale, of one young man, who was ambitious to have his name stand well up on the list, that, when asked what was the occupation of his father, replied that he was a member of the bench. So his name was placed among those of the judges' sons at the head of the list. When, at length, the real facts of the case came out it was found that his father was a member of the bench only in the sense that he was accustomed to sit on the *bench* of a *shoemaker*. Mr. Rossiter's name, on the triennial catalogue, stands just above the middle — seven above him and nine below him. Of the seven above him not a single one is set down as having acquired any distinction whatever ; but of the nine below him one became a judge and eight became clergymen. So that the relative social positions of the families were completely reversed in a single generation.

Mr. Rossiter was licensed to preach by the New London Association Nov. 18, 1742, and began to supply the pulpit in Preston on the 21st of the same month. He received a call to settle, in March, 1743 ; accepted the same in the October following ; and was ordained March 14, 1744, Dr. Benjamin Lord of Norwich Town, preaching the sermon, and Mr. Treat, the retiring pastor, offering the ordaining prayer. Mr. Rossiter's ministry was accomplished in troublous times. During the 37½ years of its continuance the country was engaged in war just about half the time. First came the first French and Indian War, from 1744 to 1748, then the second French and Indian War, from 1755 to 1763 ; and, at length, the Revolution, from 1776 to 1783. These three wars covered some 18 or 20 years. The peace of the church, too, was greatly disturbed by the rise and progress of the Separate movement. A large number of the members, resisting what they regarded as an unjust and oppressive law, which required them to support the church by the same rule of taxation under which they supported the civil government, and aspiring, too, to a higher degree of spirituality than they conceived to exist in the church of the standing order, seceded, and, at length, established a Separate church, so called, which had its house of worship erected some two miles south of this village. This Separate movement began before Mr. Rossiter came here, and the troubles which grew out of it continued through the whole of his ministry. Much of the time the Separate church was apparently more prosperous than the church from which it had separated. There were many additions to the one, while there were but few additions to the other. Sometimes there would be a period of half a dozen years or more in which not a single addition to this church would be made. This state of things continued up to the time of Mr. Rossiter's death, which occurred Nov. 17, 1781, in the 66th year of his age, and the 38th of his ministry. Mr. Rossiter baptized some 370 persons, and married about 160 couples. He lived in the house known as the Dr. Downer house, now occupied by Mrs. Charles Palmer and her daughter. He had six children — four sons and two daughters. Among his descendants now living in this region are Mr. Lucas Witter and his sisters, and Mr. Punderson Geer, in the south part of this town, Mr. Charles Smith and Miss Margaret Smith in Norwich, and Mr. Asher Rossiter Herrick and his sister, Mrs. Stark, in Central Village.

### JONATHAN FULLER

was the third pastor of the church. He was born in Mansfield, Aug. 17, 1763; was a son of Jonathan Fuller, M.D., and Sibyl Meacham, a grandson of Rev. Daniel Fuller of Willington, Conn., also a grandson, on his mother's side, of Rev. Joseph Meacham of Coventry, Conn. His first ancestor in this country was Thomas Fuller of Dedham, Mass., who came to America in 1635. The subject of this sketch was a graduate of Yale College in the class of 1783, the class which contained such men as Hon. David Dagget, Chief Justice of the Supreme Court of Conn., Hon. John Cotton Smith, Gov. of Connecticut, and Rev. Richard S. Storrs, D.D. He was ordained here, Dec. 8, 1784. He died Feb. 22, 1786, in the 23d year of his age, and the 2d of his ministry. A tradition has come down to us that he was a young man of great promise, and that his untimely death was a heavy blow to the church which had just abandoned the half-way covenant plan, and was starting, apparently, upon a new career of prosperity. Mr. Fuller was married to Anna May. A child of theirs was baptized "Anna Lockwood," March 13, 1785. This child, probably, died young. Sometime after the death of Mr. Fuller, Mrs. Fuller was married to Jesse Townsend, and among her descendants now living is a lady who has filled with becoming dignity and grace a high and honored position at the National Capital, being the wife of Hon. Grover Cleveland, Ex-President of the United States.

The fourth pastor of the church was

LEMUEL TYLER.

He was a son of Elnathan and Lucy [Bissel] Tyler; and was born at Northford, Conn., Aug. 17, 1761. His ancestors, who were among the earlier settlers of the town of Branford, came originally from Scotland. He was graduated from Yale College, at the age of 19, in the class of 1780. Among his twenty-seven classmates were Rev. Samuel Nott, D.D., of Franklin, and Gov. Roger Griswold of Lyme. Mr. Tyler was occupied in teaching for several years after graduation. He then prepared for the ministry and was licensed to preach by the New Haven Association in 1785. He was ordained pastor of this church May 7, 1789, Dr. Benjamin Trumbull of North Haven, the historian of Connecticut, preaching the sermon. He held the office till the time of his death, which occurred Sept. 18, 1810,—a period of twenty-one years. Early in his ministry, at the request of the church, he copied, in a beautiful hand, all the previous records of the church,—from the time of its formation up to the time that the work was done. From this time for about seven or eight years the records of his own ministry are kept in the same systematic order, and in the same beautiful hand, on to about 1797-8, when they abruptly close. So that nothing whatever appears upon the church records from 1798 to 1813, when the next minister began his work.

Mr. Tyler evidently had not lost his skill in clerical work, for I find that he frequently served as clerk of the New London Association through the whole period of his ministry,— more frequently indeed than any other man. I find also that he served as clerk of the General Association of the state as late as 1804. I think it probable, therefore, that the missing records were kept in some other book than that which has come down to us.

Mr. Tyler has been spoken of by those who remembered him as an excellent preacher,— as a fine singer, and very fond of music, as a thorough disciplinarian in his family, training his children from their earliest years to habits of industry and economy. A high compliment was paid to him by a leading man in his church when he said, "Mr. Tyler is wise in the things of this world as well as in the things of the world to come." Mr. Tyler was married the same year that he was ordained to Miss Ruth Fowler of Northford. The fruits of this marriage were two sons and two daughters. Mrs. Tyler died April 18, 1796, aged 34. In September, 1797, he was married to Miss Sally Crary of Preston. By her he had two sons and two daughters. During the earlier years of his ministry he lived in the house which stands quite near to this church, now occupied by Mr. Standish. He then built the Dr. Downing house, so-called, now occupied by Mr. Main, beginning it in 1798, 100 years ago — and moving into it in 1800. Mr. Tyler has descendants living in this and neighboring states. A grandson, who bears his name, Lemuel Tyler, is with us to-day. So also is a great-great-granddaughter, Miss Buckingham, who will assist in the service of song.*

For nearly two years after the death of Mr. Tyler the church was without a pastor.

### REV. JOHN HYDE

was then called, and in due time inducted into office. He was a native of Franklin, originally a part of Norwich, bearing the name of West Farms. His ancestor, Wm. Hyde, was one of thirty-five men who, with their families, came from Saybrook and settled Norwich in 1660. The subject

---

* See Note at the close of this paper.

of this sketch, the oldest son of Vaniah and Rebecca [Barker] Hyde, was born in 1776. He fitted for college with his pastor, Dr. Nott, and was graduated from Yale in 1803. He spent two or three years in studying theology, and was then ordained pastor of the church in Hamden, Conn., April, 1806. After a pastorate of some five years in that place he came to Preston, where a call was extended to him May 26, 1812. He remained here fifteen years and was dismissed May 28, 1827. In the same year he was installed at North Wilbraham, Mass., where he remained five years. His residence during the later years of his life was in Franklin, where he died Aug. 14, 1848, at the age of 72. He was married the same year that he was ordained to Susan, a daughter of Dr. Nott. They had six children, three sons and three daughters. While in Preston they lived in the gambrel-roofed house west of the Baptist Church, now occupied by Mr. Frank Fitch. Descendants of Mr. Hyde are living in Norwich, in Buffalo, N. Y., and other places.

The sixth Pastor of the Church was

REV. AUGUSTUS B. COLLINS.

He was a son of Gen. Augustus and Mary [Chittenden] Collins. He was born in North Guilford in 1789. He was for a time a student in Yale College, but did not graduate. He studied divinity, and was licensed by the Hampden, Mass., Association in 1816. He was ordained Pastor of the Church in Andover, Conn., in 1818, and dismissed in 1827. He was installed Pastor of this Church, Jan. 16, 1828, Rev. Chauncy Booth, of Coventry, preaching the sermon. The Council met the day previous, and, after the opening prayer, "Voted, that from a desire to give all their influence in favor of the cause of temperance, and in accordance with their former practice, they would dispense with ardent spirits and wine on the occasion." This vote indicates that the members of the Council were coming into line with the great temperance movement which had already begun, and which presently swept over the land, producing the most beneficent and far-reaching results. Into this movement Mr. Collins heartily entered. And though some of the leading members of the Church were not at first in sympathy with him, he succeeded at length in organizing a Temperance Society, and had the satisfaction in the course of a few years of seeing the names of nearly all the young people in the parish affixed to the pledge, and the sales of ardent spirits in this village reduced from over 100 hogsheads a year to almost nothing. Mr. Collins was Pastor of the Church between 19 and 20 years, being dismissed in 1847. There were repeated revivals of religion during his ministry, and large accessions to the Church, the whole number added by profession and letter being 150. After leaving Preston he had a pastorate of about four years in West Stafford, and shorter ones in Barkhamstead and Long Ridge. The closing portion of his life, for over 20 years, was spent with his daughter, Orra Ann, Mrs. Bishop, in Norwalk. Here in the beautiful home of Mr. Bishop, Mr. and Mrs. Collins spent their declining years, which were apparently some of the happiest years of their lives. Mrs. Collins, whose maiden name was Elizabeth P. Bishop, of Berlin, died in 1867, aged 75. Mr. Collins died in 1876, aged 87. They had four children, one son and three daughters. Their grandson, Charles O. Collins, lives in Rahway, N. J. He writes me that his family contains the only living descendants of Rev. A. B. Collins, that he has two daughters, but that his only son died a few years since. Mr. Collins, as I remember him, was a short, thick-set, fleshy man, with a bald head, and a very full, round face. He had a strong, loud voice, with which he continued to "sound the Gospel trumpet" (to quote his own language), till near the close of his long and useful life. He built the house now occupied by the family of the late Chester S. Prentice; and this was the home of the family during the greater part of the time that they resided in Preston.

### REV. NATHAN S. HUNT

was the seventh Pastor of the Church. He was a son of Ebenezer and Anna [Strong] Hunt, and was born in Coventry, July 5, 1802. He was graduated at Williams College in 1830, and at Andover Seminary in 1833. He was ordained at Abington, Conn., in 1834, and dismissed in 1845. He was Acting Pastor at Montville, 1846–7. He was installed here Oct. 20, 1847, and dismissed, April 1, 1858. From here he moved to Bozrah, and was Acting Pastor there from April, 1858, to April, 1870. He continued to reside in Bozrah up to the time of his death, which occurred April 30, 1882, when he was nearly 80 years of age. Mr. Hunt, as many of us remember, was a large man, with quite a dignified bearing, with a countenance which was thought by many to bear a striking resemblance to that of the Hon. Daniel Webster. During the greater part of the time that he lived in Preston he occupied the house now owned by Mr. R. P. Woodmansee. He was married, in 1842, to Miss Rhoda L. Mason of Lebanon. They had no children.

### REV. ELIJAH W. TUCKER

became the Acting Pastor of the Church in January, 1859, and closed his labors here in March, 1865. He was a son of Dea. Atherton Tucker, of Dorchester, Mass., where he was born March 31, 1810. Though blessed with pious parents and a godly ancestry, he did not commence the Christian life till he was about 20 years old. Having then taken this step, he at once began to think of the ministry as his future calling, and pretty soon entered upon a course of study preparatory for it. He was graduated from Brown University in 1838, and Andover Theological Seminary in 1841. He was ordained Pastor of the Church in New Market, N. H., in 1841, and dismissed in 1845. From 1846 to 1852 he was Pastor of the Church in Chatham, Mass., where his labors were attended by a powerful revival of religion. In 1852, he supplied the Church in Essex, Conn. Then he was called to Lebanon, Goshen, where he was installed in 1853, and dismissed in 1858. His labors in Goshen resulted in an extensive revival, and large accessions to the Church. From Goshen he came to Preston, and served the Church till his removal to Northfield, Conn. He was Acting Pastor of the Church in that place from 1865 up to the time of his death, which occurred, Aug. 6, 1866, at the age of 56. He was married in 1841 to Miss Hannah W. Robinson, of Dorchester. They had no children. While in Preston they lived in the same house that had been occupied by Mr. Hunt.

This closes the list of those who have finished their earthly work and gone to their reward. I will not speak *at length* of the living, presuming that most, if not all of them will speak for themselves. A few facts, however, in regard to each of them may be fittingly stated.

### REV. ASHER H. WILCOX

was born at Norwich Town and educated at Yale College and Andover Seminary. He was ordained here in '65, and served the church on to '72. He has also ministered to the churches in Westerly, Plainfield, Central Village, Bozrah, and other places. Early in his ministry here the parsonage was built, and, from that time to the present, it has been the home of the ministers' families.

### REV. ANDREW J. HETRICK

was from Pennsylvania, graduated at Princeton College, and Union Theological Seminary. He was ordained at Westport, Conn. His ministry here was in the years '72-'74. He has since labored in the West, and, for a number of years past, in Canterbury. He is now City Missionary in Norwich.

### REV. GEORGE A. BRYAN

is a native of Waterbury, and a graduate of Yale College and Yale Divinity School. He was here in the years '76-'84. He had previously had pastorates in Cromwell, West Haven, and Westbrook, and afterward had them in Wapping and Scotland.

### REV. RICHARD H. GIDMAN,

the present pastor, was born in Stamford, England; graduated at Wesleyan University and Union Theological Seminary. Before coming here he had pastorates in Bangor and Lisle, N. Y., and Morris and North Madison, Conn. He began work here in Oct. '84, and so has just completed a pastorate of 14 years.

As we look back over these twelve pastorates, covering the 200 years which we this day review, the time seems long, very long. Yet, when I was a child there were a good many people living here in Preston whose lives began before that of Mr. Treat had closed — people who had distinct recollections of the first pastor of this ancient church, *e. g.*, my great-uncle Dea. Amos Avery, whom I remember very well, was a boy seven years old, when Mr. Treat was dismissed. And he was a young man, twenty-five years old, when Mr. Treat died. So that, through the life of Dea. Amos Avery and the life of Mr. Treat, some of us can look back through this century and the *last* century, and into the century before the last to within fifty-two years of the landing of the *Mayflower*, when some of the *Mayflower* pilgrims were still alive. When we think of the country as it was in that distant past, and then look around us and see what it is in the living present, well may we with adoring gratitude, contemplate the changes that have been wrought, wrought very largely through the influence of our Christian Churches, with their educated ministers. And well may we exclaim with the Psalmist, "This is the Lord's doing; it is marvelous in our eyes." Surely "the Lord hath done great things for us, whereof we are glad."

### NOTE.

With the reference of Mr. Avery to Miss Buckingham, whose assistance in singing added much to the enjoyment of the day, it is of interest to have Prof. Hewitt's word of introduction before one of the parts of the music of the afternoon.

"Tradition relates that the Rev. Lemuel Tyler, the fourth pastor of this church, was a fine singer and very fond of music. It is one of the pleasant felicities of this occasion, as well as a good illustration of the principle of heredity, that the lady who is to sing the solo which is announced as the next part on the program, is a great-great-grand-daughter of Mr. Tyler, and also a lineal descendant of Dr. E. B. Downing, who, for more than a quarter of a century, was leader of the choir in this church. The solo will be rendered by Miss Maude Buckingham of Norwich."

Miss Buckingham gave a delightful rendering of the solo: "The Holy City."

V

THE ORIGINAL MEMBERS

# THE ORIGINAL MEMBERS.*

### BY AMOS A. BROWNING, ESQ.

The twelve persons who united to form the church in Preston, on November 16, 1698, were Thomas Park, Thomas Tracy, John Richards, Hopestill Tyler, Jonathan Tracy, Samuel Leonard, Robert Park, John Park, Caleb Forbes, Joseph Morgan, Ebenezer Witter, and John Welch. They were leading citizens in the new township, land-owners, and enterprising. All had been members in full communion of other churches. Eight of their number were among the petitioners for the incorporation of the town, and four were named in the deed of Owaneco, dated March 17, 1687, conveying to the inhabitants of "New Preston" a tract of land five miles wide, extending from Stonington to Norwich. Following is a brief notice of each of the twelve:

The name of THOMAS PARK is first in the recorded list of members of the church, suggesting the esteem in which he was held by his associates. He must have been more than threescore and ten. His wife Dorothy, daughter of Rev. John and Alice Thompson of Preston, England, was sister of the wife of Rev. Richard Blinman, pastor of the first church of New London. His brother, William Park, was a deacon in the church at Roxbury, Mass. Thomas Park himself had been a deacon of the New London church and became one of the first deacons of the church in Preston. As remarked by Mr. Blake, in his history of the New London church, "there seems to have been the stuff that deacons are made of in the Park family."

---

\* This paper was not given at the anniversary. It has been prepared since by Mr. Browning, who has gathered the facts with no small assiduity and research. It is welcomed as an interesting and valuable contribution to the contents of this history.— ED.

Mr. Park was the son of Robert and Martha (Champlin) Park, who emigrated from Preston, England, in 1630. The son removed with his father to Wethersfield in 1635, and from thence to New London in 1650. After residing at the town plot for half a dozen years, they transferred their home to the banks of the Mystic. Here, in 1664, Robert Park died, aged 84 years, and was buried in Whitehall cemetery. Prior to his death, it is said, he purchased 1,000 acres of Gov. Winthrop for his son Samuel, on the Mystic river, and as many more near Avery's pond for his son Thomas. Dea. Thomas was collector of taxes for New London in 1681, and later located on the tract above referred to in Preston.

He died July 30, 1709, and, with his wife, was buried, it is believed, in the Avery cemetery, although no stones can be found inscribed to mark the spot. Thomas Park's children were: Martha, b. at Wethersfield in 1646, m. Jan. 18, 1668, Isaac Wheeler of Stonington; Thomas, b. at Wethersfield in 1648, m. Mary Allyn of Norwich; Dorothy, m. April, 1670, Joseph Morgan of Preston; Alice, m. March 16, 1673, Greenfield Larrabee; Nathaniel, m. Sarah Geer, daughter of George and Sarah (Allyn) Geer; Robert, m. (1) Rachel Leffingwell, and (2) Mary Rose; William, m. (1) Dec. 3, 1684, Hannah Frink, (2) Oct. 3, 1707, Hannah Plimton, and (3) July 11, 1716, Mary ——; John, m. Mary ——.

THOMAS TRACY, second son of Lieutenant Thomas and Mary (Mason) Tracy, was born in 1644, probably at Saybrook. His father, born in 1610, was a native of Tewksbury, England, and after emigration resided for a time at Salem and then at Saybrook. He was one of the original settlers and land proprietors of Norwich in 1660, which place became his permanent home. Thomas Tracy was a freeman of Norwich in 1683, a constable in 1684, and one of the petitioners for the incorporation of Preston in 1686. Of his brothers, aside from Jonathan, spoken of later, John was one of the original proprietors of Norwich, and represented that town in six sessions of the colonial assembly. Another brother was Dr. Solomon Tracy, who married Sarah, daughter of Dea. Simon Huntington of Norwich. Thomas Tracy died in April, 1721. His children were: Nathaniel, b. Dec.

19, 1675; Sarah, b. Dec. 17, 1677; Jeremiah, b. Oct. 14, 1682; Daniel, b. March 3, 1685; Thomas, b. June 15, 1687; Jedediah, b. Sept. 24, 1692; Deborah and Jerusha, b. Sept. 24, 1697.

JOHN RICHARDS was one of the early deacons of the new church, and in the town records his name never appears without the title. His ancestors, his previous church connection, and his earlier residence, research has failed to disclose. In 1697 he acquired twenty-five acres of land on Stoney brook, adjoining the Norwich line, and in the deed he is described as of Preston. Several later purchases of land were made by him, all apparently located in the western part of the town. William Richards was not his brother, as Miss Caulkins thought probable, but, in the language of a recorded deed, his "well-beloved son." The latter married, Oct. 16, 1707, Lydia Adams, and died May 16, 1724. His other children, so far as known, were: John, a resident of Preston, m. June 17, 1707, Abigail Woodward, died Sept. 18, 1756; Nathaniel, a resident of Norwich as early as 1716, his lands being on the easterly side of the Shetucket; and Mary, m. Aug. 21, 1711, Jonathan Tracy. Deacon Richards survived his son William, and died prior to 1743.

HOPESTILL TYLER was the village blacksmith and resided in the forest a mile east of the church. A part of the dwelling-house erected by him, including the stone chimney, still remains, the rest of the building having been burned and rebuilt. He was the son of Job and Mary Tyler of Andover, Mass., where he was born in 1645. The father, according to tradition, was from Shropshire, England, and first appears in Andover about 1640. Hopestill Tyler was made a freeman in Mendon, Mass., in 1673, was driven by the Indians to Roxbury, and at length returned to Andover. An old record says that he was apprenticed a blacksmith, and in 1687 his native town "granted him liberty to set up a shop in ye street near his house." Soon after this the witchcraft persecution began, and Mrs. Tyler and two daughters were imprisoned at Salem. They were acquitted, however, in 1693. Perhaps, in part, because of this persecution, in 1697 he sold his land and removed to Preston. The value of the smith's craft to the community in the early days is illustrated by the vote of Preston in 1693, offering fifty acres of land to a smith who should settle there, upon certain conditions, one of which was that " he doe ingage to supply the town with smith work five yere." That Mr. Tyler availed himself of this offer, when he removed to Preston four years later, does not clearly appear. He survived his wife, who died March 3, 1732, and died at Preston Jan. 20, 1733. Both were interred in the public cemetery at Preston City.

Mrs. Tyler was Mary Lovett, daughter of Daniel and Joanna (Blot) Lovett of Braintree, Mass. The marriage occurred at Andover January 20, 1668. Their children were: Mary, m. June 30, 1693, John Farnum; Hannah, m. Dec., 1697, Robert Busswell; Daniel, m. May 28, 1700, Anna, dau. of George and Sarah (Allyn) Geer; Martha, m. Apr. 3, 1700, Robert Geer; John, b. Feb. 19, 1678, settled in or near Boston; Joanna, b. Nov. 24, 1681; James, born Dec. 28, 1683, m. (1) Oct. 8, 1705, Hannah Safford, and (2) Sept. 2, 173-, Sarah Juel, resided in North Preston (now Griswold); Hopestill, b. 1684 or 1685, m. Anna Gates, Jan. 25, 1710, remained on the homestead in Preston; and Abigail, b. about 1687, m. Daniel Fitch. John Tyler, son of the above James, rendered conspicuous service in the Revolution and became a brigadier-general. Professor Moses Coit Tyler is also a descendant of the Griswold branch.

JONATHAN TRACY, one of the fifteen persons named in the act of 1686 creating the town of Preston, was born at Saybrook, Conn., in 1646, and thus was 52 years of age at the time of the formation of the Preston church. He was son of Lieut. Thomas Tracy, already referred to. Jonathan Tracy was the first recorder or town clerk, and continued to hold the office till his death, a period of eighteen years. He was the first lieutenant of the train band, a justice of the peace from the incorporation of the town till his death, a selectman in 1698, and deputy from Preston in the colonial assemblies of 1699, 1700, and 1710. His first wife was Mary Griswold, born Aug. 26, 1656, a daughter of Lieut. Francis Griswold of Norwich, whom he married July 11, 1672. She united with the Preston church immediately after its formation. Her death occurred April 24, 1711, her age being 55 years. His second wife was Mary Richards, daughter of Dea. John Richards, whom he married Aug. 21, 1711.

His children were: Jonathan, b. Feb. 21, 1675, d. Feb. 25, 1704; Hannah, b. July 8, 1677; Christopher, b. May 1, 1680; Mary, b. Sept. 7, 1682; Mariam, b. April 23, 1685; David, b. Sept. 24, 1687; Frances, b. April 1, 1690; Sarah, b. Aug. 2, 1692, d. Sept. 6, 1693; and Samuel, b. June 6, 1697.

SAMUEL LEONARD, or Leonardson,* was born at Duxbury, Mass., prior to 1645. His father was Solomon Leonard, born in Monmouthshire, England, in 1610. He removed first to Leyden in Holland, and emigrated to America not far from 1630. He was a settler in Duxbury when the town was incorporated. Samuel Leonard's first wife was Abigail Wood, daughter of John and Sarah Wood of Plymouth, to whom he was married prior to 1676. He was early a proprietor of lands in Worcester and removed to Connecticut about 1695, because here had located Josiah and Miles Standish, Caleb Forbes, and other Duxbury friends. Mr. Leonard's second wife was Deborah, perhaps daughter of John Leonard of Springfield. She was admitted to full communion in the Preston church Nov. 4, 1716. They lived near Pachaug, and upon the formation of the church there in 1720, he became one of its constituent members. He died soon afterwards. Some of his real estate in Griswold has continued to be owned by descendants of the name until a recent period.

His children were, of the first wife, Mary, m. 1700, Edward Newton; Mercy, m. Richard Adams, d. Dec. 24, 1749; Elizabeth, m. July 10, 1703, Thomas Clark; and Samuel, b. about 1683, m. Lydia, d. May 11, 1718. Of the second wife, the children were Abigail, m. July 4, 1722, Isaac Reed; and Phebe, bapt. Oct. 17, 1703.

ROBERT PARK was the son of Dea. Thomas and Dorothy (Thompson) Park. He married Nov. 24, 1681, Rachel

---

* The widely-scattered family bearing the name Leonard, as now usually written, were formerly more often called Leonardson, and the name appears in the latter form in the Preston church and town records.

Leffingwell. His homestead was in the town of Groton, now Ledyard, and he owned a farm also at Pachaug. Mr. Park's connections had been with the Road church in Stonington, where two of his children were baptized. His second wife was Mary Rose, who was received into communion with the Preston church May 1, 1715. Mr. Park died in 1707.

His children, of the first wife, were Rebecca, b. in Norwich Sept. 7, 1682; James, b. 1685; and Joanna, b. 1692. The children of the second wife were Hezekiah, b. 1695; Jemima, bapt. in Stonington July 15, 1694; Robert, bapt. in Stonington, Oct. 10, 1697; Keziah, b. 1700; Margaret, b. 1702; Dorothy, b. 1703; and Rose, b. 1706. Elder Park of the Separate church was a great-grandson of Dea. Thomas Park through his son Robert, and Chief Justice John D. Park was in turn a great-grandson of Paul Park. Professor Roswell Park and his great-grandson, Dr. Roswell Park of Buffalo, N. Y., are descendants of this branch of the family.

CAPTAIN JOHN PARK, son of Dea. Thomas Park and a brother of Robert, resided in Norwich east of the Shetucket River as early as 1680. He and his wife Mary were members of the church in Stonington, and his daughters, Abigail and Dorothy, were baptized there. He was one of the petitioners for the incorporation of the new township. He died in 1716, and in the partition of his estate the widow received that "part of the farm on which Deacon Thomas dwelt by the pond." His widow subsequently married Rev. Salmon Treat.

Captain Park's daughter Abigail married, Dec. 19, 1704, Christopher Avery, and died in 1713. His daughter Dorothy married, June 19, 1708, Ebenezer Avery.

CALEB FORBES, the son of John and Constant (Mitchell) Forbes of Duxbury and Bridgewater, Mass., was the owner of land in Norwich as early as 1672. His first wife was Sarah, daughter of John Gager of Norwich, whom he married June 30, 1681. In 1684 and 1685 he was constable east of the river. He was one of the petitioners for the incorporation of the town of Preston and became a settled inhabitant of the new town.  He had several grants of land from Owaneco, chief of the Mohegans, one of which bounded on Connoughty brook. In all the early records, the name is written Fobes. He was a deacon of the Preston church, was frequently elected selectman or townsman, held the office of town treasurer for many years, and was often called upon to lay out lands and highways and to transact other public business. Dea. Forbes' second marriage occurred prior to the formation of the church, and his wife Mary joined before the first communion. He died August 25, 1710.

His children, so far as known, were Sarah, b. in Norwich June 24, 1684, m. Samuel Bishop of Newent in 1706; Caleb, m. Abigail Gates May 21, 1713, d. May 7, 1728, in his fortieth year; Mary; John, m. Ruth Brewster, January, 1718, d. Feb. 18, 1738; and Elizabeth.

LIEUTENANT JOSEPH MORGAN was the son of James and Margery (Hill) Morgan of Roxbury and Groton. James Morgan and his brothers, John and Moses, emigrated to New England in 1636 from Wales. Joseph Morgan was born Oct. 29, 1646, probably at Roxbury, Mass., and married Dorothy, daughter of Dea. Thomas Park, in April, 1670. He was probably connected with the New London church, of which his father was a member. He was one of the petitioners for the separation of the town of Preston from Norwich, and was also one of those to whom Owaneco deeded the town territory. His farm was that owned recently by Albert G. Ayer, and now by the latter's grandson. He had one son, Rev. Joseph Morgan, and six daughters who grew to maturity. The male line of his descendants is probably extinct. He died April 5, 1704.

His children were Joseph, b. Nov. 6, 1671; Dorothy, b. Feb. 25, 1673, died young: Dorothy, b. Feb. 29, 1676, m. May 5, 1693, Ebenezer Witter; Anne, b. Nov. 10, 1678, m. Sept. 7, 1714, Thomas Atwell; Martha, b. March 22, 1681, m. May 22, 1700, Joseph Perkins; Hannah, b. Dec. 3, 1683, d. Aug. 8, 1697; Margaret, b. July 28, 1686, m. March 10, 1709, Ebenezer Herbert; Abigail, b. Feb. 10, 1689, d. May 28, 1695; Deborah, b. May 31, 1694; and Hannah, b. Dec. 16, 1697.

EBENEZER WITTER, born in Lynn, March 25, 1668, was

son of Josiah and Elizabeth (Wheeler) Witter of Lynn, Mass., and Stonington, Conn. He was a grandson of William Witter, who emigrated to America in 1629 and settled near Lynn. He married for his first wife Sarah Tefft, daughter of Samuel and Elizabeth (Jencks) Tefft of Portsmouth and Kingston, R. I., and resided for a time on the Pettasquamscott Purchase, now South Kingston, removing to Preston in 1692. His second wife was Dorothy Morgan, whom he married in Preston, May 5, 1693. They were admitted to the Stonington church March 21, 1696, and his sons, Josiah and Joseph, were baptized there in 1698. He was chosen deacon of the Preston church between 1707 and 1711. His death occurred Jan. 31, 1712, and that of his widow March 9, 1750, in her 85th year, and both were interred in the Avery cemetery, where their tombstones may still be seen. Mr. Witter purchased eight acres on the south side of Wesquedus hill, bounding on Poquetannock brook, where he erected a grist mill which, until recently, was owned by his descendants. He subsequently increased his purchases to several hundred acres.

Mr. Witter's children were Sarah, of first wife, b. in Rhode Island; Elizabeth, b. March 3, 1694, m. Oct. 16, 1713, Benjamin Brewster; Mary, b. March 2, 1696, m. Oct. 13, 1713, Jeremiah Tracy; Josiah, b. June 10, 1698, d. Sept. 20, 1698; Joseph, b. June 10, 1698, m. Aug. 13, 1722, Elizabeth Goss; Ebenezer, b. Nov. 30, 1700, m. March 25, 1729, Elizabeth Brown, and after her death, Nov. 6, 1760, Mrs. Mary Avery of Groton; Dorothy, b. Dec. 11, 1702, m. Dec. 19, 1727, Daniel Brewster; Hannah, b. Feb. 26, 1705; William, b. May 24, 1707, d. Sept. 9, 1798; and Abigail, b. Jan. 24, 1711, d. Feb. 16, 1711. Ebenezer Witter, son of Joseph, was captain of a company from Preston in the Revolution. Jonah Witter and Lucas Witter, late of Preston, were grandsons of Ebenezer Witter, Jr. William Witter (1707-1798) was a lieutenant in 1641, represented his town in several sessions of the general court, and was further distinguished as owner of the first carriage in Preston. The late William P. Witter was his descendant.

JOHN WELCH resided in Preston at the time of the organization of the church there in 1698, but was admitted a freeman in Norwich in 1705, which appears subsequently to have been his place of residence. His ancestry and earlier home are unknown, although the family name is not an unfamiliar one in the New England records. Moses Coit Welch was a distinguished doctor of divinity, residing at Mansfield in Windham County, a century ago. Mr. Welch's early land holdings were near the Quinebaug River in Preston, while land purchased by him later was situated near Poquetanuck in Norwich. His wife's Christian name was Sarah, but her family is unknown. Mr. Welch died May 6, 1728.

Their children were Sarah, b. Nov. 15, 1698; Ebenezer, b. April 29, 1703; Joseph, b. May 13, 1706, probably married Lydia Rudd and died Dec. 1, 1734; Experience, b. April 14, 1708; Mary, b. April 14, 1711; Abigail, b. Oct. 25, 1712; and John.

# VI

GREETINGS

# THE MOTHER CHURCH.

THE CHAIRMAN: The relations between Norwich and Preston, both commercial and religious, have always been intimate and strong. Norwich deeded to us a part of her own territory, and since then we have been enjoying the luxury of bearing one-half the expense of building and keeping in repair the bridges over the Shetucket. Norwich passed on to us the torch of religious liberty, and, since then, we have been sending her some of the choicest of our sons and daughters. In describing the situation of the first meeting-house in Norwich, Miss Caulkins says it was "perched like a citadel upon its rocky height, with perpendicular ledges, or abrupt, stony declivities on either side." We look to Norwich as the rock whence we have been hewn. And on this 200th natal year the daughter naturally turns to the mother for the first greeting. I take pleasure in introducing the Rev. C. A. Northrop, pastor of the First Church of Norwich.

ADDRESS BY REV. C. A. NORTHROP.

DEAR DAUGHTER: When, upon the appearance of the program of this your bi-centennial anniversary, it was intimated to your old mother that you were not her daughter, she consulted her records, and behold, you were not there! The reason is apparent. It came out this morning. You came into existence through the co-operation of several Christian people, almost all of whom lived adjacent to the Nine Mile Square, and some of whom had been in the habit of worshiping with the old First Church on the Norwich Green. In those days we claimed everything and everybody within the bounds of the original purchase, and had our spiritual eyes upon the region beyond. Although our earliest records are lost, it is quite possible that some of your first members were actually members of the First Church, and were dismissed to help form the new organization, but if not, they were by no means strangers within our gates, and so, ours before they were yours. Even if you did not colonize from the old hive, your spiritual ancestors, we are quite sure, used to feed on its honey before they swarmed.

In any case, having heard the story of your early days, and gone over with you this morning the deeply interesting history of your trials and successes, we recognize enough of spiritual kinship to welcome you heartily as a long lost daughter. We gladly accept the relationship in which your hearts and program put us, and rejoice greatly because of your history.

One of the earliest companies to gather a church, you are in the line of an illustrious succession of churches built up around and mostly from the mother church of Norwich. We look with pride upon the history of them all, and, though distance of time may lend enchantment, we do not believe that the effective work for the kingdom of God done by them has been overstated. It is the good things that survive, and the traditions and histories of all our children fill us with gratitude and thanksgiving to the Father of us all.

We can scarcely estimate the amount of good done by these churches during these two centuries. To have belonged to the number of them in those pioneer days is to have had grand, rich opportunities.

We are pleased with the history of your younger days, and the days of your trial with the Separatists show both your weakness and your strength: weakness, in making it possible for them to arise; strength, in furnishing the stamina that made them arise — and depart. Your treatment of them was kindlier than was that of our and your English fathers in the matter of the would-be and actual Separatists of the previous century — the Puritans and the Pilgrims.

In your present prosperity, in your good sense, so like that of your mother, in keeping your ministers a long while, especially the last; in your spiritual work, kept warm and vigorous in spite of rural conditions, scattered homes and improvable roads; in your wider, all-around interest in education and other things, we, of the old mother church, take ever fresh delight. In these we see the reproduction and the enlargement of the plans and purposes and achievements of the original settlers about the Green.

We are not sorry that you set up for yourselves. The long horseback rides, and trudging, floundering walks through the swamp and around by the hetucket fords, to get to the old Town Church, must have been tedious and trying to the faith and the clothing of the Preston pilgrims.

We do not want to forget your work, nor to seem at all indifferent to your welfare. We like these anniversary days; we are going to have one ourselves soon. Our 250th anniversary will occur in 1910, and we cordially invite you to come and be with us then. The necessity of fording has gone by. By that time, let us hope the necessity of walking over muddy roads will also have gone by, and you may be able, with quick and glad footsteps, if not in electric carriages, to glide over the long stretches of macadam road that will separate and join mother and daughter.

Till that time comes we wish you well. We know that you will do well. God bless you, dear old girl!

# THE DAUGHTER CHURCH.

THE CHAIRMAN: Next after the mother we turn to the daughter, and as we do so we recall the words of the Psalmist, "Children are an heritage of the Lord." For nearly a century the church in Pachaug was in our own town, and so is connected to us by the ties both of kinship and of neighborhood. In view of the noble record of that church in raising up ministers of the gospel, we might not inappropriately adapt to this offspring the line of a Roman poet, "O daughter, more lovely than thy lovely mother!" With a motherly regard we welcome to-day the Rev. F. E. Allen, pastor of the daughter church.

### ADDRESS BY REV. F. E. ALLEN.

We beg to present our sincere congratulations to you, our mother church, upon this notable occasion. The grandmother has spoken — the church of Norwich Town — speaking out of an experience of 238 years. You yourself reach to-day a history of 200 years, and the first church of Griswold is not far behind, having attained a history of 178 years. This is a remarkable meeting of this trio, and suggests the familiar query, When shall we three meet again? Perhaps in 1910, at grandmother's quarter millennial in Norwich Town. Or, if not then, at least in 1920, at the granddaughter's bi-centennial in Griswold under the oaks. At any rate, we take this opportunity, so as to be in season, of extending to you a cordial invitation to participate with us upon that occasion. And we hope that grandmother will be there, too.

To-day we congratulate you, beloved mother, upon the prosperity which has been vouchsafed to you, both spiritual and material. The daughter notes with pleasure your outward dress, which is in quite more modern fashion than that in which she herself stands arrayed there on the banks of

Pachaug river. But we have perceived that you have a way of doing it,— when you want new clothes *you burn your old ones.* We have had reason from the start to be proud of you, our mother. For the records of the past which touch upon that separation of mother and daughter are pleasant reading. There was no quarrel — naught but good feeling, and you sent us away with your benediction.

Another thing, it has seemed to us, must be credited in good part to you. It is this: the church at Griswold has the reputation of having stood during the Separatist agitation foursquare to the winds of controversy. She did not lose her head, but following after the things which make for peace and things whereby one may edify another, she poured oil on the troubled waters. And thus it was that one said of us, recently — one of another communion than ours — as he rose from examining the church records, " Your Dr. Hart was as tender as a mother in dealing with the consciences of those Separatists."

Now, if such is the daughter's reputation, where did she inherit it from, but from mother. Blood will tell. Like mother, like child. And as it has been, so may it be. In the words of the immortal Lincoln, "with malice toward none, with charity for all," may we press on to do the right as God gives us to see the right. And then when, in some future day, you meet to commemorate your tri-centennial or quadrennial, may you not only have children around you, but grandchildren and great-grandchildren,— a host to mingle their praises and thanksgivings with yours around the common hearthstone.

# THE BAPTIST CHURCH.

THE CHAIRMAN: We should fail in our duty to-day if we did not illustrate in our exercises one of the important phases of the religious life of the present, namely, the tendency by which the various denominations of Christians are gradually coming into closer union. The mutual relations of the two churches in this village have tended more and more, year by year, I think, to illustrate the spirit of the Psalmist,—"Behold how good and how pleasant it is for brethren to dwell together in unity." To-day we extend the cordial hand of welcome and of greeting to our brother, — the Rev. C. L. Eldredge, pastor of the Baptist church,— whom I now take pleasure in introducing to you.

### ADDRESS BY REV. C. L. ELDREDGE.

It is said that the Puritans in this State once upon a time, passed these two resolutions: *Resolved*, 1, That the Saints should rule the earth. 2, That we are the Saints.

I presume that upon this memorable occasion we shall have to concede to our friends of this church the embodiment of all the requirements of these resolutions. Doubtless these resolutions, if proposed by Congregationalism present to-day, would hardly fail to secure a unanimous vote in this audience, including many adherents of other isms as well.

As pastor of the Baptist church in this village, and in behalf of its membership and congregation, allow me to extend Christian greeting to you this day. This is a *unique event*. Individual birthdays are distant from each other a twelve-month at least; anniversaries, in the common acceptance of the term, are of still rarer occurrence. Comparatively seldom is it that, in the history of organizations, we are able to celebrate the consummation of the two-hundredth year of continuous existence. Posterity may celebrate anniversaries still more memorable, but the present occasion is full of interest and meaning to the living; it will be described to children of the future; it will live in memory for many years; it will be embodied in your history. We are confronted to-day with the fact of faithful ministration and loyal adherence. During the past two hundred years the true relation of pastor and people must have had frequent, perhaps has had continuous, exemplification. The fact of continued existence and this celebration to-day evidence not only the sustaining power of God, but also faithful human activity. You must have had ministers who were not only expounders of God's word, but doers of His will in manifold ways as well. Faithful men have doubtless been numbered among your pastors, men to whom duty was no cross, men who had a true conception of the worth of a human soul, men who labored assiduously in the vineyard; sowing, pruning, reaping: by precept, by counsel, by example seeking to set before their people the desirability of a spirit-filled life. Who can estimate the benefit, to a community, of a prayerful, sympathetic, active ministry?

And they cannot labor successfully alone or in dependence solely upon God. The Christian minister may exert himself ever so strenuously, but if he has not the support of at least a portion of his people the extent of his usefulness is sorely circumscribed. He can perform but a fraction of what he ought to be able to accomplish. This church, in some periods of its history at least, must have presented to the world examples not only of a faithful ministry, but of a faithful people. Not invariably it may be, but surely at certain periods of its history, this church must have possessed a people earnest and active, quick to respond to the suggestions and behests of its shepherd, sharing his anxieties and burdens, ready to sustain the various departments of church work, harmonious and charitable. Ten score years of continuous existence are not without an adequate cause. God is not alone responsible. Zion is beloved by Him. Because of the activity of His Spirit His church moves forward to victory. But He intrusts to His ministers and His people the daily duty (however, at times, apparently insignificant) of the dissemination of His teachings, the prosecution of all legitimate endeavors to alleviate human sorrow and suffering, and to construct characters which shall be found worthy by and by to share with the King in the triumphs of His Kingdom.

It has been said, by Mr. Emerson, I believe, that no man attains success who goes through life with his head over his shoulder. And that is true; and yet it is well to look back at times.

The retrospective glance to-day should afford both pleasure and profit. Faithful ministration and loyal adherence there have doubtless been.

With respect to the history of these years, whether as influences long since sent forth, or as memories revived to-day, shall we not as a community cherish whatever is praiseworthy, uplifting, and helpful?

Once more in behalf of my church and congregation I extend to you Christian greeting, and in the words of the Apostle: "And my God shall fulfill every need of yours according to his riches in glory in Christ Jesus."

## VII

THOSE WHO HAVE GONE FORTH
FROM THE CHURCH

# THOSE WHO HAVE GONE FORTH FROM THE CHURCH.

THE CHAIRMAN: The anecdote is related of Daniel Webster that, when he was once visited by a friend from the South and was asked by his guest what the people raised in this rocky New England, his prompt reply was, "We raise men, sir." It has sometimes been remarked that Preston and North Stonington are good towns to migrate from. When, just one generation ago, I wandered out to the distant state of Michigan, I found myself making my home within a few miles of the former residence of one who years before, after graduating at Trinity College, had gone from this town and made himself prominent in the affairs of Michigan when it was a territory, and after its admission as a state, became its first representative in Congress, Gen. Isaac E. Crary. I am about to introduce to you a nephew of Gen. Crary and son of one who was, for many years, an honored pillar in this church, a gentleman who, after taking his degree at Yale College, remained in his native state to achieve distinction for himself and for this church. We are happy to welcome back to the old home to day Judge Samuel O. Prentice, of Hartford, who will speak of "Those who have gone forth from the church."

### ADDRESS BY JUDGE SAMUEL O. PRENTICE.

*Mr. President, Ladies and Gentlemen :* This is a day devoted to retrospect. For the time being we have withdrawn our thoughts from ourselves and our daily cares and concerns, and are turning them backward over two centuries of time to the little band of men and women who first here gathered themselves together into a church of Christ. Let us pause a moment to review the scene and the persons who appear in it.

Our scene is laid upon the frontiers of civilization. The persons in it are pioneers, pushing forward to the outposts of a new world in search of homes for themselves and their children.

The scene lies among these familiar hills; but the conditions and surroundings are quite other than those which we now behold after two centuries of habitation. To us of the Western world, two centuries are a long time. They carry us well back toward the beginnings of things in this country as the home of civilized man. Two hundred years ago the frontiers of settlement had not long been pushed into this region. The town was less than twelve years of age. The population was small and scattered. Signs of the wilderness were everywhere. Here were all the conditions of the frontier life of a new community springing into being.

Of the persons concerning whom we are speaking, the records tell us that thirty-six names were borne upon the rolls of the church during the first year of its history. These thirty-six represented eighteen different family names — Park, Tracy, Tyler, Forbes, Morgan, Witter, Richards, Leonardson, Welch, Williams, Treat, Brewster, Standish, West, Davison, Larribee, Whitney, Branch.

These were plain and simple folk. With rare exceptions they were descendants of members of the early Plymouth colony, or of men who had participated in the great Puritan immigration which covered the years from 1630 to 1640. They were descendants, therefore, of representatives of the best type of the great English middle class — thrifty, industrious, and intelligent. They had been born and reared amid struggles, privations, and dangers. Luxury and ease had not been their cradles. Stern necessity had rather taught them to earn their daily bread by the sweat of their brows. They had little of the polish and few of the graces of cultivated society. To us to-day they would quite likely seem somewhat too angular, too narrow, too grim, too unbending, to attract us to them. But they possessed a rare complement of rugged virtues. They were genuine, sincere, and true men and women, holding fast to themselves a religious faith that was as pure and ennobling as it was severe, and political conceptions which came as a revelation to the world. Character, virility, and force were their marked characteristics. They were of the strong and sturdy stuff of which the true pioneer is made — of that rare stuff which made them and their fellow New Englanders the ideal stock for the colonizers of a new hemisphere, the moulders of a new society, and the builders of a new nation.

A few of their characteristics it is within my purpose to notice.

They were a prolific race. Those who have given any attention to genealogical study must have been struck by this feature of our early New England life. Families were uniformly large. Thus the old stock multiplied rapidly. Let us look to the south of us for examples. At the time of which we speak, or shortly before, there were to be found five men, all early settlers — Jonathan Brewster, James Avery, John Gallup, George Denison, and Thomas Stanton. We all know many of their descendants, if, indeed, we are not of that number ourselves. But we do not stop to realize that thousands, I might almost say tens of thousands, have inherited their name and blood, and that a multitude whom no man can number — more than 100,000, doubtless — scattered all over this broad land, have first and last been able to trace their ancestry to these men. The same thing has been true, only in a somewhat lesser degree, of the early fathers and mothers of this church. The immediate sons and daughters of the household have been many. Those whose ancestry have led to this spot would make a mighty host, indeed.

Again, our forefathers here and elsewhere in New England were thoroughly imbued with the colonizing spirit which is so characteristic of the Anglo-Saxon race. The Englishman has been the world's greatest colonizer; and our forefathers were English through and through. They had in their composition a touch of restlessness, a fondness for adventure, and a keen relish for conflict and struggle. They were ambitious. It was no part of their creed, in whatsoever state they were therewith to be content. They were ever looking for some way to better themselves; for new opportunities for advancement or achievement. Therefore it was that their footsteps were ever turning from the quiet farms and villages of their nativity toward the larger centers of habitation, and the ever-changing frontiers of advancing civilization. This outward march has been constant from the earliest days. From these hillsides and the other hillsides of New England there has ever been going forth a steady stream of men and women to take their places and do their duty hither and yon in our growing new world.

Nothing has been more characteristic of our New England communities and churches than this centrifugal force which has kept them shorn of accumulating numbers. One of the chiefest chapters in their history might well be that of "The Exodus." This exodus has naturally carried with it many of the choicest and best. It has even swept away whole families from the places which once knew them. But it has not meant destruction or extermination. It has only signified a transplanting into new and generally greater or more receptive fields of influence. These new fields were very often the new communities of the frontier. The frontier seems to have had a peculiar attraction for the New Englander. Its privations and hardships drew, rather than repelled, him. Self-reliant and lion-hearted, he went manfully forth to face the difficulties, seeing the opportunities which lay behind him. And so, with his face ever turned towards the future, his feet have kept step with the drumbeat of advancing civilization.

This characteristic of our fathers is strikingly exemplified in the history of this church. The founders of it were not original immigrants seeking their first settlement. With few exceptions, their fathers or grandfathers had sought homes in the new land. Most had followed the tide of immigration from Massachusetts to Connecticut. In following this tide, many reached this region by a circuitous route of successive settlements in the older communities of Wethersfield and the shore towns. The Parks came by the way of Cambridge, Wethersfield, and Groton; the Tracys by way of Salem, Wethersfield, Saybrook, and Norwich; the Morgans by way of Roxbury, Boston, and Groton; the Tylers by way of Andover, Roxbury, and Mendon; the Standishes by way of Plymouth and Duxbury; the Treats from Wethersfield; the Brewsters from Plymouth; the Larribees from Saybrook; the Branches from Scituate, and so on through the list.

Let us now look at the other side of the picture. The present membership of this church includes only three persons, and the limits of this society only seven, I believe, who bear the surname of any of the members of the church prior to the year 1700. These early families are by no means extinct, as we have seen. Their members must be looked for elsewhere than here. The fathers followed the advance guard of settlement in its march from Massachusetts hither. The sons soon turned their pilgrim steps northward into Vermont, New Hampshire, and Maine, then to the westward into New York, and then on and further on to the great Western sea. If you look for them and their descendants to-day, you will find them scattered as wide as the continent.

Again, our early fathers and mothers held strong convictions. Whether the subject was their religious faith, their conceptions of the social order, or their theory of government, they stood for positive and vitalizing principles. At first seeking self-government and freedom for themselves alone, there came to them as an inevitable, although unforeseen consequence, the doctrine of freedom for all — religious freedom, political freedom, personal freedom — freedom under the law. A mighty wonder-working principle this to emblazon upon the banner of a people.

Again, our fathers and mothers were a forceful, aggressive people. They were not the kind who let things drift. They were of the masterful kind, who are accomplishers. They left the impress of their ideas and their personality wherever they went. They felt that they were the instruments of the Almighty to work out a foreordained, heaven-born destiny. They deemed themselves soldiers in the army of the great Jehovah, given a warfare to wage and a victory to win, and they bore themselves as soldiers should — heroically, persistently, aggressively.

These observations concerning our fathers will suffice to enable me to emphasize, as I wish to do, an aspect of the history and work of this church and community which is too often overlooked. The year 1700 found here a new and scattered community, and a small church, upon the very threshold of its existence. It was not destined that either community or church should assume great numerical proportions. The onward march of our country's growth and progress, so wonderful to contemplate, was to pass by these borders. The fast-rising tide of trade, manufacture, and commerce was to beat against other shores. This was to remain a rural community, even as it was planted — a rural community of sparse population quite apart from the busy scenes of a busy, bustling people.

But for all this, it must not be conceived that the history of this church is a history of small things. It must not be conceived that this history is made up of only that which has transpired here. This church has had a higher mission. It has done a far nobler and more wide-reaching work than is admitted by this conception.

This church, like the hundreds of other New England churches of the olden time, has been a veritable nursery of men and women who have gone forth from it to help mould and fashion a puissant nation fast springing into life. Its sons and daughters have gone forth as missionaries of the great principles and ideals to which our fathers held, carrying them with the zeal and vigor of the true New Englander into numberless communities, and leaving their indelible impress wherever they went. So has this church drained its own life that it might invigorate the life of our country. If we focus our glass upon this church in this spot, we fail utterly to obtain a correct view of it. Our vision must take wider range, and follow out the many radiating lines of influence proceeding from this Zion, through her children and her children's children down to this hour. Who can measure that influence?

History, I fancy, presents few so striking and interesting phenomena as the part which the early New England stock has played in our country's development. By the year 1640, at the close of the great Puritan immigration, about 26,000 persons had settled in New England. From these it has been estimated that fully 15,000,000 of our country's present population have sprung. Whether or not this estimate is a correct one, certain it is that New England and New England ideas have been wonderfully potent in fashioning our national life and character. Whether we look at our people, our social conditions, or our political institutions, we find that they have in a marvelous way been assimilated to the New England type. Verily, the little one has become a thousand, and the small one a strong nation. In this development of our national character the sons and daughters of this church have done their part,— by no means an insignificant one. This part belongs to the history of this church.

It is my office to-day to speak for those who have gone out from this place. I shall not seek to dignify that office by assuming to represent that far greater body who trace their lineage to those who have worshiped here, and who thus, in greater or less measure, may be said to have inherited some of the influences which have flowed from this spot. I shall rather undertake to speak for those who, like myself, are in the strictest sense entitled to call themselves children of this household, although they no longer sit by the fireside. To such, a day like this comes with peculiar interest. It carries our thoughts back, not only to the early days, but to those more recent ones when these scenes were ours. It conjures up sweet memories of childhood and youth. It recalls familiar forms and faces. The fathers and mothers of the older and the later time mingle in the vision which comes to us of this church as the home for two centuries of unassuming, godly men and women who have worshiped their Master here. Even as we look, the vision unfolds itself, and we can see something of what these fathers and mothers have wrought for the world and for us. In the presence of this vision we reverently bow our heads in thankfulness for what has been, and in prayer that this sanctuary may long continue, as in the past, to be a nursery of men and women who, both here and elsewhere, shall act a worthy part for themselves, their country, and their God.

# VIII

## THE LOCAL CONFERENCE

# THE MINISTRY.

THE CHAIRMAN: One of the churches of this local Conference is looking forward to its bi-centennial. In fact, the times of the birth of the church in Plainfield, and of this in Preston, were so nearly the same that we might almost call them twins. It seems very fitting that the local Conference should be represented on this occasion by one who is at the same time secretary of the Conference and pastor of the venerable sister church in Plainfield. The Rev. H. T. Arnold will now address you.

## ADDRESS BY REV. H. T. ARNOLD.

The Conference of Churches in northern New London County and vicinity extends its congratulations to this church on its 200th anniversary. This is the oldest of the six churches, the Plainfield coming next, on Jan. 3, 1705. Seventy-eight years after the landing of the Pilgrims, and seventy-eight years before the Declaration of Independence, this church was formed, just two centuries ago.

At the organization of the Conference, April 23, 1862, the church in Preston City responded to the invitation of Rev. B. F. Northrop of Griswold, and was represented by its pastor, Rev. E. W. Tucker, with other members of the church. For 25 years the meetings here were held in January, but in 1887 the meeting was made a part of the services at the dedication of this building on the 22d of February, and the usual meeting was held in September. Since that time the meetings have been in October, sometimes on the first Wednesday, but usually on the second or third Wednesday. Once the meeting was held in November, in exchange with the Plainfield church, and now again. The January storms were often violent at the time first appointed. On one occasion nearly two feet of snow blocked up the roads, and not a person from abroad was present. Still, the meeting was held as usual, the exercises being conducted entirely by the people of Preston.

The original plan of the meeting has been faithfully carried out, that, after some time spent in prayer and praise and Christian conference, a sermon should be preached. Then after an hour given to refreshments, social intercourse, renewing old friendships, and forming new ones, the Conference engages in the discussion of some question or subject that has been chosen.

It is to be observed that in earlier times more laymen took part in these exercises than of late. In 1876, on the topic, "How can churches prepare the way for the revival of religion," a fifteen minute address was made by Brother J. E. Leonard of Griswold, and five minute speeches by Deacons Richards, Andrews, Avery, and David A. Allen, and by Brother W. A. Browning of Griswold.

The topics discussed at our meetings here in this church have been practical, relating twice to the work of the Christian, six times to the revival of the churches, at other times to the Church Covenant, the Sunday-school, public worship, encouragements to the country church, the family, and society. Other topics have been the Holy Spirit, the blessing needed, the eternal life.

The minutes for the early years are deficient. Sometimes because of very stormy weather, the sermon has been omitted. Once, instead of the sermon, an address was given by Deacon H. L. Reade of Jewett City, on "Spiritual prosperity." Of the sermons preached here, seven were founded on texts in the Epistles, six in the Psalms, and six in the Gospels, two in the Acts, and one in the Revelation; while two were from historical books in the Old Testament, one of these with two texts. Perhaps some of the members of the Conference can recall these sermons; but certainly the influence of them has been good. Great truths have been set before us in warm, glowing accents. They have penetrated our souls, and kindled new affection, new purpose and effort in the service of our Lord.

The first sermon at the organization of the Conference, was preached by Rev. T. L. Shipman of Jewett City, and frequently afterwards did he fulfil this part. Of the preachers at the meetings here, seven named belonged to the Conference, thirteen were from Norwich, and four from elsewhere. We have been nourished up in sound doctrine. These words have been like apples of gold in baskets of silver, enriching the life of our Conference.

Meantime this church has annually furnished substantial entertainment in bountiful repasts, and has delighted the eye with clusters of autumnal flowers and foliage dyed in gorgeous colors.

At the dedication of this beautiful edifice in 1887, the Conference was represented in an address by Rev. Charles H. Peck, who was then our scribe. We met in Plainfield in 1891, with the Windham County Conference, and in the spring of the same year with the Hanover Church, at its 125th anniversary. And now, on this auspicious and happy occasion, we meet here in Preston City, for the 36th time, and hold with this venerable church, on its bi-centennial celebration, our 217th meeting. The God who planted these churches, and has so long nourished them and made them fruitful, will continue to bless them. Their work is not yet done. The glad tidings must yet be preached; the churches walking in the fear of the Lord, and in the fellowship and comfort of the Spirit, must continue to show forth the power of the truth, and the life that the gospel of the grace of God brings to men.

# THE LAITY.

The Chairman: Preston City has never been jealous of the younger city that has sprung up on the banks of the Quinebaug. Authentic history states that up to 1816 the town of Griswold was part of Preston. We have always taken a motherly interest in the territory that once was ours, and a grandmotherly interest in the church at Jewett City. There is present to-day as representative of that church, Deacon H. L. Reade, who will speak for the Laity as well as for the granddaughter.

## ADDRESS BY DEACON H. L. READE.

*Mr. Chairman and Friends:* I am glad to bring you the greetings of the lay members of the Local Conference. Thirty-three times within the last thirty-four years, when the woods were brilliant with their Autumn coloring, and the falling leaves began to carpet the paths that led hither, we have come to this spot to live a day with the church and society whose record has had such a creditable telling to-day. We have always received a cordial welcome. The pulpit and other decorations, always timely and beautiful, told of beforehand thought. The "old hymns" sung linked the golden past with the hopeful present. The table, as to-day, has always been set by Lady Bountiful; and, best of all, never have we gone away without taking something with us that could be built, if we would, into a better, a higher and more valuable life.

But the days of the Conference have been few as compared with all the days in which this church has been making history. Think of it! For two hundred years, summer and winter, through heat and cold, as the Sabbaths have come and gone, one generation after another has seen the morning and the midday and the sunset of life. First, the child brought into the sanctuary, and, held in its father's arms, the mother with often wet eyes and always a throbbing heart, standing beside him, heard with uncomprehending ears: "I baptize thee in the name of the Father and the Son and the Holy Ghost, Amen," and then the prayer that lived in the parents' thought, vivid and long. Then, as the child grew, and the years of understanding and thought and purpose came, at some Sabbath service the thrilled parents and the hushed and sympathetic congregation heard a confession that meant for the one who made it, Christ now and forever; then, in the flush and exuberance of early man and womanhood, in the red farm house where the bride was cradled, two were made one, the good minister lifting his hands over the bowed heads in sweet and loving benediction; then a man and a woman, a father and a mother doing in their sphere, be that sphere narrow or wide, their simple honest best; training those whom God had given them; ministering to those in need as ability and opportunity enabled; serving God in the family, in society, and in the church; winning men for the right by word and example both; then, gray hairs and a tottering step, and a dim eye and a dull ear; then, the tolling of the old church bell; then, "ashes to ashes" here, but all the time the echo of a welcome heard by family and neighbors and friends, there.

This is what this church has been doing for two hundred years — training men and women for heaven, and a host of the trained ones have gone on. Their bodies sleep in yon churchyards, but they are with the sanctified, the glorified.

And what the church has done for these two centuries it purposes to do to the end. Connection must be had with events of the times — that is a part of this earth life. The church must be "in it"; but in all and over all and greatest of all, is taking the boy at the mother's knee, leading him on and up, until by-and-by, after a life well lived, heaven opens and the saved man enters forever in.

IX

ADDRESSES BY FORMER PASTORS

# ADDRESSES BY FORMER PASTORS.

THE CHAIRMAN: Doubtless many in the audience have noted the fact that the clerical element in our program is a predominant one. Now, before introducing any more reverend gentlemen, I wish to remind you of our pedigree, and to show you that the fact noted is not without its significance. All are aware that we get the name of our town from old England, but I presume few know that the site of the English town was occupied by the Phœnicians one thousand years before the Christian era, that subsequently it became the seat of Druid worship, and that in the tenth century, in the reign of Athelstane, the whole district was granted to the Cathedral Church of York. On account of this ecclesiastical connection, the capital of the hundred came to be known as Priest's town, afterward changed to "Preston." The arms of the English town, a paschal lamb supporting a cross, point to the same religious motive. Very fittingly then, our program suggests the priestly significance of our name.

I consider it a great compliment to our town and church, that all three of the surviving former pastors have made their homes in that suburb of Preston City, namely, Norwich. We are glad to welcome back to-day one whom many of you will remember as the tenth pastor of this church, the Rev. A. J. Hetrick of Norwich, who will now address you.

### ADDRESS BY REV. A. J. HETRICK.

As one of the former pastors of this ancient church, I am glad to take part in the services commemorating its two-hundredth anniversary. I came to Preston first in the autumn of 1872, a little more than twenty-six years ago, and after preaching two Sundays was called to the acting pastorate. I had then just given up my first parish at Westport, which I served nearly eight years, and moved directly from that to this. I well remember how cordially the people here received me, how freely they took their teams to Norwich and conveyed my library and household goods, how much they helped to arrange them in the parsonage, and how well they supported me in my ministry among them. This was considerably shorter than that of my predecessor, Rev. Asher H. Wilcox, who was a hard man to follow; nevertheless, a goodly number, especially of young people, was added to the church in the course of it, and when it came to a voluntary end, the work was taken up by my immediate successor, Rev. George A. Bryan.

The parish was even then an ancient one, and, of course much more so now; and those who founded it were excellent men and women of a hardy race, who, in coming to this region and planting their homes in it,

> "Said to their Lord, as if afraid,
> Here is my talent in a napkin laid,
> But labored in their spheres, as those who live
> In the delight that work alone can give."

And, pray, what have the years that have since intervened been to them and their successors? Ah, me! Who can tell?

Most of them, I believe, began life in this now great, free country, on the threshold, or within the precincts of the Church of Christ, surrounded with the beneficence and splendor of an open Bible and a preached Gospel. Soon after they appeared in the world, the seal of the covenant was ready and some of them were baptized, receiving the emblems of the blood of sprinkling.

Godly parents and ministers early taught them "the old, old story," and as their minds expanded the Book of all books was put into their hands, and therein they read for themselves of the mercy which snatcheth from death, and of the love which brings Salvation. True, they did not all become Christians, but many of them did; and all enjoyed the blessings of Divine Providence, and He cared for all.

I bring up before me, too, in more or less distinct review,

scenes in which they participated while tabernacling here, diversions, toils, cares, afflictions. I fancy how many of them anxious and sad stood by the sick couches of loved ones, and, helpless and overwhelmed, saw them die. I recall the joyful greetings and pleasant visits of kinsfolk and friends, and especially the interesting occasion when lovers, with some degree of trepidation, stood up in pairs in the old parlor among the happy company assembled, or before the pulpit, and pledged to each other their sacred troth. I call to mind too, the humble beginning of their housekeeping, the unpretending homes they set up, their earnest efforts to improve them, their struggles to gain an honorable livelihood, the joyful advent of their children, the happy hours spent together by their own firesides. I think of all these things, and moreover of the many changes since they moved out of their rude cabins into their stately farm houses, of the great and most wonderful improvements that have been made in the manner of living, in the comfort of homes, and also in our meeting-houses, since this church was founded, and of greater ones still, as I believe, to be made in the not distant future, and I ask, should not the Church proper keep pace with these improvements, this progress, quite as fast, at least, in numbers and holiness if not in other things? Aye, it should, and most assuredly will, if all who love its Great Head will co-operate with Him, and work zealously for Him.

But I must hasten to a conclusion. In looking over this audience I miss from it many who were here when I served this parish in the ministry, old familiar faces that I would gladly see now, and that I understand I shall not be permitted to see on earth again. Of the older men and women who were here then, I find strongly emphasized that

> "The tree of life has been shaken,
> And but few of them linger now,
> Like the prophet's two or three berries
> In the top of the uppermost bough."

And while I feel sad that they are not here on this joyous occasion, I am glad that the parish has so fine a church edifice, one in every way so much better than the one it had when I served it, and I congratulate it on its possession; and the town on its beautiful soldiers' monument, and on the library building that is being finished for its benefit, and pray that this church may go forward and prosper in its grand mission, not only two centuries longer but to the end of time.

THE CHAIRMAN: It is a noteworthy fact that seven of the twelve ministers of this church, and all of the first five, received degrees from Yale College. The first settled pastor of this church — the Rev. Salmon Treat — had the rare distinction of being one of four ministers to receive an honorary degree from Yale at its first Commencement in 1702. We are further reminded of our indebtedness to that venerable institution by the fact that we have present to-day two representatives of the Class of 1843, — a class distinguished, among other things, for the fact that more than thirty of its members became ministers of the gospel. One of these representatives gave the interesting sketches of pastors this morning. The other representative was the eleventh pastor of this church, and as he entered into a sort of permanent alliance with this congregation, we still claim him as one of ourselves. I think we are entitled to hear from all the former pastors to-day, and I will now call upon the Rev. George A. Bryan of Norwich.

## ADDRESS BY REV. G. A. BRYAN.

I am sure you will all unite with me in felicitating this church upon the life of two hundred years, which it completes to-day. It has been, in one view, a long life — long as compared with the years allotted to the individual life of man upon the earth — and entitles it to something of the respect and honor which we accord to the hoary head, to something of the venerableness which attaches to antiquity.

It is also a circumstance worthy of grateful mention that this life of the church has been, for the most part, both a peaceful and a prosperous life, answering to St. Paul's figure of the harmonious action of the different members of the human body. That it should have been so ought not, perhaps, to be a matter of surprise. Why not? we ask. And yet, as a matter of fact, we know that differences and dissensions do sometimes arise, greatly distracting the church and ending, it may be, in its utter rupture. There are emergencies in which the powers of evil seem leagued against her, or when other communions seek to build themselves up upon her ruin. This church has not been without experiences of this sort.

It is therefore matter for grateful recognition that this church has survived all the perils of both its earlier and later history,—that it is to-day strong in the strength of its own unity, and beauteous with the garment of peace. While she has the venerableness of age, she has not its decrepitude. Her pulse beats full and strong.

With pleasure also we note that this church, along with other churches planted by the fathers of New England, has kept the faith—the faith of our Puritan ancestry, the faith of the reformers in the sixteenth century, the faith, as we believe, of the Apostolic age. Not that the formularies of the faith have undergone no change. In some respects Christian theology of to-day holds a different language from that in which the theology of even a century ago expressed itself. Statements in matters of a speculative nature which were then held to be sound and even essential to orthodoxy, are no longer accepted, and have given place to more liberal, not to say more enlightened, views. There is less of the old-fashioned Calvinism in the preaching and in the creeds of to-day. But these changes, though important, have been of minor importance. They have not touched the substance of the faith,—only the accretions which human wisdom has gathered about it. Christians of this church and sister churches hold to the great fundamental truths with as firm a grip as did the fathers. We believe in the same God, infinite in power, wisdom, goodness, and truth; in the same Christ, who is at once Son of God and son of man; in the same gospel of salvation through repentance and faith and a spiritual regeneration; the same ultimate, glorious destiny of all redeemed souls. The church of to-day stands for rights. In the person of its ministry and also its membership it inculcates the law of rights, and it seeks to exemplify that law. It has a high ethical standard, and it does not willingly tolerate any serious departure from that standard. It is the standard of Christ and his apostles, and no higher can be conceived. The church does not claim that she has attained, either is already perfect. She may have unworthy members. Those who best represent her spirit and aim confess that they fall short, but they deplore their defects and pray for the grace that shall enable them to put on the new man after the pattern of Christ. We do not believe that the standard of Christian living, taken as a whole, is any lower than it was 200 years ago, and we may confidently claim that it is far superior to that of the irreligious world.

One other thought is suggested by this bi-centennial celebration. It is of the long procession of men and women who, in their several generations, received the instructions of this church, joined themselves to its goodly fellowship, gave it their love, their support, and their prayers, worshiped in its sanctuary, received its sacraments, sought to conform their lives to its holy precepts, and having finished their course with joy, passed on to the great Beyond in assured hope of a blessed immortality. Many of them were the fathers and mothers of those now among the living, who both revere their memories and endeavor to walk in the footsteps of their worthy example. May we not think of them as with us to-day,— spectators of these proceedings, mingling their rejoicings with our rejoicings, and bestowing upon us their benedictions?

In the observances of this day we have had our faces turned toward the past. Its record has been spread before us. But what of the future,— what of the future of this church? That is a question, may I not say, of supreme importance, and what the answer shall be must largely depend upon the fidelity and devotion of you who have inherited its traditions, and in turn are to hand over to succeeding generations the sacred trust you have received. We are encouraged to believe that you, pastor and people of this church, will not be wanting to your duty. Your responsibilities will be all the greater because so many of those who have long stood at the front have been taken from your fellowship to join, we trust, the church triumphant, and of the younger generation, so many find their sphere of occupation and duty in other localities; and so it results that heavier burdens rest upon those who remain. But you will bear them, will you not, with such bravery and resolution as by the help of God shall not only ensure the perpetuity of this church, but shall secure to it a future of greater promise and grander achievement than have pertained to any period in the past. Then shall she "look forth as the morning, fair as the moon, clear as the sun, terrible as an army with banners."

# X

## STATISTICS OF THE CHURCH

# STATISTICS OF THE CHURCH.

### ORGANIZATION AND THE REVEREND SALMON TREAT'S MINISTRY.

1698. A church was embodied in Preston, Nov$^r$ 16$^{th}$, A.D. 1698. The Elders who embodied the church & performed ordination were the Rev'd James Noyes, Pastor of Stonington, the Rev'd Moses Noyes, Pastor of Lyme, and the Rev$^d$ Gurdon Saltonstall, Pastor of New London. The messengers from neighbouring churches: Deacon Gershom Palmer of Stonington, Deacon Peck of Lyme, Daniel Witherell Esq$^r$ & Deacon Douglass of New London; and Deacon Simon Huntington of Norwich.

They who offered themselves as matter for a church, having been members of other ch'hs, in full communion were brought into order by giving their consent to articles of faith & renewal of Covenant. The persons were:

Thomas Park,              Robert Park,
Thomas Tracy,             John Park,
John Richards,            Caleb Fobes,
Hopestill Tyler,          Joseph Morgan,
Jonathan Tracy,           Ebenezer Witter, &
Samuel Leonardson,        John Welch.
                                    12 persons.

N. B. — As there appears to be no other account of Mr. Treat's ordination than that above, it is probable he was ordained Nov$^r$ 16$^{th}$, 1698, or the day following. — L. T.*

1699. William Park received into full communion with the church, Jan'y 1$^{st}$ 1699.

Charles Williams received into full communion also, Jan'y 1$^{st}$.

Before the first sabbath of communion at the Lord's supper joined to communicate

Dorothy Treat, wife of S. Treat.
Dorothy Park, wife of Thomas Park.
Mrs. Standish.
Dorothy Morgan, wife of Joseph Morgan.
Mrs. Tracy, wife of Thomas Tracy.
Mrs. Tracy, the wife of Jonathan Tracy.
Marah Fobes, the wife of Caleb Fobes.
Mrs. Brewster, the wife of Daniel Brewster.
Mrs. Mary Park, widow.
Dorothy Witter, the wife of Ebenezer Witter.
Mrs. Standish, the wife of Josiah Standish.
11 of them who adjoined by renewal of their Covenant.

---

* L. T. are the initials of Rev. Lemuel Tyler, who copied this record and all the following records down to his ministry, from the originals into the present book of records.

## ADMISSIONS.

1699. Feb'y 12th, Francis West & his wife.
Mar h 5th, Thomas Davison.
" " Thomas Larribbee.
" " John Larribee.
April 23d, Joshua Whitney of Plainfield.
" " Mary, the wife of Jno. Park.
" " The wife of Peter Branch.
June 16th, The wife of Hopestill Tyler.
" " Thomas Williams.
Sept r —, Lois Standish.

1700. Aug. 4th, Anna Walbridge, wife of Henry Walbridge of Quinnabaug.
Sept r —, James Bessex of Preston.
Sept r —, Peter Davison.
Sept r —, Anna Davison, the wife of Peter Davison.
Sept r —, Mary, the wife of William Johnson.
Nov r 10th, Mary Pierce.
Dec r 25th, Josiah Standish.

1701. May 4th, Mary, the wife of Edward Spaldin.
Anna, the wife of Jno. Spaldin.
Sept 28th, Mary, wife of John Rude.
Sept r 28th, Thomas Rude's wife.
Sept r 28th, Sarah Standish.
Dec. —, Goodman Palmer and his wife of Plainfield.

1702. Jan y 14th, Joseph Johnson's wife living at Plainfield.
Joshua Whitney's wife of Plainfield.
April 5th, Daniel Brewster.
April 5th, Jno. Rude.
April 8th, Goodwife Richards.
Sarah Gile,* the wife of John Gile.
June 4th, Joseph Benjamin's wife.
Abigail Knite, a maid living in Plainfield.

1703. Jan r 24th, The wife of Joshua Wedge.
April 25th, The wife of Thomas Park baptized & admitted.
Sept r 1st, Susannah Smith, the wife of John Smith of Plainfield.
Sept r 1st, James Rix, by letter from Salem.
Sept r 1st, Margaret Rix, his wife, by letter from Salem.
Sept r 26th, the wife of Thomas Averill, by letter from Windham.

1704. Jan y 25th, Jonathan Tracy, Jun r, and his wife Anna.
Jan y 30th, Allice Laribee, a maid.
Mar. 5th, Martha Geers, wife of Robert Geers.
July 23d, Lydia Coy, wife of Samuel Coy.
Nov r 15th, Israel Standish and Elizabeth his wife.
Nov r. 15th, John Parish and Mary his wife, by letter from Ipswich.

1705. Feb. 24th, Anna Herrick.
April 1st, Miles Standish.
May 20th, Phebe Laribee.
May 27th, Goodman John Renolds.
June 24th, Samuel Herrick, by letter from Beverly.
July 8th, Hannah Prentice, wife of Joseph Prentice.
July 8th, Martha Standish.
July 22d, Hannah Buswell, the wife of Robert Buswell.

---

* The full record is as follows: "Sarah Gile, wife of John Gile brought to us a letter of dismission & recommendation from the church in Haverhill, & submitted to our discipline & was received a permanent commun't with us some time after the day & date of her letter which was written for her Nov. 17 1701."

## STATISTICS OF THE CHURCH. 131

1706. Jan 20th, Sarah Bishop, wife of Samuel Bishop.
April 14th, Mrs. Anna Starkweather.
June 9th, Ephraim Herrick and Judith his wife.
1707. M. Ames, the wife of Hugh Ames.
Nov^r 30th, Sarah Tracy, by letter from Stonington.
Dec^r 7th, Ezekiel Park.
1708. April 4th, Patience Starkweather.
Aug. 25th, Margaret Adams, by letter from Enfield.
1710. June 25th, Abigail, the wife of Jno. Freeman.
1711. Jan'y 24th, William Richards and his wife Lydia.
April 18th, Daniel Woodard and his wife, by letter from Cambridge.
1712. Sept^r 24th, James Park.
Sept^r 24th, Mehetabel Richards, wife of Nathaniel Richards.
1713. July 19th, Bridget, the wife of James Morgan.
1714. Feb. 7th, Elizabeth Branch.
June 6th, Hannah, the wife of Amos Woodard.
Oct^r 3d, Hopestill Tyler, Jun^r, and his wife Anna.
Oct^r 7th, Dorcas, the wife of Nicholas Williams, by letter from Winham.
1715. Mar. 20th, John Fobes.
April 29th, Sarah, the wife of David Tracy.
May 1st, Mary Park, widow of Robert Park.
July 17th, Deborah, wife of Samuel Partridge.
Sept^r 4th, Mary, the wife of Jonathan Geers.
Oct^r 16th, Hannah, the wife of Daniel Geers.
1716. Mar. 4th, Judith, the wife of John Ford.
April 1st, Mary, the wife of John Renalds.
April 8th, Abigail, the wife of John Richards.
April 29th, Joseph Prentice.
May 6th, Judith, the wife of Jacob Burton.
June 3d, Abigail Standish.
June 3rd, Elizabeth, the wife of Benjn. Brewster.
Aug. 5th, Hannah, the wife of John Wilkeson.
Aug. 12th, Thomas Kinne, by letter.
Aug. 12th, Elizabeth, the wife of Samuel Killum.
Sept^r 16th, Elizabeth, the wife of Francis Tracy.
Sept^r 16th, Nathaniel Laribee, in Norwich bounds.
Sept^r 16th, Richard Adams and his wife.
Oct^r 28th, The wife of Benjamin Fitch, in Norwich bounds.
Nov^r 4th, the wife of Samuel Leonardson.
1717. July 4th, Sarah Rose, wife of Joseph Rose, baptized and admitted.
Aug. 22d, Samuel Renolds and Susannah his wife.
Oct^r 3d, Mary, the wife of Caleb Gates.
1718. Feb. 23d, Jacob Elliot.
Feb. 23d, John Hill, in Stonington bounds, baptized & admitted.
Mar. 2d, Elizabeth, wife of John Hill.
Mar. 30th, Mercy Standish.
Mar. 30th, Mary Brewster.
April 3d, Sarah, wife of Nathaniel Laribee
Sept. 11, Caleb Fobes.
Sept. 11, Prudence Hamblin.
Sept. 14, Mary, the wife of Joseph Park.
Nov. 2, Abigail, wife of Caleb Fobes.
Dec. 7, James Laribee.

## STATISTICS OF THE CHURCH.

1719. Feb. 15, Samuel Standish.
April 2, Deborah, the wife of Samuel Standish.
Aug. 2, John Cook.
Sept. 27, Hannah, the wife of Stephen Gates, Jun$^r$.
Oct. 4, Anna, the wife of Thomas Polly.
Nov. 8, William Billins, Jun$^r$.

1720. May 15, James Minor of Stonington.
May 15, Mrs. Experience Robinson.
July 17, Matthew Huntington.
Oct. 30, Prudence Smith, baptized & admitted.
Nov. 17, John Brown, Esq$^r$, and his wife Elizabeth.
Nov. 17, Isaac Averill.
Nov. 20, Joseph Minor of Stonington and his wife Sarah.

1721. Jan. 15, Mr. Peter Robinson, by letter from Tisbury.
April 16, Elizabeth Fobes.
June 4, John Branch.
June 11, Ruth, the wife of John Fobes.
June 18, Joseph Freeman & Hannah his wife.
June 18, Margery, the wife of Hezekiah Park.
July 9, Thankfull, the wife of David Lamb of Stonington.
July 27, Mary, the wife of Robert Park.
July 30, Hez$^h$ Park.
July 30, Margaret, the wife of Jed$^h$ Tracy.
Aug. 20, Elizabeth Averill.
Sept. 3, Elishib Adams.
Sept. 3, Abigail Tyler.
Sept. 10, Deborah, the wife of Elishib Adams.
Oct. 15, Mercy, the wife of Ezekiel Park.
Dec. 17, Daniel Brewster and Elizabeth his wife.

1722. Jan'y 28, Ruth Gates.
March 30, Sarah, the wife of John Killum.
July 15, Mary Parish.
Sept. 9, Mary, the wife of William Dennison, in Stonington.
Oct. 7, Sarah Robinson baptized & admitted.

1723. Feb. 3, Jonathan Brewster.
Mar. 3, Abigail, the wife of Peter Yarrinton.
Mar. 31, Ebenezer Witter.
Apr. 7, Mary, the wife of John Fisher.
Sept. 1, Joseph Witter.

1724. Apr. 10, Sarah, the wife of John Meech, Jun$^r$.
May 17, Susannah Welch, the wife of John Welch, Jun$^r$, baptized and admitted.
June 28, George Woodburn.
June 28, Hannah, the wife of Dan$^l$ Meech.
July 26, Margaret, the wife of George Woodburn.
Aug. 2, Susannah, the wife of John Swan of Stonington.
Sept. 3, Elisabeth Harris.
Sept. 13, Samuel Gordon.
Sept. 27, Mary, the wife of Richard Starkweather.
Dec. 4, John Meech, Jun$^r$.

1725. Jan. 3, Archibald McDowell.
Feb. 28, Sarah Branch.
June 6, Benjamin Fitch, in Norwich bounds.
July 11, Increase Billings and his wife Hannah of Stonington.
Aug. 1, Jedidiah Tracy.
Sept. 19, Abigail, the wife of Samuel Park.
Sept. 26, Rachel, the wife of Amos Richardson.

## STATISTICS OF THE CHURCH. 133

1726. Apr. 17, Lydia Tracy, widow.
Apr. 24, John Richards.
Apr. 24, Nath*l* Tracy, son of Nath*l* Tracy of Norwich.
Aug. 12, Rebecca Fuller.
Aug. 14, Abigail, the wife of John Park.
Sept. 18, Lydia, the wife of Jonathan Ayrs, by letter from the 2nd ch'h.
Sept. 23, Rudalphus Fuller.
Oct. 2, Jane, the wife of Daniel Tyler.
Nov. 13, John Park, son of William Park.
Dec. 23, Jurusha, wife of John Park.
Dec. 23, Lydia Richards.

1727. Jan'y 27, John Brewster and his wife, Dorothy.
Jan. 27, Elisabeth Safford.
Apr. 9, Abigail, the wife of Isaac Morgan.
Oct. 8, Elisabeth, the wife of Joseph Witter.
Nov. 19, Sarah Tyler, on confession.

1728. Jan. 16, Ephraim Smith of Stonington, baptized and admitted.
Oct. 10, Thomas Branch and Zipporah his wife.
Oct. 13, Jonathan Aires.

1729. Feb. 9, Prudence Park, daughter of Thomas Park.
June 27, Thomas Park.
Oct. 5, Hannah, the wife of Ephriam Smith.
Dec. 14, Ammi Meech, the wife of Daniel Meech.

1730. Jan. 16, John Kimball and Sara his wife.
Apr. 5, Rose Meech.
May 17, Ammi Standish.
June 21, Patience, the wife of John Kimball of Stonington.
Sept. 25, Mary Mainor.

1731. Mar. 21, Abigail, the wife of John Killum.
Apr. 4, Jabez Cary and Hannah his wife, by letter from Windham.
Sept. 5, Elisabeth, the wife of Robert Park.
Sept. 24, David Morgan.
Sept. 24, Dorothy, the wife of David Morgan, baptized and received.

1732. Feb. 27, Dorothy, the wife of Thomas Woodward.
Nov. 12, Mary Crandal, baptized and admitted.

1733. Feb. 18, Abigail, the wife of Nathaniel Tracy.
June 8, Daniel Morgan and his wife Elisabeth.
Sept. 2, Jacob Kimbal and Mary his wife.
Dec. 2, William Wedge.
Dec. 23, Joseph Freeman.

1734. Jan. 11, Robert Park.
May 5, Abigail, the wife of David Tracy, by letter from Newent.
June 2, Elizabeth, the wife of Ebenezer Witter.
June 23, John Avery, by letter from Groton.
July 14, Lucy, the wife of Thomas Stanton, by letter from Groton.
July 28, Anna, the wife of John Avery.

1735. June 22, Nathaniel Tracy, Jun*r*.
July 20, Jemima, wife of Thomas Smith, by letter from Newent.
Aug. 8, Elisabeth, wife of Christopher Tracy.
Sept. 21, Margaret, wife of Epraim Jones.
Oct. 5, Martha, the wife of John Branch.
Oct. 26, Joseph Branch.

## 134 STATISTICS OF THE CHURCH.

1736. Feb'y 15, Ephraim Jones, baptized and admitted.
Apr. 4, Zerviah, the wife of William Witter, by letter from Canterbury.
May 2, Rebecca Treat.
June 11, Bethiah Richards, daughter of Deacon Wil^m. Richards.
July 23, Isaac Kimbal.
Aug. 15, James Freeman.
Oct. 31, Joseph Morgan and Ruth his wife.
1737. May 1, Sarah, the wife of Josiah Park.
May 29, Josiah Smith was baptized and received with his wife Ammi.
Aug. 14, Experience Staples.
1738. Jan'y 13, Dorothy, the wife of Sam^l Hill in Stonington.
Feb. 12, Bethiah, the wife of Ephraim Hodges, by letter from Norton.
Mar. 26, Ephraim Hodges, husband of the above.
June 4, Zipporah, the wife of Caleb Freeman.
July 16, Eliphall, the wife of Eleazer Park, baptized and admitted.
Sept. 29, Mary, the wife of Robert Little.
1739. Mar. 30, Eleazer Bellows, by letter from Southborough.
July 6, Christopher Avery and his wife Eunice, by letter from North Groton.
July 6, Patience, the wife of Will^m White, by letter from Norton.
Aug. 5, Daniel Park.
Sept. 9, Paul Park and Sarah his wife.
Nov. 18, Anna, the wife of Joshua Whitney.
Dec. 23, Abigail, the wife of Thomas Tracy.
1740. Feb. 7, Mary Fox.
Feb. 10, Prudence Treat.
Mar. 21, Sarah, the wife of Saml. Partridge and daughter of Salmon Treat.
May 30, Mehitabell, the wife of Joseph Freeman.
July 11, Samuel Treat, son of Salmon Treat, Past^r.
Oct. 5, William Witter and Hannah his wife.
Nov. 30, Jerusha, the wife of Jedidiah Tracy.
1741. July 19, William Richards and his wife Rebecca.
July 24, Simon Fobes.
Aug. 9, Mehitabell Richards.
Sept. 4, Samuel Branch.
Sept. 4, Beulah, mulatto, maid of Capt. Jno. Brewster and his wife Dorothy, my daughter, baptized and received.
Oct. 9, Simeon Fobes.
Oct. 9, Lemuel Tracy.
Oct. 9, Abigail Tracy.
Oct. 9, Hannah Meech.
Oct. 9, Abigail Tyler.
Nov. 26, Bridget, the wife of Joseph Gates.
Nov. 29, Mrs. Hannah Bellows, being an old woman.
1742. Sept. 12, Daniel Starkweather.
Dec. 26, Mary, the wife of John Ruid.

THE REV^d MR TREAT'S MINISTRY — CONTINUED — RENEWAL OF COVENANT ETC.

1698. Thomas Davison renewed covenant & submitted to discipline Dec^r 25^th.

1700. Elisabeth Experience & Martha Moor of Windham all being adults were baptised & submitted to discipline May 26^th.
The husband of Mary Pierce voluntarily confessed & submitted to our discipline Nov^r 10^th.

## STATISTICS OF THE CHURCH.     135

1701. The wife of Robert Geers was admitted to the privilege of baptism for children July 2d.
Josiah Haines submitted to our discipline Nov[r] 2[d].

1702. Abigail Knite, a maid living in Plainfield, was baptised & submitted to discipline & covenanted according to our usual practice before baptism June 28th.

1703. The wife of Joseph Prentice owned the covenant & submitted to our discipline, Mar[h] 14th.
The wife of Daniel Geers owned the covenant & submitted to discipline Aug[t] 1st.

1703. The wife of William Park & Thomas Clark owned the covenant Sept[r] 19th.

1704. James Morgan & Bridget his wife owned the covenant Mar[h] 26th.

1706. Joseph Keeney & his wife renewed their covenant & submitted to discipline Sept[r] 15th.
Mehitabel the wife of Tim[y] Starkweather was baptized & owned the covenant Sept[r] 29th.

1707. John Stanton & Mary his wife openly owned their covt & submitted to discipline Feb'y 3[d].
Eprahiam Herrick & Tabitha his wife renewed covt & personally resigned up to our discipline Feby.
Benjamin Parish & Mary his wife owned the covt of grace & submitted to discipline Feby 23[d].
Ezekiel Park renewed the covenant of grace & submitted to discipline Mar[h] 30th.

1707. James Tyler & his wife renewed covenant & submitted to discipline to Xts visible governm[t] July 2[d].
Samuel Sterrie renewed his covenant & submitted to our discipline or govorment Oct[r] 27th.

1708. Lydia the wife of Sam[l] Leonardson Jun[r] renewed cov.t. & submitted to discipline Nov[r] 7th.

1709. Richard Adams & Mercy, his wife renewed covt & rec[d] the privilege of baptism for children. Jan[y].
Samuel Gile owned the covenant & submitted to the govornm[t] of Christ openly Nov[r] 27th.

1710. Deborah the wife of Jno. Clark renewed covt openly, & submitted to Chh. discipline April 2[d].
Phebe Park, an adult, daughter of Nath[l] Park submitted to discipline & was baptised June 25th.
Joseph Freeman & his wife Hannah renewed covt & submitted to discipline Nov[r] 19th.

1711. Abigail, the wife of John Richards, renewed covt & submitted to discipline July 1st.
Hopestill Tyler & Anna his wife renewed covt & submitted to displine Oct[r] 21st.

1712. Samuel Standish & his wife renewed covt & submitted to discipline June 22[d].
Deborah, the wife of James Park, renewed covt & submitted to discipline Sept[r] 24th.

1713. David Tracy & Sarah his wife renewed covt & submitted to discipline Aug[t] 2[d].
Joseph Park & his wife Mary were baptised & submitted to displine Oct[r] 25th.
John Dane & his wife renewed covt & submitted to discipline in the chh Nov. 15th.

## STATISTICS OF THE CHURCH.

1714. Joseph Billings & his wife Comfort renewed covt and submitted to discipline Jan^y 17th.
Joseph Gates renewed covt & submitted to the discipline of the church Jan'y 17th.

1714. Christopher Tracy & his wife owned the covt & submitted to discipline Mar^h 7th.
Sarah, the wife of John Greenslit owned her covt & submitted to discipline May 30th.
Edward Stallin & his wife renewed covt & received privilege of baptism for their good Aug^t 11th.
Jerusha Smith, being an adult was baptised & submitted to discipline Nov^r 29th.

1715. Hannah, the wife of Stephen Gates owned her covt April 17th.
Thankfull, the wife of Dan^l Woodward renewed covt & was baptised Aug^t 7th.
Thomas Bennett & his wife Anna renewed covt & submitted to discipline Dec^r 11th.

1716. Jedidiah Tracy & Margaret his wife renewed covt & submitted to discipline Feby 12th.
Caleb Fobes renewed covenant & submitted to discipline in the church May 6th.

1718. Anna the wife of Hezekiah Fitch renewed covt & subm^d to discipline Nov^r 23^d.

1719. Ann, the wife of Thomas Polly entered into covt & was baptised May 17th.

1720. Margery, wife of Hez^h Park, renewed covt & submitted to discipline Nov^r 6th.

1724. James Frink renewed covt & submitted to discipline May 24th.

1726. Dan^l Smith of Stonington entered into covt & was baptised April 17th.
Thomas Robinson & Anna, his wife, renewed covt & submitted to discipline April 17th.
Thomas Woodward entered into covt & was baptised & submit^d to discipline July 31st.

1727. Hannah, the wife of John Clark Jun^r renewed her covenant Aug^t 25th.
John Eddy renewed covenant & submitted to our discipline Nov^r 12th.

1730. Lucy, the wife of Jed^h Frink, renewed her baptismal covenant Sept^r 20th.

1732. Lucy, the wife of John Swan, renewed covt & submitted to discipline April 16th.

1732. Esther & Susanna Smith, daughters of John Smith, were baptised & owned covt May 14th.

1741. Elijah Stanton & his wife, Elisabeth, renewed their baptismal covt. Aug^t 9th.

1742. Sarah, the wife of Benj^m Brewster, brought a certificate from the Rev^d Benjamin Lord of her having owned the covt & been admitted to the privilege of having her ch. baptised & was received under our watch & care & admitted to the same privilege here. July.

## STATISTICS OF THE CHURCH. 137

Rev. Mr. Treat's Ministry Continued. Baptisms of Children.

1698. Nov. 20, Zebadiah, son of Thomas Mix.
Nov. 27, Joseph, son of Jonathan Brewster.
Dec. 25, Jonathan, son of Thos Davison.
Dec. 25, A child of Charles Williams.
Dec. 25, Thomas, son of Peter Branch.

1699. Jan. 1, Sarah, daughter of John Welch.
Feb. 12, Mercy, daughter of Francis West.
Apr. —, David, son of Jno. Lamb in Stonington.
May 7, Mary & Lydia daughters of Thos Ruid.
May 7, Martha, daughter of William Park.
June 4, Anna Hutchinson.
June 4, Daniel, son of John Meech.
 Anna Treat at Stonington.
June 16, Bridget, daughter of Thos Stanton.
Nov. 4, Thomas, son of Henry Walbridge.
Dec. 1, James, son of Salmon Treat, Pastor.

1700. Jan. 19, Baptised at Plainfield Thomas, Joseph, Ebenezer & Nathan, children of Thos Williams. Ebenezer, Mary & Elizabeth, the children of Thomas Pierce, also Joseph, son of Jacob Warren. Philip, son of Edward Spalding. Elizabeth, Susanna and Mary, children of William and Mary Johnson.
Feb. 2, Dorothy, child of Peter Davison.
May 10, Mary, daughter of Jno. Meech.
June 1, Jonathan, son of William Park.
July 20, Mary, daughter of Robert Geers.
Sept. 28, Jerusha, daughter of Thos Laribee.
Nov. 2, Joshua, son of Josiah Haines.
Dec. 11, At Plainfield Mary and Abigail, the children of Samuel Cleveland. Nathaniel, son of Timothy Pierce. Abigail, daughter of Matthw Burton. Isaiah, son of Thomas Williams.

1702. May 10, Cyprion, son of Thomas Stevens, & Abiel, son of Wiliam Douglass, both the above at Plainfield.
May 31, Sarah, daughter of Thos Stanton.
 Joseph, son of Goodman Gile.
June 7, Joseph and Obed, sons of Joseph Benjamin.
 Jabez, son of James Fitch.
 A child of Robert Park.
 Bethiah, child of Daniel Brewster.

1703. Jan. 10, Dorothy, child of Ebenezer Witter.
Feb. 21, Joseph, son of Peter Davison.
March 7, Thomas, son of Thomas Davison.
March 14, Dorothy, child of Salmon Treat, Pastor.
 Joseph, son of Joseph Prentice.
 A child of Jacob Warren of Plainfield.
May 23, Abigail Witter was baptised.
 Mehetabel, child of Jonathan Ruid.
May 30, Samuel, son of Samuel Herrick.
June 6, Margaret, child of Jno. Safford.
June 13, Ebenezer, son of Jno. Welch.
July 3, Mary, daughter of widow Davison.
Aug. 1, Jonathan, son of Daniel Geer.
 Prudence, child of Thomas Gates.
Aug. 29th, Sarah, daughter of Jno. Ames.

138    STATISTICS OF THE CHURCH.

1703. Sept. 12, at Plainfield John, Henry & Rachel, the children of Josiah Cleveland & Susanna and Ruth, children of Jno. Smith. Timothy, son of Samuel Cleveland. Also John, son of William Douglass, and Jedidiah, son of Timothy Pierce.
Oct. 17, Phebe, child of Goodman Leonardson.
Dec. 5, Eliphalet, son of Thomas Laribee.

1704. Jan. 23, Jonathan & Anna, child$^n$ of Jon$^n$ Tracy Jun$^r$.
Feb. 13, Elizabeth, child of Joseph Benjamin.
Mar. 12, Anna, daughter of Jno. Stanton.
Apr. 10, William, son of Goodman Hanks.
Apr. 23, Martha, daughter Robert Geers of Pequonnock.
Apr. 30th, Dorothy, daughter of Robert Park.
June 18, A child of Thomas Averill.
June 18, A child of John Brown.
Sept. 17, Sarah, daughter of Daniel Tyler.
Sept. 24, Abigail, daughter of Thomas Park.
    Elisabeth, daughter of Joshua Wedge.
Oct. 15, Jonathan, son of Jonathan Fellows of Plainfield.
Oct. 22, Sarah, daughter of Peter Branch.
Dec. 3, Mary, daughter of John & Mary Parish.
Dec. 10, Jerusha, daughter of Salmon Treat, Pastor.

1705. Feb. 4, Mary & Theophilus, children of widow Elisabeth Stanton.
Mar. 18, Hannah, daughter of Josiah Standish.
    Noah, a child of John Ruid.
    Priscilla, daughter of Ephraim Herrick.
Mar. 25, Benjamin, son of Goodman Woodward.
    Hannah, daughter of Ebenezer Witter.
Apr. 22, William, son of Peter Davison.
May 27, Nathaniel, son of Goodman & Goodwife Hanks.
June 10, Jonathan, son of Lieut. Daniel Brewster.
June 24, Daniel, son of Ephraim Davis of Norwich.
July 1, Ebenezer, son of Henry & Anna Walbridge of Norwich.
    Susanna, Hannah, Sarah and James child$^n$ of George Halkin.
July 8, Isaac, son of Isaac Wedge of Norwich.
    Dorothy, daughter of Jonathan Geers.
    Christopher, son of Daniel Geers.
July 15, Hannah, daughter of Robert & Hannah Buswell.
Oct. 14, Nathaniel, son of Josiah & Hannah Prentice.
Dec. 16, Samuel, son of James & Bridget Morgan.

1706. Feb. —, Stephen, son of Samuel Herrick.
March 3, Hannah, daughter of Joseph Benjamin.
March 17, Abigail Plummer.
Apr. 28, John, son of Daniel Tyler of Groton.
June 9, Hannah, daughter of William Billings.
June 16, Joseph, the child of John Welch.
June 28, Isaac, the son of Isaac Morgan.
    Christopher, son of Thomas Davi—.
July 2, Anna, the daughter of John Ames.
July 14, Joseph, the child of John Safford.
    John, son of Thomas & Mary Averill.
Aug. 4, Phebe, daughter of John & Phebe Benjamin.
Sept. 15, Abigail, daughter of Joseph Kinne.
    Mary, daughter of Thomas Clark of Norwich.
Nov. 10, Abiel, a child of Charles Williams.
Nov. 24, Prudence, daughter of Salmon Treat, Pastor.
Dec. 1, Prudence, daughter of Thomas & Hannah Park.

## STATISTICS OF THE CHURCH. 139

1707. Jan. 12, Moses, the child of John Meech.
Feb. 3, John, the child of John Stanton.
Feb. 16, Benjamin, son of Timothy & Tabitha Herrick.
Feb. 23, Benjamin, son of Benjamin & Mary Parish.
Mar. 30, Daniel, son Ezek$^l$ Park.
Mar. 30, Rose, child of Robert Park.
Apr. 20, Anna, daughter of Benjamin Hanks.
Apr. 27, Booz, the child of Charles Williams.
May 4, Robert, son of Robert Geers.
May 4, Thankful, child of Tho$^s$ & Anna Stanton.
May 18, Nathaniel, the son of Nathaniel Tracy.
June 1, Sarah, the child of Joseph Geers.
June 13, Ephraim, the child Ephraim Herrick.
June 22, William, son of Eben$^r$ Witter.
June 22, Eunice, child of Dan$^l$ Woodward.
June 29, James, the child of James Morgan.
July 13, Daniel, the child of Thomas Gates Jun$^r$.
July 20, Moses, the child of James Tyler.
July 27, Jacob, the son of Joseph Kinne.
July 27, Mary, child of Thomas Averill.
Aug. 10, Rachel, the daughter of Peter Yarrinton.
Oct. 27, Joseph, the child of Peter Branch.
Hannah and Samuel, the children of Samuel Sterry.

1708. Feb. 29, Joseph, the child of Benjamin Parish.
Mar. 21, Hannah, daughter of Joseph and Hannah Prentice.
Mary, the child of Benjamin Hanks.
Apr. 4, Robert, daughter of Thomas & Patience Starkweather.
Apr. 11, Ebenezer, son of Dan$^l$ Geers.
Apr. 11, Sarah, child of Joseph Benjamin.
May 2, Jemima, daughter of John Benjamin.

1708. May 16, Mary, child of Josiah Standish.
May 16, Thomas, son of Tho$^s$ Clark.
May 23, Abigail, child of John Parish.
June 6, Roger, son of William Billings.
June 6, Cyprian, son of Sam$^l$ Sterry.
July 11, Experience, child of John Welch.
July 11, George, son of George Halkins.
July 18, Elisabeth, Patience & Jerusha, children of Tho$^s$ & Patience Starkweather.
Hannah, the daughter of Isaac Wedge.
Aug. 1, Gideon, the child of John Safford.
Aug. 12, William, the child of Ephraim Herrick.
Aug. 29, Desire and Thankfull, twin daughters of Timothy Herrick.
Sept. 12, Margaret, daughter of John Ames.
Sept. 19, Sarah, daughter of Salmon Treat, Pastor & Dorothy, his wife.
Oct. 3, Aaron, the child of John Meech.
Oct. 10, Daniel, the child of John & Mary Stanton.
Nov. 7, Lydia, daughter of Samuel Leonardson Jun$^r$.

1709. Jan. 2, Daniel, the child of Samuel Herrick.
Jan. 2, Elisabeth & Richard, children of Richard & Mercy Adams.
Feb. 20, Hannah, child of James Morgan.
Feb. 20, William, son of Joshua Wedge.
Feb. 28, Daniel, the child of Nathaniel Tracy.
May 8, Zipporah, daughter of Joseph Kinne.
June 26, Josiah, the child of Joseph Park.
June 26, Elisabeth & Joseph, the children of Benjamin Ellice.
July 10, John, the child of Thomas Davison.

140    STATISTICS OF THE CHURCH.

1709. Sept. 11, Moses, the child of Robert Buswell.
Peter, son of Peter Davison.
Sept. 11, Dorothy, child of Jnº & Abigail Freeman.
Sept. 25, Elisabeth, child of Jno. Brown.
Sept. 25, Mercy, child of John Benjamin.
Oct. 23, Jonathan, son of Jonathan Rood of Norwich.
Oct. 30, Thomas, son of Thomas Gates Junʳ.
Oct. 30, Mary, child of Benjⁿ Parish.
Nov. 20, John, the child of Benjamin Hanks.
Nov. 27, Mercy, the daughter of Samuel Gile.

1710. Apr. 16, Ebenezer, the child of Francis Plummer.
Apr. 23, Joseph, son of Isaac Morgan.
Apr. 23, Grace, child of Joseph Benjamin.
Apr. 23, Deborah, & Dorothy, daughters of Jno. & Deborah Clark.
May 8, John, the son of John & Deborah Clark.
Joseph, son of Jno. Stanton.
Ebenezer, son of Samˡ Leonardson Junʳ.
May 14, Ammi, the child of Israel Standish.
June 11, Dorothy, the daughter of John Parish.
July 2, Rebecka, daughter of Salmon Treat, Pastor.
July 23, Benajah, son of Nathaniel Tracy.
July 23, Rachael, the child of James Morgan.
July 29, Ebenezer, the child of Peter Yerrinton.
Aug. 6, Timothy, the child of Timothy Herrick.
Oct. 1, Jonas, the child of Samuel Prentice in Stonington.
Oct. 22, Jerusha, the child of Daniel Brewster Senʳ.
Nov. 5, Ichabod, the son of William Billings.
Nov. 5, Joseph, son of Timy Starkweather.
Nov. 19, Joseph, the child of Joseph Freeman.
Dec. 17, Allice, the daughter of John Laribee.

1711. Feb. 14, Abigail, the daughter of Deacⁿ Ebenezer Witter.
Mar. 4, Abigail, child of Joshua Wedge.
Mar. 4, Margaret, the child of Henry Walbridge.
Apr. 1, Mary, the daughter of John Starkweather of Stonington.
Apr. 22, Sarah, daughter of Samuel & Sarah Bishop of Norwich.
Esther, the daughter of John & Sarah Ames.
May 6, Joseph, son Samuel Herrick.
May 6, Elisabeth, child of Thoˢ Clark of Norʰ.
July 3, Eliphalet, the child of John Benjamin.
June 10, Prudence, child of Israel Standish.
June 10, Mary, child of Samuel Gile.
July 1, Hannah, the daughter of Benjamin Parish.
July 1, John, Daniel & Abigail children of John & Abigail Richards.
July 8, Daniel, the child of Joseph Kinne.
July 22, Mary, child of Thomas Park.
July 22, Robert, son of Samˡ Sterry.
Aug. 19, Mary, daughter of John Welch of Norwich.
Sept. 23, Solomon, the child of Samuel Parish of Norwich.
Oct. 21, Joseph, the son of Hopestill & Anna Tyler.

1712. Jan. 2, Jacob, son of John Brown.
Jan. 2, Hannah, child of James Tyler.
Feb. 6, Isaac, son of Ephriam Herrick.
Feb. 6, Rachel, child of Henry Hodge.
Apr. 13, Hannah, child of Thoˢ Davison.
Apr. 13, Lydia, child of Jno. Starkweather.
May 4, Joseph, son of Nathaniel Tracy.
May 4, Daniel, son of Joseph Freeman.

## STATISTICS OF THE CHURCH. 141

1712. June 1, Daniel, the child of James Morgan.
June 22, Deborah, the daughter of Samuel & Deborah Standish.
June 22, Samuel, son of Sam$^l$ Leonardson.
June 22, Joseph, son of John Clark.
June 29, Esther, daughter of Samuel Prentice of Stonington.
July 6, John, the child of Francis Plummer.
July 20, Elihu, son of Joseph Prentice.
July 20, Arthur, son of Tim$^y$ Starkweather.
July 27, Samuel, the child of Salmon Treat, Pastor.
Lydia, the child of John Stanton.
July 27, Olive, child of Thomas Stanton.
Aug. 10, Elisabeth, the daughter of Thomas Rose Jun$^r$.
Aug. 17, Jedidiah, the child of Joseph Benjamin.
Sept. 23, Olive, the daughter of Isaac Morgan.
Sept. 23, Aaron, son of James Park.
Oct. 5, Abigail, the daughter of James Rix Jun$^r$.

1713. Jan. 1, Paul & Ichabod, children of Thomas Averill.
Feb. 22, Esther, child of Sam$^l$ and Sarah Bishop of Norw$^h$.
Feb. 22, Rebecca, child of Jno. Richards.
Mar. 22, John, son of John Freeman.
Mar. 22, Joseph, son of George Halkins.
Apr. 26, Nathaniel, son of Samuel Parish of Norwich.
May 10, Robert, son of Timothy Herrick.
May 10, William, son of Dan$^l$ Geers.
May 31, Elisabeth, the daughter of William Billings.
June 28, Zerviah, the daughter of Samuel Sterry.
Aug. 2, Abigail, the daughter of Henry Hodge.
Aug. 2, a child of Benj$^n$ Parish.
Aug. 2, Sarah & Mary, daughters of David & Sarah Tracy.
Sept. 20, Ebenezer, child of Deacon Brewster.
Sept. 20, Isaac, Miriam and Eunice, children of Isaac Clark of Norwich.
Oct. 18, a child of Joseph Kinne.
Oct. 18, John, son of Samuel Gile.
Oct. 25, Sarah, the daughter of Joseph & Mary Park.
Nov. 15, Silas, John & Anna children of John Dane of Groton.
Dec. 20, Esther, the daughter of Samuel Prentice of Stonington.
Dec. 24, Martha, daughter of Mr. Cogsdell.
Dec. 24, Hannah, child of Tho$^s$ Averill.

1714. Jan. 3, Thomas, the child of Joshua Wedge of Norwich.
Jan. 6, Josiah, son of Thomas Rose Jun$^r$.
Jan. 6, Rachel, child of James Park.
John, son of John Benjamin.
Elisabeth Mackquithy.
Jan. 17, Ammi, the son of Joseph and Comfort Billings.
Jan. 25, Elisabeth, the daughter of Joseph Gates.
Feb. 7, Prudence, daughter of Thomas Starkweather.
Joseph and Rachel children of Joseph Park.
Feb. 11, Samuel, the child of Samuel Standish.
Feb. 21, Hannah, the daughter of John Ames.
Feb. 28, Hannah, the daughter of Joseph Freeman.
Mar. 7, Jonathan, the child of Christopher Tracy.
Mar. 21, Elisabeth, the daughter of William Richards.
Apr. 4, Joseph, the child of Thomas Clark of Norwich.
May 30, Jerusha, the child of John Clark.
May 30, John, son of John and Sarah Greenslit.
June 27, Dorothy, daughter of Amos & Hannah Woodward.
Benjamin, son of Nathaniel & Mehitabel Richards.
July 4, Joseph, surnamed Williams son of Allice wife of Sam$^l$ Ames.

1714. July 4, Samuel David, Mary & John, children of Sam¹ & Allice Ames.
Nathaniel the son of James Rix Jun'.
July 18, Thomas, son of Thomas Park.
July 18, Joannah, child of David Ruid.
Aug. 1, Edward, the child of Edward Stallin.
Sept. 26, Benjamin, the child of Isaac Morgan.
Oct. 31, Abraham the son of Sam¹ Gile.
Oct. 31, Daniel, son of Joseph Benjamin.
Nov. 7, Mary & Mehitabel, children of James Tyler.
Elisabeth, child of Hopestill Tyler.
Priscilla, child of Jno. Richards.
Nov. 29, Jemima, daughter of Salmon Treat, Pastor.

1715. March 6, Barzillai, the child of John Dane.
April 3, Elijah, the child of Thomas Stanton.
" 10, James, the child of Joseph Geers.
" 17, Caleb, son of Sam¹ Bishop of Norwich.
" " Hannah, child of Step'' Gates Jun'.
" 25, Nathaniel Cogswell.
May 22, Kezia, child of Sam¹ Herrick.
" " Mary, child of Joseph Park.
" 29, Jacob, son of Amos Woodward.
" " Mary, child of Tim'' Starkweather.
June 12, Hannah, daughter of Henry Hodge.
" 19, David, the child of Joshua Wedge.
July 10, Benajah, the child of Thomas Starkweather.
" 17, Hannah, and Thomas, children of Sam¹ & Deborah Partridge.
" 24, Dorothy, child of Tho⁵ Park.
" " Margaret, child of Tho⁵ Gates Jun'.
Sarah, child of Sam¹ Prentice.
Wait-still, son of Tim'' Herrick.
Aug. 7, Thankfull & Daniel, children of Dan¹ & Thankfull Woodward.
" 28, Anna, daughter of John Starkweather of Stonington.
Sept. 4, Nehemiah, son of Sam¹ Parish of Norwich.
" 18, Sarah, daughter of Joseph Billings.
Oct. 9, Thomas, son of Thomas & Phebe Beeman.
" 16, Samuel, son of Tho⁵ Davison.
" " Jacob, son of Jacob Burton.
Dec. 11, Thomas, the child of Thomas & Anna Bennit.

1716. Feby. 12, Jedidiah, the son of Jedidiah & Margaret Tracy.
" 19, Lucy, the daughter of Christopher Tracy.
March 11, Lois, child of Sam¹ Standish.
" " John, son of Benj'' Fitch of Norwich.
April 1, Eunice, the daughter of Joseph Kinne.
" 8, Caleb, the child of Joseph Freeman.
" 15, John, the son of Sam¹ & Deborah Partridge.
Nathan, son of Nicholas Williams.
Judith, child of John & Judith Ford.
" 29, Esther, daughter of Isaac Clark of Norwich.
May 6, Abigail & Joshua, children of Caleb Fobes.
" Mary, the daughter of John Renolds Jun'.
" 13, Abiel, the child of Samuel Ames of Stonington.
June 23, William, the son of Benj'' & Elizabeth Brewster.
July 22, Huldah, the daughter of John Stanton.
Aug. 5, John, the child of John Wilkeson.
" 12, Deborah, daughter of James Park.

STATISTICS OF THE CHURCH. 143

1716. Sept. 9, Asa, Anna, & Ephraim children of Widow Elisabeth Harris.
" " Jabez, the son of Widow Phebe Benjamin.
" 16, Elisabeth & Isaac, children of Francis & Elizabeth Tracy.
" " Tamson, child of Benj$^n$ Parish.
" " Zipporah, child of David & Sarah Tracy.
" 23, Naomi, the daughter of John Richards.
" 30, Hannah, the daughter of Amos Woodward.
Oct. 28, Anna, child of Mr. Robinson of Norw$^h$.
" " John, son of George Halkins.
Nov. 4, William, son of Will$^m$ Richards.
" " Lucy, child of David Andross of Norw$^h$.
Dec. —, Ebenezer, the child Jeremiah Tracy.

1717. Jan. 3, Joseph, son of Jos$^h$ Gates.
" " Charity, child of Jedi$^h$ Tracy.
Feb. 10, Amasa, son of Dan$^l$ Mix of Norw$^h$.
" " John, son of John Reed of Norw$^h$.
" 17, Anna, child of Hopestill Tyler.
" " Habbijah, child of Tho$^s$ Averill.
Mar. 31, James, son of John Freeman.
" " Priscilla, child of Obed Cook of Norw$^h$.
Apr. 7, Joshua, the child of Samuel Bishop of Norwich.
" " Grace, child of Benj$^n$ Brewster.
" " Francis, son of Francis Tracy.
" 21, Hannah, daughter of David Andross of Norwich.
" 28, Abiel, the child of Joseph Benjamin.
May 19, Susannah, a child of Joseph Geers.
" 26, Elisabeth, child of Joseph Park.
" " Sarah, child of Dan$^l$ Woodward.
June 2, Deborah, daughter of Sam$^l$ & Deborah Partridge.
" 12, Mary, daughter of Thomas Rose Jun$^r$.
" 23, Joseph, son of Edward Stallin.
" " Nathaniel, son of Isaac Morgan.
July 7, Elisabeth, daughter of Samuel Killum.
" 28, Judith, daughter of Edward Cogswell.
Oct. 3, Eunice, child of Caleb & Mary Gates.
" " Nathan, son of Sam$^l$ Leonardson.
Nov. 17, Sarah, child of Joshua Wedge.
" " Robert, son of Joseph Rose.

1718. Jan. 15, Eunice, daughter of Samuel Prentice of Stonington.
" 26, Sarah, daughter of Caleb Fobes.
Feb. 2, Elisabeth, daughter of Clement Chamberlain.
" 9, Habbijah, the child of Benjamin Fitch of Norwich.
" 23, John, the son of John Starkweather of Stonington.
March 2, William, the son of William & Jerusha Park of Stonington.
" 13, Stephen, son of Stephen Gates Jun$^r$.
" " Joseph, son of James Tyler.
" 23, Lydia, the daughter of John Ford.
Apr. 13, Jacob, son of Jacob Elliot.
" " Abigail, child of Sam$^l$ Standish.
" 27, John, son of Henry Hodge.
" " Ebenezer, son of Amos Woodward.
May 4, Joseph, son of Joseph Kinne.
" " Zebulon, son of Eben$^r$ Park.
June —, Abigail, the daughter of Richard Adams.
July 13, Reuben, son of Eben$^r$ Hibbard.
" " Deborah, child of Benj$^n$ Parish.

144    STATISTICS OF THE CHURCH.

1718. Aug. 3, Bethiah, the daughter of Christopher Tracy.
"    "  Robert, son of James Park.
"    "  Benajah, son of Thomas Park.
Sept. 14, Ebenezer, the child of Thomas Bennit.
"    27, Grace, the daughter of John Andross of Norwich.
Oct. 30, Phinehas, the child of Joseph Freeman.
Nov. 23, James, son of Hez$^h$ & Anna Fitch.
"    "  Margaret, child of Jed$^h$ Tracy.
1719. Jan. 25, Thankful, child of Francis Tracy.
"    "  Jerusha, child of Nath$^l$ Richards.
Feb. 1, Mehetabel, child of Will$^m$ Richards.
"    "  Mary, child of David Tracy.
"    22, John, the child of Samuel Renolds.
March 19, Jabez, son of John Stanton.
"    "  Abigail, child of John Freeman.
"    29, Abiel, the child of John Hill of Stonington.
Apr. 5, Ebenezer, son of Tho$^s$ Beeman.
"    "  Hulda, child of Tho$^s$ Kinne.
"    12, Daniel, the child of Joseph Park.
"    "  John, Zachariah, Jacob, Mary & Joseph Ruid.
May 17, Martha, child of Hopestill Tyler.
"    "  Jeremiah, son of Jer$^h$ Tracy of Norwich.
May 17, Hannah, child of Sam$^l$ Killum.
"    "  Mary, child of Caleb & Mary Gates.
"    31, Daniel, the child of Thomas & Ann Polly.
June 14, Jerusha, the daughter of Jacob Burton.
"    28, Caleb, the child of Caleb Fobes.
July 5, Joseph, the child of Joseph Geers.
Aug. 2, Soloman, the child of Ezekiel Park.
Sept. 13, Daniel, the child of Mr. Gore of Norwich.
"    20, Benjamin, the child of Benj$^n$ Fitch of Norwich.
"    27, Ebenezer, the child of Isaac Morgan.
Oct. 22, Damaris, child of Joseph Gates.
"    "  Soloman, son of Tho$^s$ Averill.
"    25, Lydia, the daughter of William Parish of Stonington.
Nov. 22, Thomas, the child of Samuel Prentice of Stonington.
1720. Jan. —, Simeon, the child of John Fobes.
Feb. 14, Dorothy, the daughter of Christopher Traey.
March 13, Ammi, the child of Jane Cook of Norwich.
"    27, Hannah, the daughter of Jacob Elliot.
April 3, Samuel, the child of Hezekiah Fitch of Norwich.
"    "  Samuel, the son of John Starkweather of Stonington
"    "  Sarah, the daughter of Samuel Standish.
"    24, Hannah, child of Mr. Cogswell.
"    "  Samuel, son of James Tyler.
"    30, James, son of James Billings of Ston$^n$.
"    "  Judith, child of Nat$^l$ Cady.
May 1, Ammi, the child of John Ford now of Norwich.
"    8, James, Margaret, Isaih, children of John Cook.
"    "  Ruth, the daughter of Daniel Woodward.
June 19, Patience, child of Joshua Wedge of Ston$^n$
"    "  Perez, son of Sam$^l$ Partridge.
July 3, Daniel, the child of Benjamin Parish.
"    17, Simon, son of Benj$^n$ Brewster.
"    "  Ruth, child of John Richards.
"    24, Elisabeth, child of Peter Randall.
"    "  Israel, son of Tim$^y$ Herrick.
Aug. 14, Miriam, the daughter of Francis Tracy.
"    24, Hannah, the daughter of Joseph Rose.

## STATISTICS OF THE CHURCH. 145

1720. Sept. 4, Phebe, child of Tho$^s$ Kinne.
" " Rebecca, child of James Park.
" 25, Henry, child of Henry Hodge.
Oct. 9, Thomas, son of Caleb Gates.
" " Oliver, son of Sam$^l$ Prentice.
" 23, Mary, the daughter of David Ruid of Stafford.
" 30, James, son of Nicholas Williams.
" " Sarah, child of Jed$^h$ Tracy.
Nov. 6, Elijah, the child of Hezekiah Park.
1721. Jan. 29, Esther, the daughter of Christopher Tracy.
Feb. 12, Paul, son of Hezekiah Park.
" " Margaret Smith of Stonington.
March 26, Hannah, child of Mr. Gore of Norw$^h$.
" " Matthew, son of Mat$^w$ Huntington.
April 16, Josiah, son of Joseph Gates.
" " Bethiah, child of Will$^m$ Richards.
Keziah, the daughter of Ezekiel Park.
May 14, David, son of David Tracy.
" " Thankfull, child of John Hill of Ston$^n$.
" 21, Samuel, the child of Samuel Killum.
June 4, Lydia, the daughter of John Dane of Groton.
" 25, Hannah, the daughter of Thomas Park.
July 2, Abigail, the daughter of Theophilus Baldwin of Stonington.
" 9, John, the child of David & Thankful Lamb.
" 30, Ruth, child of Hopestill Tyler.
" " A child of Robert Park.
Aug. 20, Daniel, the child of Thomas Beeman.
" 28, Benajah, the child of Benjamin Fitch of Norwich.
Sept. 10, Thankfull, daughter of Richard Ellis of Stonington.
" 24, Nathan, the child of Joseph Freeman.
Oct. 29, Timothy, son of John Swan.
" " Esther, child of Nath$^l$ Richards of Norw$^h$.
Dec. 28, Jerusha, daughter of Elishib Adams.
1722. Jan. 21, Mary, the daughter of John Fobes.
Feb. 15, Simon, son of Caleb Fobes.
" " Daniel, son of Tho$^s$ Starkweather.
" 25, Sherebiah, the child of Francis Tracy.
April 1, Phinehas & Abner, the children of John Killum.
" 22, Deborah, child of Chris$^r$ Tracy.
" " Ruth, child of John Richards.
May 6, Sarah, daughter of David Lamb of Stonington.
" 13, Israel, son of Sam$^l$ Standish.
" " Hannah, child of Jos$^a$ Wedge of Norw$^h$.
June 17, John, the child of John Starkweather of Stonington.
July 1, Ruth, the daughter of Thomas Beeman.
" 15, Zephaniah, the son of Isaac Clark of Norwich.
Oct. 14, Mary, child of Joseph Rose.
" " Eunice, child of James Billings of Ston$^n$.
" 21, Sarah, child of Caleb Gates.
" " John, son of John Ford of Norwich.
Dec. 16, Lemuel, the child of David Tracy.
1723. Jan. 24, Elisabeth, child of Hez$^h$ Fitch, Nor$^h$.
" " Daniel, son of Joseph Gates.
Feb. 3, Mercy, the daughter of Asa Harris, deceased.
" 14, Anne, child of Sam$^l$ Killum.
" " Zadok, son of John Killum.
March 6, Deborah & Lucy, twin children of Ezekiel Park.
" 10, Margaret, daughter of George Woodburn.
" 31, Abigail, the daughter of Jedidiah Tracy.

10

1723. April 7, Judah, the child of Benjamin Brewster.
" 14, Daniel, son of David Andross.
" " Rebecca, child of Jno Laribee of Norwich.
" 21, Hannah, daughter of Deacon William Richards.
May 26, Joseph, the child of Mr. John Williams of Norwich.
June 2, Jerusha, daughter of Christopher Tracy.
" 9, Jerusha, daughter of Benjamin Parish.
July 14, Mary, the daughter of Robert Park.
Sept. 1, Samuel, the child of Joseph Witter.
Oct. 23, Mehetabel, child of Eliashib Adams.
" " Josiah, son of Benjn Fitch.
" 27, Constant, the child of Caleb Fobes.
Nov. 3, James, the child of Nathaniel Richards of Norwich.
" 8, Timothy & Abigail, twin children of Hopestill Tyler.
" 29, Benjamin, the child of Joseph Freeman.
Dec. 15, Dorothy, child of Saml Prentice of Stonn.
" " Hezekiah, son of Hezh Park.
" " John, the child of John Hill of Stonington.
" 22, Jerusha, child of John Fobes.
" " Anna, child of Thomas Bennit.

1724. March 1, Sarah, the daughter of John Richards.
April 10, Hannah, the child of John & Sarah Meech.
" 19, Silas, son of Mr. Smith of Norwich.
" " John Palmer of Norwich.
" 26, Rose, the daughter of Francis Tracy.
May 24, James & Mary, children of James Frink.
June 10, Moses, son of Joshua Wedge.
" " Sibil, child of Benjn Andross of Norh.
" " Silvanus, the child of Silvanus Wintworth of Norwich.
July 12, Barnabas, the son of John Dane of Groton.
" 26, Thomas, son Saml Standish.
" " Elisabeth, child of Soln Story, Norh.
Augt 16, Solomon, the child of Christopher Tracy.
" 30, Henry, the child of John Story of Norwich.
Septr 2, Urania, daughter of Jabez Fitch of Norwich.
" 27, Elijah, the child of Richard Starkweather.
Octr 11, Samuel, son of Mr Fox.
" " Phinehas, son of John Ford of Norwich.
Novr 1, Abigail, daughter of Pelatiah Fitch of Norwich.
" 29, Abel, the child of Isaac Clark of Norwich.
Decr 20, Joseph, the child of Joseph Witter.

1725. Jan'y 3, Ebenezer, the child of Benjamin Fitch of Norwich.
" 17, Rachel, the daughter of David Tracy.
Feb'y 1, Sarah, the daughter of John Freeman.
" 14, Rufus, the child of Peter Yarrington.
Apr. 22, David, Eunice & Susannah, children of John Welch Junr of Norwich.
" " James, son of Nathl Giddins.
" " Sarah, child of Hugh Macniell.
May 9, Sarah, the daughter of John Killum.
" 23, Abel, son of Benjn Brewster.
" " Mebell, child of Francis Tracy.
July 4, Anne, the daughter of Hezekiah Fitch of Norwich.
July 11, Deborah, daughter of Samuel Killum.
" 25, Andrew, Stephen & Increase, children of Increase Billings, Stonn.
Augt 1, Jedidiah, the child of James Frink.
" 29, Joseph, son of Joseph Rose.
" " Anne, child of John Andross.

STATISTICS OF THE CHURCH. 147

1725. Sept<sup>r</sup> 5, Abigail, child of Benj<sup>n</sup> Parish.
" " Deborah, child of Elishib Adams.
" 19, Mary, daughter of Samuel & Abigail Park.
" 26, Nathan, son of Amos Richardson.
" " Nathan, son of Rich<sup>d</sup> Starkweather.
Oct<sup>r</sup> 3, Abigail & Nehemiah, children of Sam<sup>l</sup> & Abigail Park.
" 31, John, the child of Samuel & Abigail Park.
1726. Jan<sup>y</sup> 30, Ezekiel, the child of Deac<sup>n</sup> Ezekiel Park.
Feb'y 20, Rachel, child of Nathaniel Richards.
" " Jemima, child of Joshua Wedge.
Mar<sup>h</sup> 6, Samuel, the child of George Woodburn.
" 20, Bethiah, the child of Caleb Fobes.
" " Elisabeth, child of John Richards.
April 3, Hannah, the child of Daniel Meech.
" 10, Silas, son of Hez<sup>h</sup> Park.
" " John, son of Thomas Bennit.
" 17, Reuben, son of Tho<sup>s</sup> & Anna Robinson.
" " John, son of Joseph Gates.
May 8, Mary, the child of Daniel Smith of Stonington.
" 28, Hannah, the daughter of John Fobes.
June 12, Rufus, the child of John Hill.
" 19, Thankful, daughter of John Stanton of Groton.
June 26, Caleb, the child of Hopestill Tyler.
July 3, Samuel, the child of Joseph Freeman.
" 17, Mary, the daughter of Jedidiah Tracy.
" 31, Park, the child of Thomas Woodward.
Aug<sup>t</sup> 14, Temperance, daughter of John & Abigail Park.
" 28, Sarah, the daughter of Mr. Palmer of Norwich.
Sept<sup>r</sup> 18, Abigail, daughter of John Meech.
Oct<sup>r</sup> 9, Mebell, child of Dan<sup>l</sup> Tyler.
" Abigail, child of Sam<sup>l</sup> Story, Norw<sup>h</sup>.
Nov<sup>r</sup> 13, William & Jabez, children of John Park.
1727. Jan<sup>y</sup> 27, Oliver, the child of John & Dorothy Brewster.
" 29, Avery, Thankful & Desire children of Wil<sup>m</sup> & Mary Dennison.
" Ezra, the child of Joseph Witter.
Feb<sup>y</sup> 26, Irene, the child of David Tracy.
Aug<sup>t</sup> 20, Lucretia, the daughter of Jonathan Brewster.
" 25, Abigail & Timothy, children of John & Hannah Clark.
" 30, Olive, the daughter of John Branch.
Sept<sup>r</sup> —, Eliashib, the child of Eliashib Adams.
Oct<sup>r</sup> 22, Andrew, the child of John Park.
Nov<sup>r</sup> 19, John, son of John Eddy.
" " Samuel, son of Sarah Tyler.
Dec<sup>r</sup> 6, Sarah, the daughter of John Richards.
1728. Jan<sup>y</sup> 24, Dorothy, the daughter of John Brewster.
Feb<sup>y</sup> 14, Keturah, child of Francis Tracy.
" " Amasa, son of John Killum.
April 7, Zilpah, the child of John Park.
May 5, Ammi, the child of Joseph Rose.
May 19, Nathan, the child of Widow Abigail Fobes.
June 2, Moses, the child of Jonathan Tracy.
" 23, Jerusha, the daughter of Ephraim Smith of Stonington.
July 14, Mary, child of Joseph Freem(an).
" " Abraham, son of John Hill of Ston<sup>n</sup>.
Aug<sup>t</sup> 18, Mary, the daughter of Samuel Killum.
Oct<sup>r</sup> 10, Eunice, the daughter of Thomas & Zipporah Branch.
" 13, Mary & Anna, children of Richard Starkweather.
" 27, Ebenezer, the child of John Fobes.

1729. Feb$^y$ 9, John, the child of John Renolds.
Mar$^h$ 2, Nathan, the child of Jedidiah Tracy.
" 30, Judah, the child of Benjamin Brewster.
April 27, Thankful, daughter of John Clark Jun$^r$.
May 4, Elisabeth, daughter of Joseph Witter.
Aug$^t$ 17, Thomas, the child of Thomas Branch.
Sept$^r$ 28, Hannah, the daughter of John Brewster.
Oct$^r$ 5, Elisabeth, the daughter of John Eddy.
Nov$^r$ 23, Josiah, the child of Ebenezer Witter.
Dec$^r$ 7, Christopher & John, children of William & Mary Denison.
" 28, Daniel, the child of Daniel & Ammi Meech.
1730. Jan$^y$ 4, Timothy, the child of John Park.
April 8, Ruth, child of Jonathan Brewster.
" " Huldah, child of Moses Meech.
May 10, Grace, the daughter of Ephriam Smith of Stonington.
July 3, Jerusha & Mary, children of John & Patience Kimbal.
Aug$^t$ 9, Zipporah, daughter of Peter Yarrinton of Stonington.
" 30, Abel, the son of John & Abigail Park of Stonington.
Sept$^r$ 20, Thomas & Andrew, children of Jed$^h$ & Lucy Frink.
Oct$^r$ 11, Daniel, son of Jed$^h$ Tracy.
" " Hannah, child of Dan$^l$ Meech.
Nov$^r$ 22, Hannah, the daughter of Joseph Witter.
1731. Jan$^y$ 18, Rachel, the daughter of Joseph Freeman.
Feb$^y$ 17, Rachel, the daughter of Samuel Killum.
" 28, Joseph, son of Rich$^d$ Starkweather.
" " Zipporah, child of Tho$^s$ Branch.
April 9, Lydia, daughter of John Fobes.
" 18, Daniel, son of John Brewster.
" " Samuel, son of Jon$^n$ Tracy.
June 20, Hezekiah, son of Tho$^s$ Woodward.
" " Zephaniah, son of John Eddy.
" 27, Nathan, the child of John Killum.
Aug$^t$ 22, Ephraim, the child of Jonathan Brewster.
Sept$^r$ 5, Ebenezer, the child of John Clark Jun$^r$.
" 24, Isaac, son of David Morgan.
" " James, son of James Larribe, Norw$^h$.
" 26, Roswell & James, children of Robert Park.
Oct$^r$ 10, Ebenezer, son of Jabez Cary.
" " Isaiah, son of Tho$^s$ Bennit.
Nov$^r$ 5, Nathan, the child of Ebenezer Witter.
" 21, Lydia, the daughter of Eliashib Adams.
Dec$^r$ 17, John, son of Isaac Kimball.
" " Joseph, son of Jn$^o$ Kimball of Ston$^n$.
1732. Feb$^y$ 6, Ebenezer, the child of Samuel Prentice of Stonington.
" 24, Joshua, son of John Meech.
" 24, Huldah, child of Joseph Rose.
Mar$^h$ 5, Dorcas, daughter of John Branch.
" 19, Jemima, the daughter of Joseph Freeman.
April 16, John, the child of Mr. Fox.
" " Anna, Lucy & John, children of John Swan Jun$^r$.
" 23, Eliphalet, the child of John Renalds.
May 21, Jedediah, son of Jed$^h$ Frink.
" " Simeon, son of Jed$^h$ Tracy.
June 11, Zimram, son of Peter Yarrinton, Ston$^n$.
" " Mary, child of David Morgan.
July 2, Jerusha, daughter of Joseph Gates.
" 16, Susannah, daughter of Daniel Meech of Stonington.
Sept$^r$ 17, Ebenezer, the child of Joseph Witter.

## STATISTICS OF THE CHURCH. 149

1732. Nov<sup>r</sup> 26, Elisabeth, the child of Benjamin Brewster.
Dec<sup>r</sup> 3, Elkanah, the child of Moses Meech of Stonington.
" 31, Elisabeth, the daughter of John Fobes.
1733. Jan<sup>y</sup> 26, Jemima, the daughter of William Wedge.
Feb<sup>y</sup> 18, Mary, the daughter of Robert Park.
Mar<sup>h</sup> 11, Lydia, child of James Larribee, Nor<sup>h</sup>.
" " Sarah, child of Nath<sup>l</sup> Tracy.
" 18, Moses, son of Thomas Branch.
" " Olive, child of Rich<sup>d</sup> Starkweather.
April 1, John, the child of John Kimball, of Stoningtown.
" 8, Anna, daughter of Jonathan Tracy.
" 29, Seth, the child of Ephraim Smith, Stoning<sup>n</sup>.
May 27, Sarah, the daughter of John Brewster.
June 8, Hannah, child of Dan<sup>l</sup> & Elisab<sup>h</sup> Morgan.
June 8, Moses, son of Hez<sup>h</sup> Park.
July 8, Lydia, child of Sam<sup>l</sup> Killum.
" " James, son of John Eddy.
Sept<sup>r</sup> 2, Hannah & Lucy, children of Jacob & Mary Kimball.
" 16, John, son of Eben<sup>r</sup> Witter.
" " Abel, son of Isaac Kimball.
" " William, the child of Widow Deborah Adams.
Oct<sup>r</sup> 28, Jephtha, the child of John Killum.
Dec<sup>r</sup> 27, Daniel, the child of Joseph Freeman.
1734. Mar<sup>h</sup> 24, Ezra, son of Jed<sup>h</sup> Tracy.
" " Hannah, child of John Clark Jun<sup>r</sup>.
" 31, Nathaniel, son of Nath<sup>l</sup> Tracy.
" " Elisabeth, child of Dan<sup>l</sup> Morgan.
Hezekiah, child of Daniel Meech of Stoning<sup>n</sup>.
April 14, Anna, the daughter of David Morgan.
June 9, Jonathan, son of Jon<sup>n</sup> Brewster.
" " Elijah, son of Peter Yarrinton.
July 14, Lucy, the daughter of Thomas Stanton Jun<sup>r</sup>.
Aug<sup>t</sup> 11, Isaac, the child of Isaac & Lydia Lamb.
" 25, Amos, son of Jed<sup>h</sup> Frink.
" " Zilpah, child of John Branch.
Oct<sup>r</sup> 6, Sarah, daughter of John Kimball, of Stoning<sup>n</sup>.
Dec<sup>r</sup> 1, Zilpah, the daughter of Moses Meech, of Stonington.
1735. Jan<sup>y</sup> 12, Jabez, the child of Richard Starkweather.
" 23, Dorothy, the daughter of Thomas Woodward.
April 13, Abigail, child of John Avery.
" " David Garner, son of John Renalds.
May 18, Abel, son of Josiah & Mary Gibs.
" " Keziah, child of Tho<sup>s</sup> Branch.
July 13, Isaac, son of Isaac Kimball.
" " Mary, child of Eben<sup>r</sup> Witter.
Zipporah, the daughter of Ephraim Smith of Ston<sup>n</sup>.
" 20, Amos, the child of Benjamin Brewster.
" 27, Ruth, the daughter of Deacon John Fobes.
Aug<sup>t</sup> 8, Ruth, daughter of Christopher & Elisabeth Tracy.
" 17, Mary, the daughter of Joseph Freeman.
Sept<sup>r</sup> 14, Elisabeth, child of Robert Park.
" " Prudence, child of Nath<sup>l</sup> Tracy.
" 21, Elias & Desire, children of Ephraim & Margaret Jones.
" " Sibyl, the daughter of John Brewster.
Oct<sup>r</sup> 12, Abigail, the daughter of Samuel Killum.
" 26, Joseph, the child of Joseph Branch.
Nov<sup>r</sup> 9, Amos, the child of Hezekiah Park.
Dec<sup>r</sup> 14, Jacob, son of Jacob Kimball.
" " Mary, child of Jonathan Brewster.

# STATISTICS OF THE CHURCH.

1736. Jan^y 11, Ammi, the child of Jonathan & Ammi Tracy.
Feb^y 22, Asa, the child of Joseph Branch.
" " Richard, son of Jabez Chary.
Mar^h 28, Prudence, the daughter of Thomas Stanton Jun^r.
April 11, Esther, daughter of John & Olive Freeman.
" 18, Desire, the daughter, Christopher & Elisabeth Tracy.
May 9, Amos, son of Dan^l Meech, Ston^n.
" " Desire, child of Dan^l Morgan.
June 6, Reuben, the child of Ephraim Jones.
July 4, Benjamin, the child of Ebenezer & Susannah Brewster.
" 11, Abigail, the daughter of Peter Yarrinton of Ston^n.
Aug^t 22, Thomas, the child of Thomas Starkweather, Jun^r.
Sept^r 12, Lydia, the daughter of John Kimball of Ston^n.
Oct^r 3, Hulda, child of John Branch.
" " Jerusha, child of John Clark.
1737. Mar^h 20, Elijah, the child of Moses Meech of Ston^n.
April 13, Ammi, the child of Richard Starkweather.
" 17, Daniel, the child of Thomas Branch.
" 24, Jesse, son of Isaac Kimball.
" " Amos, son of John Avery.
May 8, Jacob, the child of Ebenezer Witter.
" 25, Joseph, Benjamin & Sybil, children of Josiah & Sarah Park.
" " Jonas, the child of Thomas Woodward.
" 29, Oliver, Nathaniel, Benjamin & Jonas, sons of Jos^h & Ammi Smith.
June 5, Olive, the daughter of John & Olive Freeman.
" 26, Olive, the daughter of Joseph Morgan.
July 24, Rosell, the child of David Morgan.
Aug^t 14, Anna, the daughter of Jedidiah Frink.
Sept^r 11, Temperance, daughter of Deacon Jedidiah Tracy.
Oct^r 2, Submit, the daughter of Nathaniel Tracy.
" 16, Susannah, the daughter of Ephraim Smith.
" 30, John, the child of Deacon John Fobes.
Nov^r 6, Lois, the daughter of Jonathan Tracy.
Dec^r 18, Mehetabel, daughter of Joseph Freeman.
1738. Jan^y 13, John, son of John Brewster.
" " Ammi, child of Sam^l & Dorothy Hill.
" 21, Elisabeth, daughter of Ebenezer Witter.
Jan'y 21, Lydia & Elisha, children of Ruth Eddy.
" 29, Christopher, child of Christopher Tracy.
Feb^y 24, Zipporah, the child of Daniel Morgan.
Mar^h 19, Mary, child of Jacob Kimball.
" " Keziah, child of Peter Yarrinton.
" 26, Lydia, the daughter of Jonathan Brewster.
April 16, Hannah, the daughter of Robert Park.
" 23, Rachel, the daughter of Ephraim Hodges.
May 21, Dorothy, child of Josiah Park.
" " Zerviah, child of Joseph Branch.
July 23, Ephraim, the child of Ephraim Jones.
Oct^r 8, Mary, the daughter of Robert & Mary Little.
Nov^r 12, Ammi, the child of Daniel & Ammi Meech of Stoning^n.
" " Peter, Unice, Simeon, Asa, Abijah, Elijah & Mary, chil^n of Eleaz^r Park.
1739. Feb^y 9, John, the child of John Meech.
" " Jesse, son of Richard Starkweather.
" 25, Dorothy, the daughter of Isaac Kimball.
" 28, Hezekiah, son of John Branch.
" " Patience, child of John Clark Jun^r.

STATISTICS OF THE CHURCH.    151

1739. April 22, Isaac, the child of Joseph Morgan.
    May 13, Lucy, the daughter of Caleb Freeman.
    June 3, Anna, the daughter of John Avery.
    July 1, Levi, son of Sam$^l$ Hill, Ston$^n$.
    "   " Abigail, child of Robert Little.
    "   22, Amaziah, the child of Peter Yarrington of Stoning$^n$.
    Aug$^t$ 5, Abigail, daughter of Thomas Beeman Jun$^r$.
    "   " Lemuel, son of David & Esther Lamb.
    "   " John son of Moses Meech.
    Sept$^r$ 30, Levi, the child of John Brewster.
    Nov$^r$ 18, Lydia & Lucy, children of Joshua & Anna Whitney.
    Dec$^r$ 9, Benjamin, child of Deacon Jedidiah Tracy.
    "   23, Enoch, son of Tho$^s$ & Abigail Tracy.
    "   " Ammi, child of Chris$^r$ Tracy.
1740. Jan$^y$ 13, Eunice, daughter of Christopher Tracy.
    "   27, Deborah, daughter of Thomas Tracy.
    Feb$^y$ 7, Ebenezer, son of Nath$^l$ Tracy.
    "   " Lois, child of Tho$^s$ Branch.
    "   24, Mary, daughter of Daniel Park.
    Mar$^h$ 16, Rufus, son of Joseph Branch.
    "   " Hannah, child of Deac$^n$ Jona$^n$ Brewster.
    "   23, Mebell, child of Tho$^s$ & Sarah Partridge.
    "   " Amos, son of Josiah Park.
    April 15, Dorothy, child of Jonath$^n$ Tracy.
    "   " Hezekiah, son of Robert Park.
    May 30, Hannah, child of Ephraim Smith.
    "   " Ebenezer, son of Wid$^w$ Susanna Brewster.
    June 22, Esther & Eunice, twin children of John Kimball of Stoning$^n$.
    July 11, Elijah, son of Paul Park.
    "   " Marah Moore, child of Prudence Treat.
    "   13, John, son of David Lamb, Ston$^n$.
    "   " Ezra, son of James Freeman.
    "   29, Consider, child of Joseph Morgan.
    "   " Hannah & Ammi, twins of Jo$^h$ Freeman.
    Sept$^r$ 14, Ephraim, the child of Ephraim Hodges.
    Oct$^r$ 5, Mary, the daughter of William Witter.
    Nov$^r$ 30, Margaret, the daughter of Jedidiah Tracy.
    Dec$^r$ 31, Benajah, son of Tho$^s$ Beeman Jun$^r$.
    "   " Eunice, child of John Brewster.
1741. Mar$^h$ 3, Josiah, the child of Ebenezer Witter.
    "   20, John, son of John Clark Jun$^r$.
    "   " James, son of Nath$^l$ Tracy.
    May 3, Margaret, daughter of Capt. John Avery.
    "   10, Jonathan, son of Jon$^n$ Tracy.
    "   " Moses, son of Jacob Kimball.
    June 14, Lydia, child of Caleb Freeman.
    "   " Mary, child of Tho$^s$ Woodward.
    July 26, Phebe, child of Wil$^m$ & Rebecca Richards.
    "   " Amaziah, son of John Branch.
    Aug$^t$ 9, Joshua, son of Elijah Stanton.
    "   " Abigail, child of John Freeman.
    "   30, Elijah, the child of Thomas Tracy.
    Sept$^r$ 4, Samuel, Soloman, Cyprian, Anna & Isaac, child$^n$ of Sam$^l$ Branch.
    Nov$^r$ 26, Mary, child of David Plummer.
    "   " Hannah, child of Joseph Gates.
1742. Jan$^y$ 24, Hannah, the daughter of Thomas Branch.
    Feb$^y$ 19, Alpheus, the child of Ephraim Jones.

## STATISTICS OF THE CHURCH.

1742. April 25, Phebe, child of John Kimball.
" " Zephaniah, son of Robert Little.
May 23, Susanna, child of Josiah Park.
" " Lydia, child of Joseph Morgan.
" 30, Moses, son of Moses Meech.
" " Allice, child of Daniel Park.
July 4, Jonah, son of Benj$^n$ Brewster.
" " Esther, child of Dan$^l$ Meech.
Sept$^r$ 5, Benjamin, the child of Deacon Jedidiah Tracy.
Oct$^r$ 10, John, son of Ebenz$^r$ Witter.
" " Hannah, child of Will$^m$ Witter.
" 31, Lucy, daughter of Richard Starkweather.
Dec$^r$ 5, James, child of James Freeman.
1743. Jan$^y$ 23, Elisabeth, child of Joseph Freeman.
" " Sabra, child of Jed$^h$ H. Tracy.
Feb$^y$ 27, Lois, child of Nath$^l$ Tracy.
" " Vine, child of Sam$^l$ Branch.
Mar$^h$ 6, Esther, daughter of Elijah Stanton.
" 20, Levi, son of John Brewster.
" " Bridget, child of Joseph Gates.
April 3, Sarah, the daughter of Ephraim Hodges.
June 5, Elisabeth, child of David Plummer.
" " Sarah, child of Tho$^s$ Tracy.
" 26, John, the child of Stephen Gates Jun$^r$.
Oct$^r$ 23, Asa, son of Jn$^o$ Freeman.
" " Sarah, child of Dan$^l$ Park.
Dec$^r$ 11, Caleb, son of Caleb Freeman.
" " Jonah, son of Will$^m$ Richards.
1744. Feb$^y$ 5, William, son of Will$^m$ Witter.
" " Lucy, child of Jed$^h$ Frink.

The Rev$^d$ M$^r$ Salmon Treat resigned the pastoral office Mar$^h$ 14$^{th}$ 1744, & departed this life Jan$^y$ 6$^{th}$ 1762 in the 90th year of his age.

---

## THE REV$^D$ ASHER ROSSITER'S MINISTRY.
### March 14. 1744 — November 17 1781.

Names of Communicants at his Settlement Mar$^h$ 14$^{th}$ 1744.

#### MALE MEMBERS.

Salmon Treat,
John Amos,
Jonathan Ayer,
John Avery,
Christopher Avery,
Eleazer Bellows,
Daniel Brewster,
John Brewster,
Jonathan Brewster Dea$^n$,
Thomas Branch,
John Branch,
Samuel Branch,
Joseph Branch,
Joseph Freeman,
James Freeman,
Simeon Fobes,
Simon Fobes,
John Hill,
Ephraim Hodges,
Ephraim Jones,
John Kimball,
Isaac Kimball,
Jacob Kimball,
Isaac Morgan,
Joseph Morgan,
John Meech,
Hezekiah Park,
Robert Park,
Paul Park,
Daniel Park,
John Richards,
William Richards,
Samuel Standish,
Ephraim Smith,

## STATISTICS OF THE CHURCH.

Daniel Starkweather,
Jedidiah Tracy, Dea$^n$,
Nathaniel Tracy,
Samuel Treat,
Total males 42.

Hopestill Tyler,
Joseph Witter,
Ebenezer Witter,
William Witter.

### FEMALE MEMBERS.

Mary Treat,
Lydia Ayer,
Anne Avery,
Unice Avery,
Elisabeth Brewster,
Dorothy Brewster,
Mary Brewster,
Dorothy Brewster,
Martha Branch,
Zipporah Branch,
Hannah Bellows,
Beulah — Mulatto,
Abigail Fobes,
Ruth Fobes,
Elizabeth Fobes,
Hannah Freeman,
Zipporah Freeman,
Mary Gates,
Bridget Gates,
Hannah Gates,
Elisabeth Hill,
Bethiah Hodges,
Margaret Jones,
Elisabeth Killum,
Sarah Kimball,
Prudence Kimball,
Mary Kimball,
Patience Kimball,
Abigail Morgan,
Ruth Morgan,
Sarah Meech,
Rose Meech,

Mary Little,
Margery Park,
Hannah Park,
Eliphal Park,
Elisabeth Park,
Abigail Park,
Sarah Park,
Mary Plummer,
Abigail Richards,
Rebecca Richards,
Patience Starkweather,
Mary Starkweather,
Jemima Smith,
Abigail Tracy,
Mary Tracy,
Ammi Tracy,
Abigail Tracy,
Abigail Tracy,
Jerusha Tracy,
Abigail Tracy,
Elisabeth Tracy,
Anna Tyler,
Abigail Tyler,
Prudence Treat,
Rebecca Treat,
Hannah Wilkison,
Elisabeth Witter,
Elisabeth Witter,
Hannah Witter,
Abigail Yarrinton,
Dorothy Woodward,
Margaret Woodburn.

Total Females 64.
Total Males & Females 106.

---

NAMES OF THOSE ADMITTED TO FULL COMMUNION BY MR. ROSSITER.

1744. Sept$^r$ 30, Zerviah, wife of Joseph Branch.
" " Mary, wife of Jon$^n$ Smith.
1745. July 14, Olive, the wife of John Freeman.
Nov$^r$ 24, Edey, wife of Caleb Fobes made a publick confession to God & this church of a former breach of Sabbath & was rec'd to full communion.
1746. June 15, Anna Renolds.
1747. Nov$^r$ 15, Thankfull Fisher.
1754. Aug$^t$ 18, Elisabeth Amos.
1755. Oct$^r$ 2, Elisabeth, wife of Ebenezer Witter made confession & was restored to full communion.
1756. Mar$^h$ 14, Esther, wife of Samuel Tracy.
May 30, Jemima, the wife of Joseph Keene.

1758. April 16, Jonathan Brewster, Jun^r.
July 16, Abigail, The wife of Roger Sterry.
Nov^r 26, Betty, Negro servant of Mr. D. Lamb.
1761. June 21, Samuel Morgan, & his wife Elisabeth.
1764. Nov^r 18, Mary, the wife of David Safford.
1765. April 14, Margaret Ames.
Aug^t 24, Martha Starkweather.
1766. June 22, Simeon Tracy.
" " Abigail, wife of Peter Bowdish.
" " Jemima, wife of Ezra Tracy.
Sept^r 28, Abigail Plumer.
Nov^r 16, Lois, the wife of Simeon Tracy.
1767. Nov^r 15, Esther, the wife of John James.
1769. Jan^y 1, Zipporah, the wife of Jonathan Brewster.
Mar^h 12, Hannah, the wife of Samuel Branch.
1771. Jan^y 27, The Widow Miriam Ames.
1772. May 17, Ruth Fobes 2^d.
1776. Dec^r 1, Hannah, the wife of Simeon Morgan.
1777. Mar^h 30, Elisabeth Avery.

Names of those recommended from other Ch'h's & received &c.

1744. July 1, Anna, wife of Joseph Freeman, recommended by the Rev^d M^r Wight & the church in East Norwich, was received to communion.
Oct^r 21, Park Avery, from the first church in Groton.
Nov^r 18, Joseph Stanton & his wife Abigail, from the 2^d Ch'h in Preston.
1745. Jan^y 6, Esther, wife of Daniel Park, from the second Ch'h in Preston.
Feb^y 17, Lucy, wife of Ephraim Smith from the 2^d Ch'h in Stonington.
1751. Sept^r 1, Mary, wife of Thomas Tracy from the 1^st Ch'h in Canterbury.
1753. Sept^r 2, Lucy, wife of Eben^r Avery from the 1^st Ch'h in Groton.
1756. May 30, Joseph Keene.
1758. Nov^r 12, Doct^r Benj^n Blodget from second Ch'h in Stonington.
1760. June 1, Elisabeth Witter from the Ch'h in Newent.
Nov^r 17, Constant Searl, from the Ch'h in Little Compton.
1761. Feb^y 21, Mary, wife of Deac^n Joseph Freeman from the Ch'h in Norwich.
May 30, Oliver Crary & his wife from the Ch'h in Westerly.
1764. Anna MacFarlin from the Ch'h in Reading.
1771. June 21, Mary Avery from the first Ch'h in Groton.
1780. June 30, Samuel MacFarling from the Ch'h in Wrentham.

Names of those who owned their Covenant.

1754. Nov^r 17, Nathan Freeman.
1755. April 20, Jonathan Brewster & his wife Zipporah.
May 4, Zipporah, the wife of Joseph Smith.
July 13, Elij^h Starkweather & wife Esther.
" Mebel wife of Joseph Williams.
Oct^r 26, Elisabeth wife of Caleb Ruid.
1756. June 20, Jemima Wells, confessed & owned Cov^t.
" 27, Abigail Sterry.

STATISTICS OF THE CHURCH. 155

1757. April 17, Andrew Gates & wife Olive confessed, owned Cov$^t$ & he baptised.
Sept$^r$ 25, Joseph Johnson & his wife.
" " Joseph Park, & his wife.
1759. May 6, Elisha Dennison, & his wife.
June 17, Zilpha, wife of Isaac Morgan.
" " Hannah, wife of Step$^n$ Starkwe$^r$.
Dec$^r$ 16, Simeon Tracy & his wife Lois.
1760. Feb$^r$ 24, Samuel Leonard Jun$^r$ & his wife Mary.
1761. April 19, Esther Tracy Jun$^r$.
June 21, Mary, the wife of John Safford.
1763. Jan$^y$ 9, Elijah Barns & wife Lucy confessed & owned Cov$^t$.
June 5, Eunice Bundy confessed & owned Cov$^t$.
1767. July 19, Temperance, the wife of Nathan Fobes.

NAMES OF PERSONS MARRIED BY HIM.

1744. Sept$^r$ 27, Rufus Yarrington & Lucretia Brewster.
1745. Jan$^y$ 2, Benjamin Freeman & Abigail Tracy.
Mar$^h$ 26, Samuel Johnson of Plainfield & Abigail Meech.
Dec$^r$ 17, Christopher Dennison & Abigail Tyler.
1746. Mar$^h$ 13, Park Woodward & Zilpha Park.
May 22, Sherebiah Tracy & Hannah Wentworth.
Dec$^r$ 3, Samuel Witter & Sarah Calkins.
" 26, Jacob Tyler & Elisabeth Clark, widow.
" 31, John Hill & Thankful Clark.
1747. Jan$^y$ 15, Negro Sharp & Negro Betty servants of Eph$^m$ Smith & Dan$^l$ Lamb.
May 19, Jonathan Tracy & Lucy Avery.
Sept$^r$ 30, Andrew Davis & Eunice Kimbal.
" Nov$^r$ 5, Daniel Geers & Mary Starkweather.
" " 25, Elijah Bliss & Mary Tracy.
1748. Jan$^y$ 4, Timothy Clark & Mary Rude.
" Oct$^r$ Simeon Fobes & Ruth Brewster.
1751. Oct$^r$ 22, Nathan Starkweather & Dorcas Hamlinton.
" Nov$^r$ 5, Andrew Gates & Olive Starkweather.
" " 20, Joseph Smith & Zipporah Branch.
1752. April 2, Hezekiah Lord & Jerusha Gates.
" July 30, Solomon Story & Dorcas Branch.
" Nov$^r$ 9, Zephaniah Spicer & Sarah Starkweather.
1753. Nov$^r$ 1, Thomas Davison & Rachel Rude.
" " 15, Nathan Witter & Kesiah Branch.
" " 28, Asa Park & Rachel Park.
1754. Jan$^y$ 2, Joseph Williams & Mabel Meech.
" " 3, Joseph Witter Jun$^r$ & Hannah Davison.
" Feby. 13, Nathan Kimbal & Margaret Rix.
" May 15, John Utley & Desire Tracy.
" " 23,, James Rix & Hannah Safford.
" Aug$^t$ 7, Jonathan Calkins & Jerusha Clark.
" " 15, Samuel Hill & Silence Rude.
1755. Feby. 3, Ebenezer Clark & Eunice Calkins.
" May 15, Joshua Gates & Anna Branch.
" June 5, Moses Tracy & Esther Tracy.
" Sept$^r$ 17, Amos Story & Hannah Renolds.
" Dec$^r$ 25, Sam$^l$ Leonard & Mary Freeman.
" " 25, George Brown & Huldah Lari(    ).

1756. Jan^y 29, David Ames & Abigail Butler.
" Feb^y 26, Samuel Renolds & Ruth Tracy.
" May 6, Enos Tracy & Lydia Whitney.
" Nov^r 4, Jacob Robinson & Anna Tracy.
" Dec^r 1, Doxie Lane & Esther Freeman.
" " 15, Jedidiah Frink Jun^r & Esther Pierce.
1757. May 26. Jacob Stephens & Elisabeth Leonard.
" Dec^r 22, Benjamin Kenedy & Olive Rude.
1758. Jan^y 5, John Branch & Priscilla Tracy.
" Mar^h 23, Christopher Tracy & Rose Tracy.
" Sept^r 13, Simeon Tracy & Lois Branch.
" Oct^r 5, Simeon Bundy & Unice Meech.
" Nov^r 22, Allen Leet & Rachel Morgan.
1759. Mar^h 15, John Safford & Mary Johnson.
" Oct^r 4, John Geer & Jerusha Park.
1760. Mar^h 5, Isaac Branch & Susanna Weakly.
" Dec^r 4, Rossel Morgan & Martha Downer.
1761. Sept^r 16, Thomas Partridge & Zipporah Freeman
" Nov^r 4, William Brewster & Olive Morgan.
" " 15, Caleb Gates & Elisabeth Branch.
" " 26, Ebenezer Benjamin & Phebe Benjamin.
" Dec^r 10, Edward Mott & Sarah Kinne.
" " 16, Abijah Park & Elisabeth Morse.
1762. Feb^y 25, Asa Partridge & Eliphal Geer.
" " 25, John Putnam & Martha Woodward.
" Joshua Downer & Huldah Crary.
" April 22, Ebenezer Prentice & Lucy Cary.
" May 13, Will^m Robinson & Anne Blake.
" " 13, Elijah Barnes & Lucy Kinne.
" June 10, Reuben Park & Sarah Rockwell.
" " 17, Oliver Spalding & Mary Witter.
" " 17, Oliver Sisson & Mary Park.
" " 24, Ames Leonard & Mary Partridge.
" " 24, Henry Herrick & Unice Putnam.
" July 1, Benajah Tracy & Lucy Herrick.
" Aug^t 26, Simeon Morgan & Hannah Morgan.
" Oct^r 28, Daniel Rix & Rebecca Johnson.
1763. Feby. 10, Ezekiel Bundey & Ama Starkweather.
" May 5, Nathan Fobes & Temperance Tracy.
" Aug^t 18, Elijah Morgan & Dorothy Morgan.
" Nov^r 3, James Tracy & Phebe Richards.
" " 6, John Anslay & Eunice Bundey.
" " 10, Elisha Eddy & Bersheba Pierce.
" " 17, Nathan Fobes Jun^r & Elisabeth Fobes.
" Dec^r 8, Silas Sterry & Olive Killam.
1764. Jan^y 12, Nathan Leonard & Hannah Branch.
" April 5, Moses Meech & Elisabeth Plummer.
" Nov^r 21, Jeremiah Kinne & Elisabeth Plummer.
1765. May 12, Moses Porter & Sarah Park.
" Nov^r 24, Samuel Mott & Abigail Rosseter.
1766. Mar^h 30, David Benjamin & Esther Wibourn.
" May 1, Nathan Geer & Jerusha Tracy.
" Sept^r 18, Asa Branch & Elisabeth Tracy.
" Nov^r 20, Newman Perkins & Abigail Dennison.
1767. Jan^y 4, Joseph Jeffers & Ruhama Downing.
" Mar^h 12, Nathan Ayres & Desire Tracy.
" April 9, Abel Partridge & Eunice Story.

## STATISTICS OF THE CHURCH. 157

1768. Jan<sup>y</sup> 7, Jonas Brown & Mary Clark.
" April 13, William Farnham & Jerusha Starkweather.
" " 17, John Morgan & Eunice Crary.
" " 21, Asa Smith & Elisabeth Morgan.
" Dec<sup>r</sup> 25, Hezekiah Tracy & Eunice Rude.
1769. Feb<sup>y</sup> 19, David Benjamin & Lucy Park.
" " 24, John Crary & Anna Morgan.
" Mar<sup>h</sup> 9, Dan Rude & Deborah Meech.
" April 10, Jonathan Boardman & Priscilla Safford.
" " 13, Simeon Lathrop & Esther Branch.
" June 2, Hutchinson MacFarlin & Lucy Randal.
" Aug<sup>t</sup> 3, Jedidiah Wilbur & Abigail Plummer.
" Nov<sup>r</sup> 23, Jonathan Smith & Hannah Witter.
" Dec<sup>r</sup> 7, Timothy Lester Jun<sup>r</sup> & Elisabeth Kinne.
1770. Mar<sup>h</sup> 1, Elijah Tracy & Lois Smith.
" " 22, Amasa Branch & Thankful Bowdish.
" " 29, Jedidiah Fitch & Elisabeth Hillyar.
" April 1, Francis Plummer & Keziah Kinne.
" " 5, Nathan Thomas & Sarah Bowdish.
" May 14, William Whitney & Mary Fobes.
" June 10, Nathan Peters & Lois Crary.
" Sept<sup>r</sup> 13, Abraham Yarrinton & Eunice Bundey.
" " 18, James Smith & Ama Blason.
" Dec<sup>r</sup> 2, John Andros 3<sup>d</sup> & Grace Rude.
1771. April 11, Hezekiah Douglass & Esther Witter.
" Aug<sup>t</sup> 5, John Page & Ama Geer.
" " 29, Samuel Prentice & Anne Benjamin.
" Sept<sup>r</sup> 18, Abiel Benjamin & Lovisa Ellis.
" Nov<sup>r</sup> 14, Nathaniel Tracy & Miriam Ames.
1772. Jan<sup>y</sup> 1, Jonathan Rawson & Bathsheba Tracy.
" " 16, Jonas Avery & Mary Avery.
" June 1, Charles Mile & Sabra Bennit.
" " 17, Reuel Cook & Elisabeth Jones.
" Aug<sup>t</sup> 14, Jonathan Sweet & Anna Dennison.
" Sept<sup>r</sup> 24, Thomas Main & Lucy Tyler.
1773. June 23, Daniel Kimbal & Mary Sterry.
" July 29, Solomon Storey & Dorothy Rude.
" Aug<sup>t</sup> 25, Joseph Robbins & Mary Wilkinson.
" Oct<sup>r</sup> 14, Calvin Barstow & Margaret Tracy.
1775. Feby. 26, Jabez Brewster & Dorothy Park.
" April 19, Silas Bliss & Judith Freeman.
" July 20, Ziba Baldwin & Ama Brown.
" Aug<sup>t</sup> 17, William Brown & Elisabeth Tyler.
" " 31, Newport William & Mercy Cossump.
" Sept<sup>r</sup> 6, Nathaniel Stanton & Ama Avery.
1776. Oct<sup>r</sup> 4, John Potter & Elisabeth Witter.
1777. Jan<sup>y</sup> 22, Emmanuel Northrup & Phebe Brown.
" " 23, Daniel Morgan & Johannah Brewster.
" Feb<sup>y</sup> 25, David Morse & Esther Laribee.
" April 17, Thomas Wilbur & Rachel Herrick.
" May 1, Christian Gosmer & Mary Rouse.
" May 13, Rev<sup>d</sup> Aaron Putnam & Elisabeth Avery.
" June 22, Abel Cook & Elisabeth Branch.
" Sept<sup>r</sup> 9, James Rockwell & Anna Williams.
" " 25, Jonathan Daboll & Rebecca Cunningham.
" Nov<sup>r</sup> 12, Joseph Emes & Hannah Tyler.

1778. Jany. 1, Elisha York & Ama Clark.
" April 9, Levi Tracy & Lucy Frink.
" June 18, York Quomine & Phillis Hill.
" July 16, Edward Tracy & Azuba Jennings.
" Aug$^t$ 13, Avery Dennison & Prudence Brown.
" Sept$^r$ 13, Erastus Rosseter & Lydia Perkins.
" Nov$^r$ 15, Caleb Kight & Elisabeth Richards.
1779. Feby. 4, Benjamin Babcock & Desire Billings.
" Mar$^h$ 21, Rufus Park & Zerviah Laribee.
" Nov$^r$ 28, Jeremiah Wilbur & Sabra Tracy.
1780. April 13, Daniel Meech & Zerviah Witter.
" May 18, Amos Hutchinson & Lucy Kinne.
" " 25, John Starkweather & Hannah Leonard.
" June 13, Ephraim Starkweather & Rachel Clark.
" Aug$^t$ 16, Ezekiel Rude & Phebe Rix.
" Sept$^r$ 24, Nathan Johnson & Mary Maclain.
" Dec$^r$ 7, Frederick Witter & Lydia Tyler.
" " 7, Robert Crary Jun$^r$ & Cynthia Lamb.
1781. Mar$^h$ 8, Roswell Park & Eunice Starkweather.
" May 10, David Palmer & Anna 'Ray.

## BAPTISMS.

1744. April 1, Asa, son of John Branch.
" " 1, Stephen, son of Tho$^s$ Branch.
" " 8, Ama, the daughter of Isaac Kimbal.
" June 3, Margaret, daughter of Robert Little.
" " 7, Lois, the daughter of Moses Meech.
" July 1, Jerusha, daughter of Simeon Fobes.
" " 8, Paris, son of Jon$^n$ Tracy.
" " 8, Jabez, son of Nath$^l$ Tracy.
" " 15, Elijah, the child of John Clark.
" Aug$^t$ 12, Elisabeth, child of Joseph Branch.
" " 12, Asahel, son of Jed$^h$ Tracy Jun$^r$.
" " 15, Damaris, daughter of Joseph Gates.
" Sept$^r$ 2, Jonathan, child of Christopher Tracy.
" " 23, Tamson, daughter of Daniel Meech.
" Oct$^r$ 7, Asa, son of Ebenezer Witter.
" " 7, Asa, son of Widow Whitney.
" " 7, Josiah, the child of Josiah Park.
" " 21, Jasper, the child of Park Avery.
" " 28, Anna, the daughter of Ephraim Smith.
" Nov$^r$ 11, Lois, the daughter of Benjamin Brewster
" Dec$^r$ 20, Joseph, the child of Joseph Freeman.
1745. Jany. 20, Elisabeth, child of Chris$^r$ Tracy.
" " 20, Joshua, son of Widow Whitney.
" Mar$^h$ 24, Abigail, daughter of David Plummer.
" April 21, Samuel, the child of David Park.
" April 28, Amos, the child of James Freeman.
" May 19, Joseph, the child of Joseph Morgan.
" July 7, Benajah, son of Tho$^s$ Tracy.
" " 7, Susanna, child of Simeon Fobes.
" Sept$^r$ 22, Zipporah, daughter of Caleb Freeman.
" Oct$^r$ 6, Margaret, daughter of Benjamin Freeman.
" " 20, Sarah, the daughter of Elijah Stanton.
" Nov$^r$ 24, Caleb, the child of Caleb Fobes.
" Dec$^r$ 1, Phebe, child of Jon$^n$ Smith.
" " 1, Amasa, son of Joseph Branch.

## STATISTICS OF THE CHURCH.

1746. Feby. 2, Phebe, the daughter of Richard Cook.
" Mar^h 23, Zerviah, the daughter of William Witter.
" " 30, Jonah, the child of Deacon Jonathan Brewster.
" May 4, Asaph, the child of Capt. John Brewster.
" June 29, Nathan, the child of Thomas Branch.
" July 27, Elias, the child of Jedidiah Frink.
" Aug^t 10, Joseph, the child of Benjamin Fitch.
" " 17, Ebenezer, the child of Park Avery.
" " 31, Lucy, the daughter of Ephraim Smith.
" Oct^r 5, James, the child of Ebenezer Witter.
" " 26, Dorothy, the daughter of Nathaniel Tracy.
1747. Feby. 1, William, the child of Caleb Fobes.
" Mar^h 8, Abel, the child of John Branch.
" " 29, Mary, the daughter of Moses Meech.
" Margaret Ames, professed faith & was baptized.
" April 12, Martha Ames, professed faith & was baptized.
" May 3, Francis, the child of David Plummer.
" May 17, Asher, the child of Asher Rosseter, Pastor.
" " 26, Esther, wife of Sam^l Tracy, owned the Cov^t & brought her child^n Samuel, Esther, Priscilla, Elisabeth & Miriam to baptism.
" " 31, Jerusha, child of Jed^h Tracy Jun^r.
" " 31, Jerusha, ch^d of Dan^l Starkweather.
" Sept^r 20, Mary, the daughter of Caleb Freeman.
" Oct^r 18, Nathaniel, the son of Daniel Park.
" Nov^r 15, Thankful Fisher.
" Dec^r 13, Eunice, the daughter of Joseph Witter.
1748. Jany. 14, Roger, son of John Clark.
" " 14, Phinehas, son of Joseph Freeman.
" " 26, Thomas, the child of Josiah Park.
" Feby. 28, Mary, child of Simeon Fobes.
" " 28, Lois, child of Jon^n Smith.
" Mar^h 27, Mary, the daughter of Christopher Dennison.
" May 6, Margaret, daughter of Ebenezer Avery.
" " 8, Elias, the child of Benjamin Brewster.
" " 15, Rebecca Yarrinton, owned the Cov^t & her children, Jonathan & Rachel, were baptized.
" " 15, Daniel, son of Wil^m Witter.
" July 3, Appleton Walcott, son of Asher Roseter, Pastor.
" Nov^r 27, Esther, daughter of Thomas Branch.
" " 30, Sarah, daughter of Josiah Park.
" Dec^r 25, Stephen, the child of Samuel Tracy.
1749. Feby. 8, Thankful, daughter of Ephraim Smith.
" April 16, Ebenezer, son of Nath^l Tracy.
" " 16, Duella, son of Joseph Morgan.
" April 21, Moses, the child of Daniel Park.
" June 4, Rufus, the child of Jedidiah Tracy Jun^r.
" " 11, Ebenezer, child of Joseph Freeman.
" July 9, Lucy, the daughter of Caleb Freeman.
" Sept^r 3, Aaron, the child of Moses Meech.
" Oct^r 1, Eunice, the daughter of Simeon Fobes.
" " 15, Abigail, daughter of Asher Rosseter, Pastor.
" Dec^r 17, Lucy, wife of Jonat^n Tracy professed faith & was baptized.
Lucy, daughter of Jonathan & Lucy Tracy.
1750. April 5, Esther, the daughter of Daniel Park.
" May 20, Hannah, daughter of Capt. William Witter.
" July 15, Abigail, daughter of Nathaniel Tracy.
" " 22, John, the child of M^r Jonathan Jackson.

1750. Sept$^r$ 9, Asa, the child of Daniel Starkweather.
" Oct$^r$ 28, Dorothy, daughter of Ebenezer Avery.
" Nov$^r$ 27, Hannah, daughter of Jonathan Tracy.
" Dec$^r$ 2, Asahel, the child of Jonathan Smith.
1751. Mar$^h$ 17, Lucretia, daughter of Samuel Tracy.
" " 31, Timothy, the child of Asher Rosseter, Pastor.
" Dec$^r$ 22, Margaret, daughter of Jedidiah Tracy Jun$^r$.
1752. Jan$^y$ 5, Lucretia, daughter of Simeon Fobes.
" April 11, Anna, daughter of Caleb Freeman.
" " 26, Nathaniel, son of Tho$^s$ Tracy.
" " 26, Israel, son of Jonathan Tracy.
" Joanna, daughter of Benjamin Brewster.
" May 3, Isaac, the child of Daniel Park.
" Aug$^t$ 2, Erastus, the child of Asher Rosseter, Pastor.
" Aug$^t$ 16, Frederic, the child of William Witter Esq$^r$.
" Dec$^r$ 3, Ezra, the child of David Plummer.
1753. Jan$^y$ 21, Roger, the child of Daniel Starkweather.
" May 6, Ebenezer, child of Simeon Fobes.
" " 20, Esther, daughter of Ebenezer Witter.
" June 24, Asher, son of Booz Williams.
" " 24, Mary, child of Jos$^h$ Morgan.
" Oct$^r$ 14, Richmond, the child of Samuel Tracy.
1754. April 25, Lydia, the daughter of Caleb Freeman.
" " 28, Submit, the daughter of Jonathan Tracy.
" May 5, Josiah, the child of Jonathan Smith.
" " 19, Ezekiel, the child of Daniel Park.
" July 7, Levi, the child of Jedidiah Tracy.
" Aug$^t$ 18, Elisabeth, daughter of William Amos Jun$^r$.
" Oct$^r$ 29, Ama, daughter of Ebenezer Avery.
" Nov$^r$ 17, Daniel, son of Simeon Fobes.
" " 17, Daniel, son of Nathan Freeman.
1755. Feb$^y$. 11, Mary, the daughter of Thomas Tracy.
" " 23, Martha, daughter of Booz. Williams.
" April 20, Elisha, the child of Jonathan Brewster.
" May 4, Elisha, the child of William Witter Esq$^r$.
" " 10, Daniel, the child of Joseph Smith.
" " 18, Sarah, daughter of Asher Rosseter, Pastor.
" July 13, Joseph, son of Elij$^h$ Starkweather.
" " 13, Zipporah, child of Jos$^h$ Williams.
" " 13, Mehitabel, wife of Isaac Tracy, made profession, & was baptized with Isaac, Mary, Zipporah, Zaven, Bathsheba & Mehitabel, their children.
" July 20, Hannah Phillips, a mullatto, professed faith, & was baptized, with her daughter, Lydia.
" Oct$^r$ 26, Elisabeth, the daughter of Caleb Rude.
" Dec$^r$ 14, Lucy, the daughter of Nathan Freeman.
1756. Feb$^y$. 8, Joseph, the child of Joseph Smith of Stonington.
" April 4, Lucy, the daughter of Simeon Fobes.
" May 30, Joseph, the child of Joseph Kinne.
" June 6, Samuel Morgan Jun$^r$ & his wife Bethia professed faith, when he and their child, Lucy, were bapt$^d$.
" Solomon, the child of Isaac Tracy.
" 27, Mary, the daughter of Roger Sterry.
" July 7, Sabra, child of Jed$^h$ Tracy Jun$^r$.
" " 7, Martha, child of Will$^m$ Ames.
" Aug$^t$ 22, Elijah, the child of Elijah Starkweather.
" Sept$^r$ 19, Hulda, the daughter of Caleb Freeman.

## STATISTICS OF THE CHURCH. 161

1757. Feby. 20, Ruth, the daughter of Thomas Tracy.
" Mar<sup>h</sup> 3, Arthur, the child of Roger Sterry.
" April 10, Zerviah, the daughter of Jonathan Smith.
" " 17, Jerusha & Ama, daughters of Andrew Gates.
Lucy, the daughter of Joseph Williams.
" May 8, Dorothy, the daughter of Nathaniel Wells.
" June 30, Esther, daughter of Jonathan Brewster Jun<sup>r</sup>.
" Aug<sup>t</sup> 22, Jonathan, the child of Joseph Kinne.
" Sept<sup>r</sup> 25, Hannah, the daughter of Nicholas Leonard.
" " Elijah, son of Joseph Johnson.
" " Joseph, son of Joseph Park.
" " 27, Jonathan Kimbal, professed faith & was baptized.
" Oct<sup>r</sup> 16, Daniel Tracy & his wife, Mary, owned Cov<sup>t</sup> & their son, Solomon, baptized.
" Dec<sup>r</sup> 25, Samuel, the child of Joseph Johnson.
1758. Jany. 17, Walter, the child of Joseph Smith.
" Mar<sup>h</sup> 26, Lemuel, son of Dan<sup>l</sup> Tracy.
" " 26, John, son of Simeon Fobes.
" April 23, Lucy, the daughter of Elijah Starkweather.
" May 7, Seth, son of Joseph Freeman.
" " 7, Nathan, son of Nathan Freeman.
" June 18, Betty, M<sup>r</sup> Lambs servant, owned Cov<sup>t</sup> & was baptized with Prince, Kate, Pharoah, Shadrack, her children.
" July 9, Lois, the daughter of Isaac Tracy.
" Sept<sup>r</sup> 3, Eunice, the daughter of Jedidiah Tracy Jun<sup>r</sup>.
" Nov<sup>r</sup> 19, Rachel Morgan; made profession, & was baptized.
1759. Mar<sup>h</sup> 4, Mary, the daughter of Joseph Williams.
" " 11, Mehitabel, daughter of Roger Sterry.
" May 6, Simeon, son of Elisha Dennison.
" " 6, Phebe, child of Joseph Park.
Lucy, daughter of Doct<sup>r</sup> Benjamin Blodget.
" June 17, Nathan, Mary & Anna, children of Isaac Morgan.
" " Asa, the child of Stephen Starkweather.
" Aug<sup>t</sup> 5, Cesar, son of Betty, Negro, by M<sup>r</sup> Powers of Newent.
" Sept<sup>r</sup> 9, Rachel, the daughter of Daniel Tracy.
" Oct<sup>r</sup> 17, Elisha & Zerviah, children of Daniel Starkweather.
" " 28, Daniel, the child of Joseph Kinne.
" Nov<sup>r</sup> 26, Jonathan, the son of Jonathan Brewster Jun<sup>r</sup>.
" Dec<sup>r</sup> 16, Seth, the child of Simeon Tracy.
1760. Jany. 13, Thomas, the child of Daniel Starkweather.
" Feby. 24, Sabra, the daughter of Samuel Leonard.
" July 6, Zerviah, the daughter of William Witter.
" Aug<sup>t</sup> 17, Lemuel, the child of Joseph Smith.
" Oct<sup>r</sup> 5, Susa, the daughter of Isaac Morgan.
" Nov<sup>r</sup> 16, Grace, the daughter of Elisha Dennison.
" " 30, Zerviah, the daughter of Isaac Tracy.
1761. Mar<sup>h</sup> 1, Newcomb, the child of Joseph Kinne.
" " 29, Anna, the daughter of Stephen Starkweather.
" April 19, Edward, Samuel & Sybil, children of Moses & Esther Tracy.
" May 10, Jedidiah, the son of Jedidiah Tracy.
" " 17, Eunice, the daughter of Benjamin Blodget.
" " 24, Esther, the daughter of Elijah Starkweather.
" June 21, Elisabeth, the wife, & Daniel, Elisabeth, Ama & Jonas, ch<sup>n</sup> of Sam<sup>l</sup> Morgan.
Johnson, the child of John Safford.
" Aug<sup>t</sup> 30, Elim, the child of Simeon Tracy.
" Sept<sup>r</sup> 20, Lemuel, the child of Daniel Tracy.
" Oct<sup>r</sup> 11, Consider, the child of Roger Sterry.

11

1761. Nov$^r$ 22, Levi, son of Jonath$^n$ Smith.
" " 22, Zipporah, child of Jon$^n$ Brewster.
" Dec$^r$ 20, Hannah, daughter of Stephen Starkweather.
1762. Jany. 3, Vina, the daughter of Daniel Starkweather.
" May 23, Deborah, the daughter of William Witter.
" June 13, David & Jonathan, twin children of Joseph Kinne.
" " 27, Zipporah, daughter of Isaac Morgan.
" Aug$^t$ 22, Rogers, the child of Constant Searl.
" Sept$^r$ 26, Ama, the daughter of Joseph Smith.
" Oct$^r$ 3, Anna, the daughter of Moses Tracy.
" Nov$^r$ 28, Jacob, the child of John Safford.
1763. Jany. 9, Lydia, the daughter of Elijah Barnes.
" Mar$^h$ 27, Ama, the daughter of Elijah Starkweather.
" April 17, Desire, the daughter of Elisha Dennison.
" June 5, Nabby & Lucy, daughters of Eunice Bundy.
" Oct$^r$ 9, Mercy, the daughter of Simeon Tracy.
" " 28, Leah, the daughter of Daniel Tracy.
" Dec$^r$ 26, Keturah, the daughter of Isaac Tracy.
1764. Jany. 1, Metilda, the daughter of Simeon Fobes.
" May 6, Sarah, the daughter of Jonathan Brewster.
" Sept$^r$ 9, Eunice, the daughter of Elisha Dennison.
" Oct$^r$ 21, Roger, the child of Capt. Roger Sterry.
" Nov$^r$ 18, Benjamin, the child of David Safford.
1765. Jany. 7, Gager, the child of Jonathan Smith.
" April 14, Dwella, the child of Isaac Morgan.
" " 21, Samuel, the child of Moses Tracy.
" May 26, John, the child of John Safford.
" June 2, Thankful, the daughter of Isaac Tracy.
" " 16, Susanna, the daughter of Joseph Smith.
" Aug$^t$ 4, Ruth, the daughter of Constant Searle.
" " 25, Ezra, the child of Jabez Starkweather.
" Sept$^r$ 15, Bradford, the child of Joseph Kinne.
" Nov$^r$ 10, Diadama, daughter of David Safford.
" Dec$^r$ 29, Robert, the child of Daniel Tracy.
1766. May 11, Jonas, the child of Jonathan Brewster.
" June 1, Nathan, the child of Elisha Dennison.
" June 22, Abigail, the wife of Peter Bowdish.
" " " Thankful, Peter, Edward, Abigail & Asa, chil$^n$ of Peter Bowdish.
" Gilbert, Sanford & Wealthy, children of Ezra Tracy.
" Aug$^t$ 3, Asenath, daughter of Simeon Tracy.
" Sept$^r$ 28, Joseph, the child of Peter Bowdish.
" Nov$^r$ 2, John, the child of Capt. Roger Sterry.
1767. Feby. 8, Hannah, the daughter of Jabez Starkweather.
" Mar$^h$ 15, Olive, the daughter of Isaac Morgan Jun$^r$.
" June 14, Abigail, the daughter of John Safford.
" July 12, Ama, the daughter of Simeon Fobes.
" " 19, Sarah, the daughter of Nathan Fobes.
" Sept$^r$ 13, Thankful, daughter of Elisha Dennison.
" " 27, Roger, the child of Daniel Tracy.
" Nov$^r$ 15, Anna, child of John James.
" " 15, Zuba, child of Moses Tracy.
" " " Lucretia, the daughter of David Safford.
1768. Mar$^h$ 27, Betty, the daughter of Isaac Tracy.
" July 3, Susanna, the daughter of John James.
John, son of Nathan Fobes.
" " Thomas, the child of Joseph Smith.
" 10, Lois, the daughter of Peter Bowdish.

## STATISTICS OF THE CHURCH. 163

1768. Sept<sup>r</sup> 4, Asher, the child of Nathan Starkweather.
" Nov<sup>r</sup> 13, Huldah, the daughter of Jabez Starkweather.
1769. Mar<sup>h</sup> 19, Thomas, son of Daniel Tracy.
" " 19, Elisha, child of Ezra Tracy.
" " 26, Elisabeth, Solomon, Walter, William, Hannah, Sarah, Eunice & Samuel, the children of Samuel Branch.
" April 2, Abigail, the daughter of Capt. Roger Sterry.
" June 9, William, the child of John James.
" July 23, Seth, the child of Simeon Fobes.
" Oct<sup>r</sup> 22, Moses, the child of Jonathan Brewster.
1770. April 29, Joseph, the child of John Safford.
" May 27, Cloe, the daughter of David Safford.
" July 1, David, the child of Jedidiah Wilbur.
" " 29, Joseph, the child of Nathan Starkweather. Witter, the child of Samuel Branch. Samuel, the child of Peter Bowdish.
" Nov<sup>r</sup> 18, Jabez, the child of Jabez Starkweather.
1771. May 12, Jonas, son of Moses Tracy.
" " 12, Charlotte, child of Daniel Tracy.
" " 19, Septimeous, the child of Joseph Witter Jun<sup>r</sup>.
" June 16, Erastus, the child of Ezra Tracy.
" " 23, Mercy & Anna, daughter of Nathan Avery.
" July 15, Ephraim, the child of Nathan Fobes.
" Aug<sup>t</sup> 18, Ezra, Zebulon, Elijah & Susanna, children of widow Miriam Ames.
" Nov<sup>r</sup> 8, Bathsheba, the wife of Seth Mix at Newent.
1772. Aug<sup>t</sup> 2, Happy, the daughter of Samuel Branch.
" Sept<sup>r</sup> 19, Zipporah, the daughter of Joseph Smith.
" Oct<sup>r</sup> 4, Lydia, the daughter of Jonathan Brewster.
" Nov<sup>r</sup> 22, Sarah, the daughter of Nathan Avery.
1773. May 16, Deborah, daughter of Jedidiah Wilbur.
" Anna, the daughter of Ezra Tracy.
" June 20, Moses, the child of Moses Tracy.
" Dec<sup>r</sup> 5, Stephen, the child of David Safford.
1774. April 10, Elisha, the child of Nathan Fobes.
" May 22, Nathan, the child of John Safford.
" July 31, Lucy, the daughter of Joseph Witter Jun<sup>r</sup>.
1775. Oct<sup>r</sup> 20, Hannah, the daughter of Elisha Dennison.
" " 29, Margaret, the daughter of Ezra Tracy.
1776. Mar<sup>h</sup> 10, Esther, the daughter of Moses Tracy.
" June 9, David, the child of David Safford.
" July 28, Jedidiah, the child of Nathan Fobes.
" Aug<sup>t</sup> 4, Elim, the child of Jedidiah Wilbur.
" Sept<sup>r</sup> 15, Nathan, the child of Henry Williams.
" Oct<sup>r</sup> 27, Polly, child of Joseph Smith.
" " 27, Esther, child of Nathan Avery.
1777. Jan<sup>y</sup>. 8, Sally, Shubael, Mehitabel, Lucy & Simeon, the children of Simeon & Hannah Morgan.
" May 4, Erastus, the child of John Safford.
" June 9, Samuel, the child of Simeon Morgan.
" Aug<sup>t</sup> 3, Jemima, the daughter of Ezra Tracy.
1778. Jan<sup>y</sup> 11, Polly, the daughter of Nathan Avery.
" May 24, Silas, the child of Silas White of Long Island.
1779. May 30, Appleton, the child of Ezra Tracy.

1780. April 16, Hannah, the daughter of Simeon Morgan.
" May 7, Caleb, the child of Nathan Fobes.
" " 15, Zerviah, Avery & Isaac, the children of Elisha Dennison, baptized at his house.

The Rev<sup>d</sup> M<sup>r</sup> Asher Rosseter, departed this life, Nov<sup>r</sup> 17<sup>th</sup> ADomini 1781 in the 66<sup>th</sup> year of his age, and 38<sup>th</sup> of his ministry.

## THE MINISTRY OF THE REV<sup>D</sup> JONATHAN FULLER.
### December 8 1784 — February 22 1786

NAMES OF CHURCH MEMBERS AT THE TIME OF HIS SETTLEMENT.

| | |
|---|---|
| William Witter, | Abigail Sterry, |
| Samuel Mac Farlin, | Elisabeth Witter, |
| William Blodget, | Elisabeth Morgan, |
| Ebenezer Witter, | Margaret Amos, |
| Zipporah Branch, | Esther James, |
| Jerusha Tracy, | Hannah Morgan, |
| Mary Starkweather, | Betty, Negro, |
| Mary Freeman, | Kezia Rosseter, occas<sup>l</sup> |
| Elisabeth Amos, | commun<sup>t</sup>. |

NAMES OF THOSE ADMITTED.

1785. Aug<sup>t</sup> 28, Jonathan Smith & Hannah, his wife, joined in full comm<sup>n</sup>.

BAPTISMS.

1785. Mar<sup>h</sup> 13, Anna Lockwood, daughter of Jonathan Fuller, Past<sup>r</sup> by Mr. M.
" Aug<sup>t</sup> 28, Elisabeth, William & John Smith, & Abigail Rosseter, the family of Jonathan & Hannah Smith.

The Rev<sup>d</sup> Jonathan Fuller departed this life Feby. 22, A.D. 1786, in the 23<sup>d</sup> year of his age, & 2<sup>d</sup> of his ministry.

## AN INTERMEDIATE SEASON, OR VACANCY OF THE CHURCH.

1788. Mar<sup>h</sup> 23, Amos, son of Jonah & Eunice Witter, baptized by the Rev<sup>d</sup> M<sup>r</sup> Porter, of Voluntown.
1789. Mar<sup>h</sup> 9, Jonah Witter & his wife, Eunice, were received into full communion by letter of dismission & recommenation from the Pastor & Church of Christ in Brooklin.
" " 9, Doct<sup>r</sup> Joshua Downer was admitted to full communion.

## THE MINISTRY OF THE REV<sup>D</sup> LEMUEL TYLER.
### May 7 1789 — September 18 1810

NAMES OF CHURCH MEMBERS AT THE TIME OF HIS SETTLEMENT.

| | |
|---|---|
| Ebenezer Witter, | Elisabeth Amos, |
| William Witter, | Mary Freeman, |
| William Blodget, | Margaret Amos, |
| Joshua Downer, | Hannah Morgan, |
| Jonathan Smith, | Hannah Smith, |
| Jonah Witter, | Esther James, |
| Jerusha Tracy, | Abigail Sterry, |
| Elisabeth Witter, | Eunice Witter, |
| Elisabeth Morgan, | Betty, Negro. |

## STATISTICS OF THE CHURCH.

### ADMISSIONS.

1790. Feby. 28, Huldah, the wife of Doct$^r$ Joshua Downer.
" Bridget, the wife of Asa Smith, baptized and admitted.
" Mar$^h$ 21, Esther, the wife of Moses Tracy.
1791. Aug$^t$ 7, Hannah, the wife of Charles Foresides.
1793. June 9, Temperance, the wife of Nathan Fobes.
" Sept. 29, Azuba, the wife of Edward Tracy.
1795. July 26, Edward Tracy.
" " Asa Meech, baptized and admitted.
1797. Aug$^t$ 20, Calvin Barstow.

### RECEIVED BY LETTER.

1790. Jany. 3, Ruth, the wife of Lemuel Tyler, Pastor, received to full communion by letter of dismission & recommendation from the church of Christ in Northford.

### DISMISSIONS.

1789. June 22, Ebenezer Witter, dismis$^d$ & recom$^d$ to the chh. at Hanover.
" Nov$^r$ —, Jemima Tracy, dismised & recomd$^d$ to the chh. at Pittsfield.

### BAPTISMS.

1789. May 17, Lydia Ives, daughter of Lieut. Asa & Sarah Todd at Northford.
" Dec$^r$ 6, Augustus Williams, son of Stephen & Abigail Maltby at Northford.
" 6, Olive, daughter of James & Sarah Linsley at Northford.
1790. Jany. 31, Eunice, daughter of Jonah & Eunice Witter.
" Feby. 28, Bridget, the wife of Asa Smith.
" Mar$^h$ 28, Youngs, Betsey & Isaac Ledyard, the children of the above mentioned Bridget Smith by a former husband.
1790. May 30, Elisha, Sarah, Sophia & John children of Doct$^r$ Joshua & Huldah Downer.
" 30, Rebekah, the daughter of Moses & Esther Tracy.
" July 18, Fanny, the daughter of Asa & Bridget Smith.
1791. June 5, Lemuel, son of Lem$^l$ Tyler, Pastor, & Ruth, his wife, ae 1 day.
" Aug$^t$ 21, Asa, Charles, Nancy, Hannah & Chapman, the children of Charles & Hannah Foresides.
1792. June 3, Julia, the daughter of Asa & Bridget Smith.
" Asa, the son of Jonah & Eunice Witter.
1793. Mar$^h$ 31, Lucius, the son of Lemuel Tyler, Pastor, & Ruth his wife.
" Oct$^r$ 6, Amanda, Charles, Lucretia, Ralph, Betsey & Harriet, the children of Edward & Azuba Tracy.
1794. Oct$^r$ 5, Louisa, the daughter of Lemuel Tyler, Pastor, & Ruth.
" Nov$^r$ 23, Laura, the daughter of Jonah & Eunice Witter.
" " 30, Austin, the son of Asa & Bridget Smith.
1795. July 26, Asa Meech professed faith and was baptized.
" Sept$^r$ 16, Ansel, the son of Ashbel & Polly Sheppard of Greensboro, Vermont.
" " 22, Ozias & Hiram, sons of Josia$^s$ Safford, of Fairfax, S$^t$ of Vermont.
" " 23, Huldah, daughter of Truman & Lucretioe Powel of Cambridge, Vermont.

# 166  STATISTICS OF THE CHURCH.

1796.   May 15, Ruth Fowler, daughter of Lemuel Tyler, Pastor, & Ruth, his wife.

## MARRIAGES.

1789.   Sept$^r$ 20, Joseph Tracy & Elisabeth Brown, of the West Society.
"       Dec$^r$ 31, Oliver Spicer of Groton & Eunice Tyler of Preston.
1790.   Jany. 27, Blanchard Darby of Norwich & Elisabeth Benjamin of W$^t$ Soc$^y$.
"       " 28, Jesse Barns of Groton & Lucy Palmer of the West Society.
"       " 31, Benjamin Fitch & Lucy Braman of the West Society.
"       May 30, Ephraim Rix of the 2$^d$ & Martha Brown of the 1$^{st}$ Soc'y.
"       " 30, Elisha Tracy & Hannah Swaney, both of the West Society.
"       July 15, Jason Stanton & Kezia Brumley of the 1$^{st}$ Society.
"       Nov$^r$ 7, Enos Clark of Middletown Vermont & Clarissa Cook, 2$^d$ Soc'y.
"       Dec$^r$ 12, Amos Avery Jun$^r$ & Susanna Starkweather.
"       " 12, Zephaniah Rude of Granby & Betsey Meech, Preston.
"       " 30, Levi Brumley & Penelope Hall of North Preston.
1791.   Mar$^h$ 10, Shubael Morgan of Preston & Cynthia Bellows of Groton.
"       " 17, Olive Woodworth of Norwich, & Eliphal Cook of Preston.
"       " 20, Denison Brown & Mary Robbins.
"       " 27, Elijah Clark & Eunice Morgan.
"       July 1, Solomon Jones, of Lebanon & Phebe Quince of Preston, free Negros.
"       Sept$^r$ 29, Joseph Osyer & Polly Saunders both of the west Society.
"       Oct$^r$ 16, Aron Hendley from New York & Silve Avery of Preston, free Negros.
"       Nov$^r$ 24, William Witter Jun$^r$ & Hannah D. Branch.
1792.   Jany. 1, Job Wickes of Providence & Polly Braman of West Society.
"       Mar$^h$ 25, Walter Palmer & Patty Pendleton both of West Society.
"       Apr$^l$ 29, Ames Bennet & Wealthy Safford, both of 1$^{st}$ Society.
"       Oct$^r$ 4, John Sterry & Rebecca Brumley.
"       " 14, Sauney Anderson, a free negro & Tamar Smith.
"       " 18, Abiel Rath of West Soc$^y$, & Mary Stanton, North Soc$^y$.
"       Nov$^r$ 25, Edward Leet of Say Brook & Amy Morgan of Preston.
"       Dec$^r$ 24, Cyrus Punderson of Groton & Deborah Smith of Preston.
1793.   Jany. 6, Jonathan Hinckley, of Stonington & Sally Saunders, of Preston.
"       Feby. 7, John Searle of Royalton, Vermont, & Nabby Safford, Preston.
"       " 10, Eleazer Lewis & Sally Stanten Rude, both of Preston.
"       June 16, John Saunders & Lucy Daniels, both of the West Society.
"       Sept. 8, Cordilla Fitch & Joanna Mix, both of the West Society.
"       " 22, Enos Tallmage of Milton, State of New York, & Ruth Freeman, Preston.
"       Dec$^r$ 1, Gillmore Robbins & Grace Brown.
"       " 31, Beriah Green & Elisabeth Smith.
1794.   Mar$^h$ 9, Robert Sanders & Hannah Brown, both of West Society.
"       " 11, Reuben Bristol of New-Canaan, St$^e$ of New York & Elis$^h$ Starkweather.
"       " 16, Elisha Pitcher of Norwich & Jane Coombs of Preston.
"       " 20, Ezra Benjamin of the 2$^d$ Soc$^y$, & Amy Stanton of Groton.

## STATISTICS OF THE CHURCH. 167

1794. Mar[h] 23, Gershom Mott, of the 2[d] Soc[y] & Zipporah Rockwell of the West Soc[y].
" Ap[l] 1, Israel Park of Stonington & Abigail Sterry of Preston.
" " 27, Benjamin Billings & Eunice Tracy.
" Oct[r] 26, Roger Sterry & Lavinia Yarrington.
" Nov[r] 2, Reuel Cook & Amy Packer.
" " 5, Russel Rose & Polly Brown, both of North Soc[y].
" " 9, Nathan Seers, & Mercy Rockwell.
" " 27, Benjamin Baily & Lydia Gore.
" James Rouse & Thankful Brumley, both of Preston.
1795. Feb[y] 5, James Wood of Chester, Massachus[tts] & Elizabeth Brewster, Stoningt[n].
" " 22, William Butler of Norwich & Barsheba Stoddard of West Society.
" May 7, Thomas Giles of Groton & Betsy Deming of West Society.
" June 7, Stephen Payne of Lebanon & Widow Prudence Thomas, Preston.
" " 24, Stephen Congdon, of N[h] Kingston, Rhode Island & Thankf[l] Stuart, Preston.
" Aug[t] 4, The Rev[d] Solomon Morgan of Canterb[y] & M[rs] Anna Haskel of Preston.
" Oct[r] 18, William Stewart of New Lebanon, St[e] N. York & Rebecka Eells, Stoningt[n].
" " 18, John Chapman of Groton, & Bethany Button of Preston.
" Nov[r] 12, Joseph Adams & Mary Brown, both of North Soc[y].
" Dec[r] 3, Gershom Dorrance, & Sarah Rosseter, both of N[h] Soc[y].
" " 24, Daniel Palmer Stanton of Nor[h] Soc[y]. & — Roath of the West.
" " 31, Jeremiah Vincent of Westerly St[e] of Rhode[d] & Sally Kimball, Ston[n].
1796. Jan[y] 3, Joel Canfield of Saybrook & Sally Peters of Preston.
" " 3, Samuel Fagins & Nabby Sterry, people of colour.
" " 10, Daniel Kinne & Betsey Maine.
" " 10, Joshua Meech & Polly Peters.
" Mar[h] 20, Stephen Meech of Preston & Lucy Billings of Stonington.
1797. Jan[y] 8, Isaac Avery of Groton & Clarissa Button of Preston.
" " 15, William Wells of Colchester & Eunice Clark of Preston.
" Feb[y]. —, Philip Gray of Groton & Sabra Stanton of West Soc[y].
" Mar[h] 23, Andrew Lamb & Charlotte George, both free blacks of Stonington.
" April 9, Christopher Benjamin, of Burlington, St[e] of New York & Sally Fitch, Preston.
" Ephraim Fobes & Amy Fitch.
John Stanton of North Soc[y] & Lydia Olden of the West Soc[y].
Elias Woodward of Plainfield & Zipporah Cook of the West Soc[y].
Seth Fitch & Cloe Haskel, both of the West Soc[y].
Benjamin Fitch & Anna Braman, both of the West Soc[y].
Richard Fanning & Elisabeth Park.
1798. Daniel Lawrence of Voluntown & Cynthia Wilkinson, Nor[h] Soc[y].
" Feb[y] 18, George Leonard & Honor Andruss.
" Mar[h] 7, John Crary of Preston & Mary York of Stonington.

### Deaths.

1789. May 9, Alice Lathrop of Newent, at Mrs. Ben[ts], 18[ys], Slow Fever.
" July 2, Widow Elisabeth Morgan, 74[ys], Paralytic complaint.

1789. Nov$^r$ 7, The wife of Peris Prentice, 28$^{ys}$, The Dropsy.
" " 18, Jedidiah Tracy, 28$^{ys}$, The Consumption.
" Dec$^r$ 6, The Widow Prudence Stanton, 83$^{ys}$, Putrid Fever.
" " 30, A child of Amos Witter, — 9$^{mo}$, Dropsy in the head.
1790. Jan$^y$ 30, Robert Crary Esq$^r$, 73$^{ys}$, The Asthma.
" Mar$^h$ 7, A child of Pelek Freeman, 5$^{ys}$, Scalded.
" April 8, William Amos, 68$^{ys}$, Paralytic disorder.
" " 10, A child of Nathan Stanton, 2$^{ys}$, Scalded.
" July 15, The Widow Rosanna Meech, 84$^{ys}$, Sudden decay.
" " 31, A child of Thomas Prentice, Ston$^n$, — 5½$^{ms}$, Fits.
" Aug$^t$ 9, A child of Richardson Avery, 2$^{ys}$, Schirrous liver.
" Sept$^r$ 5, The widow Lydia Park, 70$^{ys}$, Consumption.
" " 14, Lucy Button, wife of Mat$^s$ Button, 40$^{ys}$, Consumption.
" Nov$^r$ 23, Ebenezer Freeman, 75$^{ys}$, Obstructed Liver.
" " 26, The Widow Margaret Jones, The dropsy.
1791. Jan$^y$. 13, The wife of Capt. Eben$^r$ Witter.
" May 10, Kezia Stanton daught$^r$ C$^r$ Brumley, 26$^{ys}$, Consumption.
" June 7, Asa Lamphere, of St$^e$ Rhod$^d$ at Capt. Airs, 17$^{ys}$, Inflamation Kidneys.
" Sept$^r$ 26, A child of Judah Brewster W$^t$ Society, — 16$^{ms}$, Rattles.
" " 29, A child of William Brown, 1$^{st}$ dy.
" " 30, —— Prentice, son of Elisha Prentice, 17$^{ys}$, Putrid Fever.
" Dec$^r$ 4, Lucy Morgan, 20$^{ys}$, Consumption.
1792. Feby. 10, The wife of Robert Crary Jun$^r$, 29$^{ys}$, The Dropsy.
" " 15, John Avery, son of Col. Isaac Avery, 17$^{ys}$, Fractured Scull.
" Mar$^h$ 6, A child of Johnson Safford, 3$^y$ 7$^m$, Scalded.
" " 6, A child of Daniel Morgan, 1$^y$, Convulsion Fits.
" April 30, Joseph Tyler, 80$^{ys}$, The Asthma.
" May 8, Beulah, Negro woman, at Gen$^l$ Motts, The Consumption.
1793. Jan$^y$. 6, Elijah Park, 37$^{ys}$, The Dropsy.
" May 1, A child of Timothy Clark Jun$^r$, — 7$^{ms}$.
" July 27, A child of Oliver Spicer & Eunice, 1$^{ys}$ 3$^m$.
1794. Mar$^h$ 9, Wife of Amos Brown, 53$^{ys}$, Pleurisy.
" April 1, Wife of Eben$^r$ Avery, Child-bed.
  William Leonard, West Indias.
  A child of Joseph Ames.
  Betty, Negro Girl, Consumption.
" July 11, Wife of Consider Sterry, Consumption.
" " 15, Sally Frink, Consumption.
" " 23, John Avery Esq$^r$, 62$^{ys}$.
  Child of Sam$^l$ Bailey, Scarlet Fever & putrid sore throat.
  Child of Sam$^l$ Bailey, D$^o$ D$^o$.
  Elijah Barnes, Fractured Scull.
1795. Jan$^y$ 12, Child of Maj$^r$ E$^d$ Mott, Scarlet Fever & put$^d$ S. Throat.
" " 13, Widow Brewster, at O. Crarys, Suddenly, without assistance.
" " 18, Child of —— Dunwell, 1$^y$ 4$^m$, Putrid Fever.
" " 19, Wife of Benj$^n$ Billings, Child bed — Consumption.
" " 21, Infant child of Benj$^n$ Billings, 5$^{ds}$, Fits.
" " 23, Infant child of Benj$^n$ Billings, 7$^{ds}$, Fits.
" " 28, Timothy Clark Jun$^r$, Consumption.
" Feby. 10, Zechariah Rude, 104$^{ys}$ 7$^m$.
" " 12, Fanny, child of Asa Smith, 4$^{ys}$, Scarlet Fever & putrid sore throat.
" " 23, Sally Rose, of Groton, 17$^{ys}$, Suddenly at a dance.

## STATISTICS OF THE CHURCH. 169

1795. Mar<sup>h</sup> 3, Child of Silas Brewster, — 9<sup>m</sup>, Consumption.
    Wife of Walter Brown.
" July 11, Doct<sup>r</sup> Joshua Downer.
    Child of Doct. Ay Downer.
    Wife of Mr. John Crary, Consumption.
1796.   Nicholas Leonard.
    Wife of Capt. Nathan Ayer, Consumption.
" April 18, Wife of Lem<sup>l</sup> Tyler, Pastor, 34, Measles.
    Child of Daniel Meech.
    Child of Thomas Prentice.
" June 6, Amy Thomson, at Mr. Crarys, Consumption.
    Wife of Simeon Morgan.
    Wife of Pomp, a negro, Consumption.
1797.   Widow Baldwin, Cancer.
    Child of Stephen Meech.
    Wife of Gen<sup>l</sup> Sam<sup>l</sup> Mott.

---

### THE MINISTRY OF THE REV<sup>D</sup> JOHN HYDE.

### May 26, 1812 — May 28, 1827.

NAMES OF CHURCH MEMBERS AT THE TIME OF HIS SETTLEMENT.

Jonathan Smith,
Jonah Witter,
Calvan Barstow,
Richard Fanning,
John Gore,
Ephraim Meech,
Betty, Negro,
Esther Tracy wife of Moses T.,
Hannah Smith wife of Jon<sup>n</sup> Smith,
Wid. Olive Tracy,
Lucy Brewster, wife of Judah,
Hannah Forsyth, wife of Ch<sup>s</sup> F.,
Bridget Smith, wife of Asa. S.,
——Gore, wife of John. G.,
Sally Meech, wife of Ja<sup>c</sup>,
Sally Smith wife of Chester S.,
Eunice Witter, wife of Jonah W.,
Wid Sally Prentice,
Wid. Rebeckah Tracy,
Elisa<sup>th</sup> Fanning, wife of Richard F.,
Wid. Esther Clark,
Betsey Brown,
Rebeckah Tracy,
Amy Meech.
Sally Hillyard,
Sophia Hillyard,
Susan Smith,
Zubab Tracy, wife of Ew<sup>d</sup> Tracy.

---

ADMISSIONS.

1812. Nov.  ——Button, the wife of Roswell Button.
1813. Sept 26, Elisha Kimball & his wife.
   " Charles Meech & his wife.
   " Shubael Meech & his wife.
  Nov. 7, Giles Capron & wife.
   " Eunice Harris.
   " Nancy Ames.
   " Widow Phebe Ames.
1814. July 24, Daniel Gore and wife.
   " Mrs. Eunice Spicer wife of Oliver Spicer.
  Sept. 4, Jacob Newton.
   " Stephen Meech & wife.
   " Anna wife of Tho<sup>s</sup> Prentice.
1815. May 20, Sabra Tracy.
  Oct. 1, William Smith.
   " Wi<sup>d</sup> Mary Prentice.
1816. Sep<sup>t</sup> 1, The Widow Lucy Meech.
   29, Julia Smith.
    Olive Rood.

## STATISTICS OF THE CHURCH.

1817. July 6, Mrs. Esther Rix.
1818. Augst. Lydia Mott.
" Lucinda Morgan.
1821. Feb 4, Polly the wife of Henry Fanning.
Sept 2, Chas. G. Clark.
" Mrs. Louisa Downing.
1822. March 17, John P. Cook.
Nov. 24, Samuel Y. Tracy.
Dec. 14, Ezra B. Smith, Chs. Smith, Azubah Tracy, & Orra Geer.
1823. Jan. 13, Amy Browning, Susan Prentice, Eliza Ann Prentice, Sally B. Meech, Elizabeth Pridde, Athelia Spicer, Diana Spicer, Latham Browning, Jonathan Smith & Alexander Rogers.
May 3, Welthy Starkweather.
1824. Jan. 4, Mary C. Meech, Ann E. Hyde, Lucretia T. Hide and Cynthia Melissa Meech.
Mar. 7, Joseph Yarrington & wife.
" Henry Fanning & wife.
" Ruth Meech.
" Amy wife of Ruel Cook, Betsey Cook, Amy Cook.
July 4, Sybel Kimball.
Aug. 5, Widow Lucretia Meech, Olive Starkweather, Rosina A. Downes Noyes B. Meech, Susan A. Ames.

### Received by Letter.

1813. May Susan, the wife of John Hyde, Pastor from the first chh in Hamden.
Nov. 5, Lucy Benjamin from the church in Royalton, Vermont.
1823. May 3, Huldah, the wife of Samuel Tracy of Hopkington, R. I.

### Dismissions.

1822. April Giles Capron & wife to the church in Red-hook, N. York.
" Daniel Gore & wife to the church in Red-hook, N. York.

### Baptisms.

1812. July John Barker, son of Revd. John Hyde.
1813. Sept. 26, Chs. Meech & wife & Shubael Meech.
Oct. 3, Polly Crary, Chs. Lamb, & Cynthia Melissa, children of Chs. Meech.
" 24, Sarah, Hezekiah Lord, Lydia, Henry, Mary, Susan, Shubael, Adaline, Edwin Butler, children Shubael Meech.
Nov. 7, Eunice Harris and Nancy Ames.
" 21, Phebe Prentice, Bradford, Curtis, Mary Tyler, Louisa, Sally Maria, Susan Augusta, Chs. Tyler chiln of Wd. Pheba Ames.
1814. July 24, Daniel Gore, also William child of Moses Hilliard.
August 7, Lucinda, Lura, Athelia, Diara, children Oliver Spicer.
" 21, Asa Park, Rachel, Mary, Daniel Chester, Clarinda Lucy, chn Dl Gore.
Sept. 4, Stephen Meech.
Oct. 9, Sally Billings, Lucy Billings, Stephen Wilcox, Sanford Billings, Noyes Billings, Lucretia Kimball, children of Stephn Meech.
" " Hezekiah, son of Ephraim Meech.
" 16, John Tyler, son of Shubael Meech.

STATISTICS OF THE CHURCH. 171

1815. Mar. 26, Samuel Nott, son of John Hyde, Pastor.
May 20, Sabra Tracy, also Sam$^l$ Capron, child of Daniel Gore.
Aug. 20, Sarah Ann, daughter Charles Meech.
Oct. 1, William, Jonathan, Betsy, Celina, Joseph Wilbur, child$^n$ of W$^m$ Smith.
1816. May 5, Chester, son of Moses Hilliard.
July 7, Harriot Newell, daughter of Ephraim Meech.
Sept. 1, Dwight Lester, son of Shubael Meech.
" 29, Olive Rood.
Nov. 3, Eunice, infant child of Stephen Meech.
1817. July 6, Mrs. Esther Rix.
" George, child of Daniel Gore.
1818. May Sally, daughter of Moses & Sally Hilliard.
Sept. 5, Eleanor, daughter of William Smith.
Sept. 5, Maria Loiza, daughter of Sam$^l$ Tracy, Hopkinton, R. I.
1819. Oct. 31, Daughter of Franklin Park.
Nov. 7, Louisa, daughter of Charles Meech.
1820. July 2, Sabra Ann, daughter of Moses Hilliard.
Sept. 3, Susan Nott, daughter of John Hyde, Pastor.
Oct. 22, Henry Austin, son of Daniel Gore.
1821. Feb. 4, Polly, the wife of Henry Fanning.
" Henry Nelson & W$^m$ Austin, children of H. Fanning.
April 7, Crista Cook, daughter of W$^m$ Smith.
Sept. 30, Lemuel Tyler, Louiza Tyler, & Helen Maria Williams, children of Dr. Eliazar B. Downing.
1822. March 17, John Cook.
July 7, Lemuel Swan, son of Ch$^s$ Meech.
Aug. 11, Hannah, daughter of W$^m$ Smith.
Oct. 13, Barnabas Bruen, son of John Hyde, Pastor.
Frederick, son of Moses Hilliard.
Dec. 14, Ezra Smith, Ch$^s$ Smith, & Orra Geer.
1823. Jan. 12, Susan Prentice, wife of Samuel H. Prentice, Amy, wife of Thomas Browning, Eliza Ann Prentice, Elizabeth Pridde and Latham Browning.
May 3, Wealthy Starkweather.
1824. March 7, Amy, wife of Ruel Cook, Polly, wife of Joseph Yarrington, Sophia, wife of Henry Fanning, Betsey Cook, & Amy Cook.
May 2, Elizer Butler, child of Dr. Downing, Celia Tyler, daughter of Ruth Meech, Mary Emeline, Luther, Lucelia, Lucy Ann, Ch$^s$ Alonzo, children of Joseph Yarrington.
July 4, Sybel Kimball.
Aug 22, Daniel Tyler, Eleazer Hyde & Susan, children of Ezra B Smith.
Sep$^t$ 5, Olive Starkweather, Rosina A Downer, & Lucy Park, child of Henry Fanning.
Oct 17, Isaac Fellows, son of William Smith.
1825. May 15, Diantha Maria, daughter of Ch$^s$ Meech.
" " Stephen Noys, son of Joseph Yarrington.
Oct 30, Elias Brewster, son of Moses Hillard.
1827. March 25, Moses, son of Ezra B Smith.

MARRIAGES.

1812. Aug 30, Allen Button & Anna A Witter.
Nov 23, Thomas Browning & Amy Prentice of North Stonington.

## STATISTICS OF THE CHURCH.

1813. Dec. 19, Henry Fanning of Preston & Mary Morgan of N. Stonington.
1813. Jan 10, Jonas Ayres & Abby Morgan.
" 31, John Prentice & Amy Meech of North Stonington.
Feb 14, John F. Fanning of Groton & Betsey Gates of Preston.
" " Avery Prentice of North Stonington & Fanny Johnson of Preston.
" 28, Charles Hewit & Eunice Witter.
Sept 19, Joseph Avery Yarrington of North Stonington & Mary P Meech of Preston.
" 30, Eleazer B Downing & Louisa Tyler.
Oct 14, Ephraim Meech of North Stonington & Sophia Hilliard of West Society.
Dec 23, Thomas M. Meech & Ruth F. Tyler.
1814. July 4, William S. Marian & Sally Palmer.
Sept 18, Jesse Main of North Stonington & Anna Benjamin of Preston.
Nov 6, Gurdon Chapman & Elizabeth Phillips of North Stonington.
Nov 27, Samuel H Prentice & Susan Baldwin of North Stonington.
" 13, Joseph Hervey & Betsey B Phillips of West Society.
Dec. 1, Cyrus Newton of Groton & Sally Spicer of Preston.
" 11, John Denison Wheeler & Lucy Prentice of North Stonington.
1815. Feb 16, Ansel Brown of Preston & Susan Smith of North Stonington.
May 10, David Boardman, North Soc'ty & Mary Brown.
July 2, Reynolds Kynion of Rhode Island & Abby McCoombs, Preston.
1816. Jan 21, Asa Witter & Betsey Clark of West Parish.
Feb 22, Joseph Gere of Groton & Lura Witter of Preston.
Oct 6, Ralph Hutchinson of Griswold & Eliza Kimball of Preston.
Nov 24, Barton D Kimball & Betsey Robbins.
Dec 24, Robert Miner of North Stonington & Alura Spicer, Preston.
" 30, Ansel D Shipman of Saybrook & Betsey Peters of Preston.
1817. June ——Alden of Stafford & Sally Giddins of Long Society.
Sept 11, John Demming & Clarisa Hilliard of Long Society.
1818. Jan 11, James Gorton of Voluntown & Sally Buddington of Stonington.
Feb 26, Jed[h] Hough of Bozrah & Betsey Starkweather of Preston.
Sept 13, Jeremiah S. Halsey & Sarah Brewster.
" 24, John Abell of Bozrah, & Lucretia Meech of Preston.
Nov 8, Lathrop Williams & Abby Prentice of North Stonington.
" " Amos Corning of Preston & Matilda Guyant of Groton.
Dec 6, Samuel Brackets of Dudley, Mass, & Esterher B. Morgan.
1819. Jan 10, Leonard Herrick of Washington, N. York & Sabra Tracy.
" 21, Ch[s] Prentice of North Stonington & Phebe P Ames of Preston.
" 24, Obadiah Corbin of Woodstock & Amanda Morgan of Preston.
June —, Sebra Benjamin & —— Standish.
Oct 11, Joseph Doane & Frances Treat.
" " Cushin Eells Cook of Griswold & Betsey Popple of **Preston.**

## STATISTICS OF THE CHURCH. 173

1820.  April 23, Joseph Utley of Griswold & Lucinda Spicer of Preston.
Oct. 1, Silas Babcock of North Stonington & Mary Cook of Preston.
Sept. 4, James Wade of Norwich & Phebe Lambert of Preston.
" 20, Caleb Bishop of Lisbon & Betsey Brown of Preston.
Dec. 11, George Prentice & Olive A. Mott.
" 14, W$^m$ P. Palmer & Fanny Crary.
1821. Jan. 11, Levi Standish & Susan Fitch of Long Society.
Russel Fitch & Julian Phillips of Long Society.
April 4, James Killum & Caroline Holden of Long Society.
Augst. 18, Harvey L. Hazen of Norwich & Sarah B. Corning of Preston.
Sept. 19, George W. Hilliard & Sarah C. Tyler.
" 30, Milton B. Weeks & Eunice A. Palmer.
Nov. 5, Darius Bingham of New Milford of Penn. & Amy Crary.
Dec. 6, Henry Fanning & Sophia Davis of Stonington.
1822. Jan$^y$ 6, Ephraim Meech of East Haddam & Eunice T. Spicer of Preston.
Dec. 8, William K. Latham & Eliza Witter.
" 26, Peter B. Gardner & Hannah Hall.
1823. Feb. 6, William Starkweather & Kezziah Benjamin.
" 13, David Baldwin of N. Stonington & Mary Brown of Preston.
Aug. 7, Rufus Prentice Jun$^r$ of Griswold & Wealthy Starkweather of Preston.
1824. March 16, Calvin B. Cook & Eunice Crary.
May 17, Cha$^s$ Rude of Preston & Mary Cook of Griswold.
July 22, Francis Young and Susan Brumly.
Sept. 16, Edwin Fitch & Lucy B. Meech.
1825. Oct. 17, James Whipple of Attleborough Mass. & Elizabeth W. Corning of Long Society.
" 27, Nathan Johnston of Griswold & Ruth L. Meech.
Dec. 29, Russel Benjamin & Sally Cook of Long Society.
1826. Sept. 28, Stephen W. Meech & Ann E. Hyde.
Nov. 15, Norman Robinson of Providence & Margaret Barstow of Preston.
" 16, Aaron B. Gates & Rebeckah M. Tracy.
" 20, Grandison Philips & Emma Williams of N. Stonington.
1827. Jan. 1, Jasper Giddings of Franklin & Sabra Button of Preston.
Mar. 7, Russel Hinkley of Hebron & Sophia Fitch of Preston.
" 8, Samuel Holden & Sally H. Brewster.
April 1, Elias Brewster of Troy N. Y. & Arabell Tracy.

### DEATHS.

1812. ——— Longwood — pauper, 99, Old age.
Infant child of John Mott.
Elisha Parks.
Wife of Daniel Meech, N. Stonington, Dropsy.
Wife of Roger Sterry, Rheumatism.
Child of Ch$^s$ Meech, 2, Consumption.
Nov. 26, Samuel Avery, Dropsy.
1813. Jan. 2, Mrs. ——— Kimball — pauper, 94, Old age.
Feb. 16, Elijah Benjamins, 41, Suicide by hanging.
March 4, Sally, the widow of Rev. L. Tyler, 37, General debility.
" 23, William Avery, Consumption.
May 3, Elliu Benjamins, North Society, Ep$^{dk}$ Fever.
" 6, Wid. Anna Palmer, 68, Epidemick Fever.
" 16, ———Parish, Gr$^d$ child of Ed Tracy, 7, Drowned.

1813. May 17, Gen. Samuel Mott, 78, Epidemic Fever.
" 21, Wid. Sally Prentice, Epidemic Fever.
" 27, Anna Rennolds — pauper, 90, Old age & Fever.
" 28, ——— Cunningham — State pauper, Epidemic Fever.
Aug. 4, Wid. ——— Partridge, 98, Old age.
" Mrs. ——— Park — pauper, 90, Old age.
" 19, Caleb Ames, 35, Dropsy, Gout, & Jaundice, with an affliction of the liver.
Sept. Mrs. ——— Giddings wife of G. ———, Consumption.
" Child of Shipley Halsey.
Oct. 11, Patty Smith, Consumption.
" 17, Polly Latham — pauper, 52, Consumption.
Nov. 9, Moses Tracy, Old age.
" 18, A child of Avery Prentice aged twelve days.
Dec. 31, ——— Morgan, the wife of Amos M. of West Society, 20.
1814. Feb. 9, The Widow of Samuel Avery, 60.
" 11, Samuel Capron, Spotted Fever.
" 16, Lucy, child of Elisha Kimball Jun$^r$, 2yr. 9mths, Throat disorder.
April 23, Bridget Smith, Consumption.
July  A child of Shubael Park, Throat disorder.
" 19, Samuel Ellis of West Society, 85, Old age.
Aug. 4, Maj. John Baldwin North Stonington, 61, Paralytick shock.
Sept. 18, Lydia, daughter of Joshua Barstow, 21mo., Throat disorder.
Oct. 5, Capt. ——— Robbins, 95, Old age.
Dec. 15, Widow of Isaac Avery, 70, Old age.
" 20, Child of Daniel Gore, 3.. 9mo., Fever, Worms.
" 21, Mrs. Corning — pauper, Old age.
" 28, Capt. Craig — pauper, 80, Old age.
1815. Jany. 15, Widow Esther Avery, 87, Paralytic Shock.
" 19, Will$^m$ Cook of West Society, 71, Consumption.
April 9, John Safford, 86, Old age.
" 14, Sally Giddings, 61, Consumption.
May 2, Sarah Gere, wife of John Gere, 67, Pleurisy.
" Wid$^w$ ——— Ames, 96, Old age.
July 6, A child of Sam$^l$ Prentice N. Stonington, 8 months, Bowel complaint.
Aug.  Dyer Frink in the poor house, 84.
Dec$^r$ 21, The Wife of Nathan Herrick, 60, Consumption.
1816. Jan. 25, Elijah Pride of West Society, 67, Asthma.
" 27, Rachel, wife of Asa Park, 83, Dropsey.
March 25, David Frink of West Society, 41, Consumption.
May 5, A son of Jeremiah S. Halsey, 5 mo., Head-disorder.
July 9, John Morgan, 74, Old age with Delirium.
Aug 20, Dolly Witter, 23, Kings Evil.
Dec. ——— Lambert, a foreigner, Fever.
1817. Jan. 21, The wife of Jeremiah S. Halsey, 32, Consumption.
Feb. 10, Henryetta, child of Ch$^s$ Smith, 3, Consumption.
" 16, Daniel Morgan, 72, Old age.
March 3, The Wife of David Moore of North Stonington, 44, Consumption.
Feb. 17, The Wid$^w$ of Caleb Tyler, Delirium.
June 8, Mr. ——— Buel, State pauper, 63, Sudden death.
" 10, Jabez Story of Long Society, 84, Palsey.
" 13, Mrs. ——— Corning of Long Society.
Aug.  Wid. of John Safford.
"  The wife of Abel Spicer.
Sept. 17, Miss Lydia Rood, 77, Consumption.

## STATISTICS OF THE CHURCH. 175

1817. Sep 26, An infant child of Ephraim Meech.
" 28, An infant child of Ch$^s$ Meech.
Dec       Chapman Forseith, Dropsy.
" 17, Asa Cook, pauper of Griswold, 82, Sudden death.
" 18, The wife of Moses Meech, pauper.
1818. Jan'y     Widow Esther Brewster, Intoxication.
April       Jeremiah Culver, 83, Sudden death.
" 23, A child of Barton D. Kimball.
May       Wid$^w$ —— Avery, Old age.
"         Daughter of —— Watson, 13, Fever.
Sep 23, Wid. Mary Tracy, 58, Liver complaint.
" 27, Almira Tracy, 17, Fever.
Oct 9, John T. Mott; 40, Fever.
Nov 10, Simeon Capron, 68, Fits.
Dec 3, Elkanah Fanning, 57.
" 10, Moses Rood, 82, Suddenly in a fit.
" 29, Minerva Witter, 22, Consumption.
1819. Feb 18, Wid Sarah Fitch, Long Society, 92, Old age.
Mar 2, John Kinne, son of Jesse Starkweather Jun., 4, Bowel complaint.
" 7, Son of Gilbert Button, 4, Dropsy in head.
     Child of Allen Button, Burn.
June 23, Nathaniel Fitch, 66.
Aug 27, Mrs —— Pollard, pauper, 86, Sudden death.
Sep$^t$ 11, The wife of Adin Cook, 32, Consumption.
Oct 17, Louisa Meech, 19, Typus fever.
" 18, Moses Meech, 74, Sudden death.
Nov 20, Martha, child of Wid. Joshua Meech, 6, Typus fever.
" 23, Amy, the wife of John Prentice, 33, Fever.
1820. Jan'y 9, The wife of Belcher Starkweather, 57, Sudden death.
" 29, Jason Rood, 21, Typus fever.
June 16, Roswell Button, 74, Gout in stomach.
" 20, Stephen Latham, 26, Consumption.
" 22, Nathan Ayers, 74.
Oct 7, Betty Lamb, a woman of color, Old age.
1821. Feb 15, Polly, the wife of Henry Fanning, 27, Consumption.
March 10, Asa Park, 89, Old age.
June 7, Widow Ziporah Fitch, Long Society, 49, Consumption.
Sept 1, Ch$^s$ Forseith, 66, Dropsy in chest.
1822. Feb 8, Nathan Herrick, 88, Gravel.
March 1, Charles Morgan, 30, Consumption.
July 27, Lemuel Swan, child of Ch$^s$ Meech, 3 m, Canker.
Aug 28, Louisa, daughter of Ch$^s$ Meech, 3, Cholera morbus.
Oct 13, Amos Prentice, 30, Typus fever.
" 21, Thomas Meech, 74, Dropsy.
1823. Jan'y     A child of Minor Grant.
" 19, Widow Dorcas Standish, 100 years & 3 months.
May       Wife of Jonathan Smith, Old age.
Sept 29, Sally, wife of Moses Hilliard, 42, Consumption.
1824. Jan'y 4, John P. Cook, 23, Consumption.
Feb 7, Nathan Peters.
March 7, Bridget, wife of Asa Smith, 70, Consumption.
1825. Oct 20, Sophia, wife Sam$^l$ Browning, N. Stonington, 34, Typus fever.
1826. Jany 2, William T. Browning, 60, —— & Dropsy.
" 15, Lydia Brewster, wife of Judah Brewster, 74.
April 21, The wife of Roswell Park, 68, Sudden death by cramp.
Aug 3, The wife of Erastus Brewster, child bed.
1827. March 26, The widow Sarah Smith, N. Stonington, 89, old age.

## STATISTICS OF THE CHURCH.

### THE MINISTRY OF REV. AUGUSTUS B. COLLINS.

January 16, 1828 — March 16, 1847.

Names of Church Members at the Time of Mr. Collins' Settlement

Jonathan Smith,
Jonah Witter,
Jacob Newton,
Elisha Kimball,
Dec. Charles Meech,
Shubael Meech,
Stephen Meech,
Dec W<sup>m</sup> Smith,
Joseph A. Yarrington,
Ezra B. Smith,
Latham Browning,
Charles G. Clark,
Alexander Rogers,
Jonathan Smith 2<sup>nd</sup>,
Noyes B. Meech,
Henry Fanning,
Wid. Esther Tracy,
Wid. Hannah Forsyth,
Wid. Lucy Meech,
Mrs Sally Meech, w. Jacob M.,
Mrs Sally Smith, w. Chester S.,
Mrs Eunice Witter, w. Jonah W.,
Wid. Rebeckah Tracy,
Wid. Elizabeth Fanning,
Wid. Esther Clark,
Rebeckah Tracy,
Azuba Tracy,
Mrs Amy Cook, w. of Ruel C.,
Mrs Betsey Wilcox,
Mrs Amy Wilcox,
Wid. Azuba Tracy,
Wid Olive Tracy,
Mrs Fanning, w. of Henry F.,
Mrs. Meech, w. of Dec. Charles M.,
Lydia Mott,
Mrs Louisa Downing, w. of E. B. D.,
Julia Smith,
Lucinda Morgan,
Mrs Spicer, w. of Oliver S.,
Wid Polly Prentice,
Mrs. Amy Browning, w. of Thomas B.,
Mrs. Esther Rix,
Mrs. Yarrington, w. of Joseph A. Y.,
Mrs Olive Geer, w. of Jeptha G — Jun.,
Wid Phebe Ames,
Mrs Prentice, w. of Thomas P. Esq<sup>r</sup>.,
Nancy Ames,
Mrs Susan Prentice, w. of Sam<sup>l</sup> P.,
Wid. Lucretia Meech,
Mrs Kimball, w. of Elisha K.,
Mrs. Meech, w. of Shubael M.,
Mrs Meech w. of Stephen M. Esq<sup>r</sup>,
Sally B. Meech,
Elizabeth Pridde,
Althelia Spicer,
Diana Spicer,
Mrs Ann E. Meech,
Mary C. Meech,
Lucretia T. Hyde,
Mrs Eliza A. Browning,
Mrs Susan Hyde, w. of Rev J. H.,
Cynthia M. Meech,
Rosina A. Downer,
Mrs. Orra Gore, w. of Amos G.,
Mrs Sybel Branch,
Susan A. Ames.

### Admissions.

1828. May 4, Mrs Lydia E. Collins, w. of Rev<sup>d</sup> Augustus B. Collins.
Sept 7, George Loring & his wife by letter from Griswold.
Nov 3, Wid. Dorcas Mix.
" Wid. Lovinia Fanning.
Dec. 7, Joshua Barstow.
Mrs. Moses Hilliard, by letter from church in Griswold. Abby Tracy.

1829. Jan 18, Wid Martha Benjamin.
" Mrs. Patty Avery.
" Katharine R. Phillips.
" Emily A. Phillips.
" Hannah Frink.
" Mrs Mehitable Morgan.
" Sarah Ann Meech.

1829. March 8, John Baldwin.
" Mrs. Anner Baldwin the wife of John B.
" Mrs Sally Holmes.
" Sally Ann Baldwin, daughter of John B.
" Daniel Swan.
" Mrs. Hannah Swan, the w. of Daniel S.
" Mrs. Katharine Prentice, the w. of John P.
" Amy Prentice, daughter of John P.
" Mary Ann Prentice.
" Samuel Prentice.
" Mrs. Amy Prentice, the w. of Samuel P.
" Chester S. Prentice, son of Samuel P.
" Thomas Browning Esq$^r$.
" W$^m$ T. Browning, son of Thomas B. Esq$^r$.
" Mary P. Browning, daughter of Tho$^s$ B. Esq$^r$.
" Mason B. Browning, son of Thomas B. Esq$^r$.
" Sally Ann Browning, daughter of T. B. Esq$^r$.
" David N. Prentice, son of Sam$^l$ H. Prentice.
" Samuel Prentice, son of Sam$^l$ H. P.
" Emily Augusta Baldwin.
" Elizabeth B. Collins, daughter of Rev$^d$ A. B. Collins.
June 7, Mrs. Lucinda Boardman, w. of Capt. Joseph B.
" Roswell Parks.
" Mrs. Mabel Parks, w. of Roswell P.
" Charles Prentice.
" Mrs. Phebe Prentice, w. of Charles P.
" Charles Swan 3$^{rd}$.
" Nancy Ann Mott.
April 15, Sophia Grinals at the house of her grandfather Morgans, a few days before her death.
Aug. 9, Capt. Joseph Boardman.
" Charles Geer.
" Mrs. Sally Ingreham.
" Mrs. Betsey Combs.
" Lucy Ann Tracy.
" Lydia Loring.
" Francis Ann Loring.

1830. Jan. 7, Mrs. Mary Woodard, wife of Mr. Appleton Woodard from the chh. in North Stonington.

1831. July 24, Capt. Jacob Meech.
" Mrs. Desire Crairy.
" Mrs. Elizabeth Parmenter.
" Sarah Meech.
" Mrs. Harriot Ames.
" Mrs. Emily Browning.
" Susan Augusta Browning.
" Arrabella Tracy.
" Erastus Morgan Jun$^r$.
" Lucy Meech Morgan.
" Charles Crairy Morgan.
" John Morgan.
" Eunice Crairy Morgan.
" Lemuel Tyler Downing.
" Louisa Tyler Downing.
" Eunice Billings Meech.
" Adaline Tuttle.
" Caroline Mariah Rouse.
Nov. 7, Mrs. Ann D. Grant, the wife of Mr. John Grant by letter from the chh. in North Stonington.

12

1835. Jan. 11, Oliver Spicer.
" Erastus Safford.
" Phebe Safford.
" Lydia Barstow.
" Widow Cartharine Browning.
" Ziporah Geer.
" Mary Rood.
" Caroline Swan.
" Eunice Avery.
" Sarah Mariah Crairy,
" George W. Phillips.
" Denison Baldwin Holmes.
" Augustus Pattison Collins.
Nov. 1, Lucy A. Loring by letter from the church in Lee Mass.
1836. March 20, Widow Lucinda Utley by letter from church in Griswold.
1837. 5, Louisa Avery, by letter from the Free Congregational church in Stockbridge Mass.
Sept. 3, Mrs. Lucretia K. Miner.
1838. March 11, Henry Prentice & Eliza Ann, his wife by letter.
May 15, Widow Dimis Swan Avery.
" Orra Ann Collins.
July 1, Andrew Smith Frink.
" Samuel Prentice Browning.
" Alexander S. Prentice.
" Mrs. Martha Witter.
" Adaline Browning.
" Catharine Browning.
" Elizabeth Hull Browning.
" Mary Eaton Prentice.
" William Henry Prentice.
Sept. 2, Fanny Witter.
1840. Sept. 6, Aaron Taylor by letter from the fourth Congregational chh. in Hartford.
1841. Sept. 5, Elizabeth Choat, she being in the ninety-first year of her age.
" Sarah Standish.
Nov. 7, Widow Sarah Bailey.
1842. Jan. 23, Widow Sarah C. Cook at her own house, she being sick.
March 6, Mrs. Eunice Meech, the second wife of Stephen Meech Esq$^r$ by letter from the first chh. in Lisbon.
" Mrs. Sabra Park the wife of S. Park.
1844. July 7, Eunice Geer Palmer.
1845. May 4, Mrs. Louisa Williams by letter.
" Mrs. Nancy Crary Browning the wife of W$^m$ T. Browning.
1846. May 10, Lucy Ann Palmer, the wife of Charles Palmer.
" Ruth Ann Palmer.
" Mary Jane C. Collins.
July 5, Clarrissa Smith.

---

## BAPTISMS.

1828. Oct. 19, Dwight, the child of Ezra B. Smith.
Nov. 3, Wid. Dorcas Mix.
Dec. 7, Joshua Barstow.
1829. Jan. 18, Wid. Martha Benjamins. Mrs. Sally Homes. Mrs. Mahitable Morgan. Katharine Phillips, Emily Phillips, Hannah Frink.

STATISTICS OF THE CHURCH. 179

1829. March 8, John Baldwin, Mrs. Anner Baldwin, W. of John B., Sally Ann Baldwin, daughter of J. B., Mrs. Hannah Swan, w. of Daniel S., Mrs. Katharine Prentice, Mary Ann Prentice, Amy Prentice, Mrs. Amy Prentice, w. of Sam$^l$ P., Chester Smith Prentice, Thomas Browning Esq$^r$, William T. Browning, Mary P. Browning, Mason B. Browning, Sally Ann Browning, children of Thomas B. Esq$^r$, Emily A Baldwin, David N. Prentice, & Samuel Prentice.
" 25, Sophia Grinals.
June 7, Mrs. Mabel Parks, Charles Prentice, Charles Swan 3$^{rd}$, Nancy Ann Mott, Mary Melissa, a child of Dec. W$^m$ Smith, & Hamilton Fowler, a child of Doc$^t$ E. B. Downing.
July 12, Charles Franklin, Mary Eaton, and William Henery children of Samuel and Amy Prentice. Adaline, Catharine, Elizabeth Hull, Harriet Augusta & Frances Adelia, all children of Thomas Browning Esq$^r$ and his wife.
Aug. 9, Capt. Joseph Boardman, Mrs. Sally Ingreham, Mrs. Betsey Combs and Charles Geer.
—— ——, Harriet Tyler, Mary Elizabeth & Emily Williams, all three children of Mr. Charles & Phebe Prentice — also Mary Jane Chittenden a child Rev$^d$ Augustus B. and Lydia E. Collins.

1831. May    George Loring, a son of Dec. Loring.
July 24, Capt. Jacob Meech, Mrs. Desire Crairy, Susan Augusta Browning, Erastus Morgan Jun$^r$, Lucy Meech Morgan, Charles Crairy Morgan, John Morgan, Eunice Crairy Morgan, Adaline Tuttle & Caroline Mariah Rouse.
Aug. 7, Henery Warren Yarrington, a child of Joseph A. Yarrington.

1832. Jan. 2, Stephen Wallbridge Meech.

1834. June 15, Cynthia Mellissa Phillips.

1835. Jan. 11, Oliver Spicer, Erastus Safford, Phebe Safford, Ziporah Geer, Mary Rood, Caroline Swan, Eunice Avery, George W. Phillips & Denison B. Holmes.
July 29, Wid. Katharine Roggers.
Sept. 6, Charles Henery, son of Charles Prentice.

1836. May 1, Phebe Angeline, a child of Erastus Safford.
" 12, George Alonzo, a child of George W. Phillips.
Sept. 4, Sarah Brewer, a child of Joseph A. Yarington.

1837. Sept. 3, Eliza Perkins and Sarah Lucretia, children of Erastus P. & Lucretia K. Miner.

1838. Jan. 27, W$^m$ Perkins, a child of Erastus P. & Lucretia K. Miner.
May 6, Sarah Hellen Crairy & Nathan Oscar Crairy children of Nathan & Sarah M. Crairy.
" 15, Widow Dimis S. Avery.
" " Nancy Amelia Phillips, a child of George W. Phillips.
July 1, Andrew Smith Frink, Samuel Prentice Browning, Alexander S. Prentice & Mrs. Martha Witter.

1840. Aug. —, Sarah Louisa, a child of George W. Phillips.

1841. Sept. 5, Sarah Standish.
Nov. 7, Ann Eliza, a child of George W. Phillips.
" " Widow Sarah Bailey.

180  STATISTICS OF THE CHURCH.

1842. Jan. 16, Widow Sarah C. Cook.
March 6, Elizabeth Brewster, a child of Silas Park.
Aug. 21, Andrew Tyler Huntington, a child of Andrew Huntington.
Nov. 15, Augustus Lyman Talcott, a child of Samuel L. Talcott & Elizabeth B. Collins Talcott, his wife.
1843. Sept. 3, Charles Crairy Phillips, a child of George W. Phillips.
1844. July 7, Eunice Geer Palmer.
1845. April 29, John Williams, an infant child of Robert A. Williams.
May 4, Nancy Crary Browning, the wife of W<sup>m</sup> T. Browning & Emma Dorothea, a child of W<sup>m</sup> T. Browning.
June 15, Norman Austin, a child of George W. Phillips.
1846. May 10, Ruth Ann Palmer.
July 5, Clarrissa Smith.
Sept. 27, Abigail Ayer, the widow of Jonas Ayer Esq<sup>r</sup>.
Oct. 4, Charles Lucian Palmer & Lydia Ann Palmer children of Charles Palmer & Lucy Ann Palmer, his wife.

MARRIAGES.

1828. Jan 15, Lucas Witter & Emily Downer, both of Preston.
Feb'y 28, Nathan A. Crairy & Sally F. Ames, both of Preston.
March 20, Bradford Ames & Harriet Meech, both of Preston.
Oct 5, Nathan Benjamin & Hannah Cook, both of Preston.
Nov 6, Oliver Austin Crairy & Mary T. Ames, both of Preston.
" 27, Avery D. Herskell & Chrissa Ann Standish, Preston.
Dec 11, Jephtha Geer & Olive Starkweather, both of Preston.
Dec 25, James R. Stetson of Lisbon & Mary Ann Brown, Preston.
1829. Feb 25, Benjamin F. Avery of Preston & Demis F. Bailey, North Stonington.
March 26, Charles Kimball & Sarah Ann Frink, Preston.
April 2, Stephen K. Safford & Thankful Killam, Preston.
" 5, Peter Brown of Grotton & Maria Yarrington, Preston.
June 8, Robbert S. Avery Esq & Nancy Crairy, both of Preston.
Sept 7, Charles Barstow & Eunice H. Geer, both of Preston.
" 22, Alfred A. Kinney, Voluntown & Athelia Spicer, Preston.
Oct 1, Charles L. Meech & Abby A. Phillips, both of Preston.
" 8, Asher P. Brown & Louisa Ames, both of Preston.
1830. ———, Nathan D. Palmer of Preston & Nancy Swan, North Stonington.
———, Latham H. Browning & Emeline Wheeler, both of North Stonington.
April 24, Zebulon R. Robbins, Norich & Charlotte Holden, Preston.
June 20, Erastus S. Turner, Norwich & Julia Ann Brown, Preston.
Sept 13, Latham H. Ayer, N. Stonington & Susan A. Ames, Preston.
" 15, Asa Kinney, Homer, New York & Diann Spicer, Preston.
Nov 7, Jonah Witter, Jun<sup>r</sup> & Eliza Halsey, both of Preston.
Dec 22, George W. Morgan, Preston & Eliza Brewster, Griswold.
1831. ———, Denison Swan & Caroline Bailey, N. Stonington.
———, Capt. Charles Smith & Emma Stanton, both of South Stonington.
Jan. 20, Thomas M. Safford & Nabby P. Hakes, Preston.
April 7, Elijah Benjamin, Lisbon & Eunice A. Weeks, Preston.
June 7, George Harkness & Frances A. Champlain, Preston.
Sept. 14, George W. Phillips & Mary C. Meech, Preston.
Dec. 11, Amos Stanton, Grotton & Ardelia Stanton, Preston.
" 18, Lee A. Bailey, Groton & Sarah Woodmancy, Preston.

## STATISTICS OF THE CHURCH. 181

1832. Feb. 8, Erastus P. Miner, Nowich & Lucretia K. Meech, Preston.
" 12, Francis H. Averil, Griswold & Mary P. Spicer, Preston.
March 12, Elisha Brewster Jun<sup>r</sup> & Lucy H. Kimball, Preston.
March 25, John M. Richmond, Exeter, R. I. & Emily Frink, Preston.
April 26, Asa L. Latham & Mary Brewster, Preston.
June 14, Joseph Brumley & Abigail Wright, Preston.
Oct. 3, John B. Clark & Abby H. Thurston, Preston.

1833. Jan. 20, Giles Gallup, Growton & Sarah O. Witter, Preston.
Feb. 17, Giles Herskell & Eliza C. Standish, Preston.
Sept. 17, Luther Pellet of Nowich & Mary Ann Palmer, Preston.
Dec. 24, John D. Geer, Griswold & Mary Ann Cook, Preston.

1834. March 17, Edwin Palmer & Harriet N. Morgan, Preston.
April 28, Samuel Whaley, Bolton & Sally Phillips, Nowich.
May 4, James R. Cozzens, Plainfield & Clarissa H. Swan, Preston.
" 5, Jonathan Slocum, N. Kingston, R. I. & Susan A. Browning, N. Stonington.
" 28, Hezekiah Kanfield of Mount Clemons, Michigan & Lucy M. Morgan, Preston.
Nov. 3, Erastus Morgan Jun<sup>r</sup> & Mary L. Morgan, Preston married by Rev<sup>d</sup> George A. Calhoun of Coventry.

1835. June 3, Andrew Huntington, Nowich City & Lydia Loring, Preston.

1836. Oct. 3, Abraham Yarrington Jun. of Norwich & Margaret Crapo, North Stonington.
Nov. 8, Doct ——— Miner of Griswold & Lucy A. Loring of Preston.
Nov. 13, George W. Richmond of Exeter, R. I. & Fanny Frink of Preston married by Rev. Edward A. Bull of Lebanon.
" 24, Isaac S. Geer & Abby J. Brewster, Preston.

1837. Feb. 22, Nathan P. Kimball & Harriet Frink, Preston.
March 23, Benjamin F. Browning of the city of New York & Eunice B. Hull of Stonington.
June 19, Edwin Gavitt of Nowich City & Abby Gavitt of Preston.
Oct. 16, Charles C. Morgan of New York City & Lucy Ann Tracy, Preston.

1838. Oct. 31, Thomas F Standish & Ruth Ann Holden of Preston.
Dec. 25, Capt. Charles L. Meech of Preston & Mary Swan of Norwich.
" 30, Capt. Bartlett Holmes of Preston & Mrs. Lucinda Utley.

1839. Jan. 27, Jedediah Corning & Rhoda Ann Buddington, both of Preston.
March 24, George W. Richmond, Exeter, R. I. & Maria Frink of Preston.
April 3, Denison Hewett, & Mary P. Browning of North Stonington.
May 3, Charles Denison & Sarah M. Crocker of Norwich.
June 20, Stephen Meech Esq<sup>r</sup>. & Eunice Averill, both of Preston.
Sept. 1, George N. Griffin of Wallingford & Sarah A. Baldwin of North Stonington.
" " Russell Griffin of Wallingford & Emily A. Hewett of North Stonington.

1840. March 8, Ellis Leonard & Phebe A. Woodward, of N. Stonington.
April 2, Henry H. Cary of Windham, & Persis C. Geer of Preston.
" 5, John P. Babcock, Salina, N. York & Abby A. Ayer of Preston.

# STATISTICS OF THE CHURCH.

1840. April 12, Warren Cook & Abby Crary of Preston by Rev. Wm R. Jewett.
June 2, Samuel L. Talcott of Coventry & Elizabeth B. Collins, Preston.
Sept. 10, Andrew Huntington of Savannah, Georgia & Louisa T. Downing, Preston.
Nov. 23, Silas Wilcox, Stonington & Emma Herskell, Preston.
Dec. 30, Wm R. Prentice & Frences M. Avery both of Preston.

1841. Jan. 6, Henry B. Hakes, Preston & Ann W. Woodard, N. Stonington.
Sept. 5, John Shaplay of Caznovia, N. Y. & Mary L. Smith of Ledyard, Ct.
Oct. 31, Oliver W. Fowler & Mary Ann Dennis of Preston.

1841. Nov. 7, Lester Fuller of Hampton & Philena Benjamens of Preston.

1842. Feb. 1, William Loring & Harriot K. Morgan, Preston.

1843. Jan. 8, Rufus S. Greenman & Hannah E. Davis of Preston.
" 9, Charles W. Holden & Rebeca C. Corning of Preston.
Feb. 22, Oliver P. Avery & Sarah Loring of Preston.
March 23, William T. Browning of North Stoninton & Nancy C. Avery of Preston.
Sept 13, Wm. C. Osgood of Norwich & Adaline Browning of N. Stonington.
" 21, Jabish Gallup of Newburgh, Ohio & Louisa Avery of Preston.
Dec. 13, Chester S. Prentice of Grotton & Lucy Crairy of Preston.

1844. July 1, William B. Palmer & Amanda M. Gallup, both of Preston.
Oct. 20, William Ingreham & Harriet F. Williams, both of Preston.
Dec. 18, Francis S. Avery & Joann T. Hinkley, both of Preston.
" 25, James D. Rogers of Nowich & Eunice G. Palmer of Preston.

1845. Dec. 16, Capt. Daniel B. Morgan & Lucy Ann Rude of Preston.
" 23, Elisha Rude of Preston & Elizabeth A. Hewett of N. Stonington.

1846. March 4, George W. Frink & Sally M. Williams of Preston.
April 15, Augustus P. Collins of Windham, Willimantic Society & Harriet P. Beckley, of Berlin.
May 10, Isaac G. Ford of Norwich & Cynthia R. Woodward of North Stonington.
" 14, Silas F. Beebe of Norwich & Mary C. Holden of Preston.
Sept. 30, Rix Rude & Amy Bromley, both of Preston.
Nov. 15, Nehemiah C. Cook of Nowich City & Almeda Barns of Preston by Rev. John P. Gulliver of Nowich City.

1847. March 21, Wm A. Collins of Nowich & Widow Dimis S. Avery of N. Stonington.

## Deaths.

1828. Jan. 18, Wid. Lucy Meech.
Sept. 5, A child of Mr. Parks.
" 11, A child of Mrs. Allen died at the poor house.
" 13, Amy Kenedy, a town pauper.
Oct. 25, Nabby Stalson, a woman of colour.
Nov. 2, Will Madison, a coloured man.
May 13, Mrs. Margaret Kimball, relict of Mr. Nathan Kimball.
Dec. 10, Mrs. Elizabeth Dorrance.
" 31, Mary Avery.

## STATISTICS OF THE CHURCH. 183

1829. Jan. 2, Mrs. Sally Avery, the wife of Robbert S. Avery Esqr.
Feb. 4, Denison Palmer Esqr.
" 18, Judah Brewster.
May 15, Sophia Grinalds.
Oct. 22, Mr. Elisha Kimball Jur.
Dec. 25, Mrs. Phebe Prentice.
" Old Mrs. Witter at the poor-house.

1830. Feb. 23, Cap$^t$ W$^m$ Palmer.
Nov. 12, Julia Ann Morgan.
Dec. 20, Wi$^d$ Fanning at Jonah's Witter's Esq$^r$.
" 25, Eliza Ann Fitch, a child of Asa Fitch.
———, Mary Ann Davis.
———, Rose, a woman of Colour.
Dec. 27, Deacon Thomas Swan.

1831. ———, Alexander Bags.
———, Mr. Belcher Starkweather.
———, A child of Capt. Charles L. Meech.
July 6, Dec. Elijah Denison.
Aug. 18, Nancy Ames.
———, Charles F. Prentice.
———, Giles Parkes.
———, Mrs. Downer, the wife of Doc$^t$ Avery Downer.
———, Asa Smith.
———, A child of Kit Brown.
———, A woman at the poor-house.
———, The wife of Caleb Woodard.
———, Luke Wheeler.
Dec. 16, Simeon Harvey's child.
" 24, Cynthia Melissa Meech.

1832. Jan. 6, Stephen Wallbridge Mech 2$^d$.
" 7, Mary Barnes.
" 14, The wife of Amacy Standish, Long Soc$^{ty}$.
" 21, John Ayer.
Feb. 11, Mrs. Avery, wife of Christopher Avery.
Mar. 12, The wife of Erastus Safford.
April 7, Sarah Perkins.
" 10, Benjamin Mortimore.
" 14, Mrs. Davis, the wife of Shory Davis.
" 17, Abby Tracy.
June 12, A child of Jonah Witter J$^{un}$.
Aug. 7, Patty Palmer.
" 22, Erastus Brewster.
25, A daughter of Mr. Crocker.
Oct. 9, Allen Button.
Dec. 28, Mrs. Witter, the wife of Jonah Witter Esq$^r$.

1833. Feb. 23, Emily Williams Prentice, a child of Charles Prentice.
March 17, Walter Palmer Esq$^r$.
———, Lucy Safford.
May 18, Elisha Kimball.
July 2, Mrs. Abby Meech, the wife of Cap$^t$ Charles L. Meech.
Aug. 8, Mrs. Eliza Witter, the wife of Jonah Witter J$^r$.
———, Two children of Charles Rood.
Nov. —, Widow Brewster.
" —, Mrs. Sharp, the wife of Leonard Sharp.
Dec. —, A child of John Gates.

1834. Jan. —, Emily Jane Crairy.
———, W$^m$ Tracy Gates.
Feb 17, Mrs. Sally Ingreham.

1834. March 15, An infant child of Washington Phillips.
" 20, A trantient person who said his name was Samuel Bemis, died in a fit of intoxication.
———, Wid. Lucretia Meech died at Waterford and was brought to Preston to be buried.
April 20, Elihu Hakes.
May 22, Francis Ann Loring.
June 9, Widow Hope Kimball, the wife of Elisha Kimball, deceased.
Aug. 1, The wife of Capt. Elisha Phillips, deceased.
" 24, Franklin Avery.
Oct. 15, Charles D. Browning.
Nov. 18, Lee A. Bailey.
———, Nancy Baldwin.
———, A child of Lyman Bailey.
———, A coulered person at the poor-house.

1835. Jan. 20, Jonathan Morgan.
Feb. 2, Sally Morgan.
March 6, Heney N. Fanning, at Lisbon but his remains were brought to Preston and buried.
June 3, Ethan Wilcox at Lisbon but his remains were brought to Preston.
" 5, The Widow Susan Baldwin.
Aug. 5, Wid. Katharine Roggers.
Oct. 11, Wid. Martha Benjamins.
" 14, Lydia Starkweather.

1836. Jan. 3, Mary Ann Avery, the wife of Capt. Elias Avery.
" 16, Mrs. Francis Treat, the wife of Capt James Treat died at Voluntown and her remains were brought to Preston for interment.
Feb. 11, A child of Mr. Baggs.
" 11, Mrs. Sally Meech, the wife of Capt Jacob Meech.
March 28, Hetty Morgan.
" 29, Old Mrs. Pride, the last member of the Congregational chh. in Long Society — formally under the charge of the Rev. Mr. Wight.
April 2, Cyrus Gates.
" 3, Arrabella Tracy.
" 23, Mrs. Combs, the wife of Edward Combs.
" 27, Ziporah Geer.
Aug. 12, Mrs. Lucy Loring, the Wife of Dec. George Loring.
Sept. 8, Ezekiel Rood.
Oct. 13, Widow Joanna Morgan.
" 18, Prosper Kimball.
Nov. 13, Joseph Ames.
Dec. 2, Widow ——— Frink.
" 3, Fanny Guile lived in Long Society.
" 7, Thomas Renolds.
—, Levi Jones, a town pauper at the poor house.

1837. Jan. 5, Mrs. Lucy Ann, wife of Albert Bennett.
" 7, Widow Kimball, the wife of Mr. Prosper Kimball deceased.
" 25, Simeon Jones.
" 26, John Starkweather.
Feb. 13, Mrs. Cleveland, the wife of John Cleveland.
" 26, Mrs. Lucy Meech, the wife of Stephen Meech Esq.
March 11, Mrs. Treat, the wife of James Treat.
" 20, Julia Ann Morgan, a child of Mr. Erastus Morgan Junr.
April 23, Nathan Brown.
May 19, William Brown.

## STATISTICS OF THE CHURCH. 185

1837. ———, Mrs. Ayer, the wife of W^m Ayer.
May 25, Samuel Prentice.
July 9, Eunice B. Meech at St. Louis.
Aug. 2, Betsey Brown.
" 31, Mr. Bushnel.
Sept. 30, Capt. Moses Hilliard of Long Society.
Oct. 30, Eunice E. Kinney, a grand-child of Capt. Oliver Spicer.
1838. Feb. —, Edward Combs.
March —, W^m Pendleton.
" 29, George Buttoff.
———, ——— A child of Mr. Dewey.
———, Mrs. Gates, the wife of Frederick Gates.
June 19, Mrs. Fanny Richmond.
" 25, Mr. Amos Williams.
Dec. —, Mr. ——— Brown.
1839. Jan. 11, Lucinda Morgan.
April 6, Widow Gates.
" 30, Thomas Prentice Esq^r.
Nov. 22, Capt. Oliver Spicer.
Dec. 1, Mrs. Nancy Phillips, the wife of George Phillips.
July —, Mrs. Hannah Starkweather.
" —, A child of Carmi Saunders.
" —, A child of Holibut Geer.
1840. Jan. 30, Mr. Adin Cook.
April —, Cyrus F. Cook.
June 6, Mrs. Mabel Park, wife of Mr. Roswell Park.
Sept. 27, Widow Polly Prentice.
" 28, Widow Hannah Tracy of Long Society.
Oct. 7, Henry E. Cook.
" 18, Almira Aaron, Collord Girl.
Nov. 25, Amos Avery.
1841. Jan. 15, W^m Henry Harrison, a child of Col Edwin Palmer.
Feb. 25, Shora Davis.
May 10, William Brown.
1842. Jan. 30, Elizabeth Swan, wife of Charles Swan Jun^r.
Feb. 1, Widow Sarah C. Cook.
———, Mrs. Renolds.
———, Mrs. Bushnel.
———, Mrs. Thomas.
April 7, Eunice Ingreham.
Nov. 3, Susan Frink.
" 26, Mrs. Gates, the wife of Noah Gates.
1843. Jan. 31, Capt. John Morgan.
Feb. 9, Elizabeth Choate, Ninety-four years of age.
" 24, George Phillips.
" 24, Sarah Moriah Gates, aged Eleven years.
" 26, Mary Eliza Gates, aged Fourteen years.
" 28, Erastus Fitch Gates, 8 years old; all children of Noah Gates; the two last of which were buried in one grave.
March 28, Hezekiah Ingreham.
April 11, Mrs. Rood, the Widow of Capt. Ezekiel Rood.
Sept. 16, Jacob Newton of Long Society.
1844. June 26, Luther C. Gates drowned in Amoses Pond.
July 26, Zipporah Abby Cazwell, a child of Joshua Cazwell.
1846. March 18, Harriet Augusta Browning.
May 30, Jonas Ayer Esqr.
June 27, Robbert S. Avery Esqr.
Sept. —, Ezra Barnes.
" 28, Abigail Ayer, the widow of Jonas Ayer Esqr. deceased.

# STATISTICS OF THE CHURCH.

1847. March 14, Latham Browning.
" 21, Capt Jacob Meech.
" 10, Nathaniel Avery.
" 24, Nancy Palmer.

## THE MINISTRY OF THE REVᴅ NATHAN S. HUNT.
### October 20, 1847 — March 31, 1858.
#### NAMES OF CHURCH MEMBERS AT THE TIME OF MR. HUNT'S INSTALLATION.

Dea. Charles Meech.
Dea. George Loring,
Stephen Meech,
Joshua Barstow,
John Baldwin,
Chester S. Prentice,
Thomas Browning,
Wᵐ T. Browning,
Roswell Park,
Andrew S. Frink,
Samuel P. Browning,
Wᵐ H. Prentice,
Henry Prentice,
Samuel Prentice,
Charles Swan,
John Morgan,
George W. Phillips,
Alexander S. Prentice,
Wid. Elizabeth Fanning,
Mrs. Cynthia Meech, wife of Dea. M.,
Lydia Mott,
Mrs. Louisa Downing, wife of Dr. D.,
Mrs. Spicer, w. of Oliver S.,
Mrs. Amy Browning, w. of T. B.,
Mrs. Prentice w. of T. P. Esq.,
Mrs. Susan Prentice, w. of Sam. P.,
Sally B. Meech,
Mrs. Eliza A. Browning, w. of S. B.,
Wid. Dorcas Mix,
Wid. Lovinia Fanning,
Mrs. Mahitable Morgan,
Mrs. Anner Baldwin,
Wid. Amy Prentice,
Mrs. Betsey Combs,
Mrs. Mary Woodward,

Sarah Meech,
Mrs. Emeline Browning,
Eunice C. Morgan,
Mrs. Lydia Barstow,
Wid. Catharine Browning,
Mrs. Caroline Swan,
Eunice Avery,
Mrs. Martha Witter,
Catharine Browning,
Elizabeth H. Browning,
Mary E. Prentice,
Mrs. Eliza Ann Prentice,
Fanny Witter,
Sarah Standish,
Wid Sarah Bailey,
Mrs. Eunice Meech,
Mrs. Sabre Park,
Mrs. Eunice G. Rogers,
Mrs. Louisa Williams,
Mrs. Nancy C. Browning,
Mrs. Lucy Ann Palmer,
Ruth Ann Palmer,
Clarissa Smith,
Mrs. Sally Yarrington,
*Mrs. Amy Wilcox,
*Julia Smith,
Mrs. Mary C. Phillips,
Rosina A. Downer,
Sally Ann Baldwin,
Mrs. Katharine Prentice,
Amy Prentice,
Mary Ann Prentice,
Sally Ann Hewitt,
Emily A. Baldwin,
Wid. Desire Crary,
Mrs. Dimis S. Collins,
Sarah M. Meech.

### ADMISSIONS.

1847. July 4, Sarah M. Meech.
1848. July 2, Mrs. Polly Meech, Wid. of ———.
1849. July 1, Mrs. Lucy Rude, wife of Nathan Rude.
1850. March 10, Mrs. J. A. Swan, wife of Ephraim Swan.
July 7, De Witt C. Prentice.

---

* Between these two names is written in different ink, "Both previously dismissed

## STATISTICS OF THE CHURCH.

1853. Nov. 6, Mrs. Esther Kimbal wife of W<sup>m</sup> Kimball.
" Mr. Henry B. Rude & Miss Louisa W. Meech.
1854. March 12, Ira A. Judd.
Nov. 5, Esther C. Cook.
1856. May 4, Mrs. Cynthia B. Benjamin.
1857. Jan. 4, Mr. Charles Palmer.
Mch. 1, Mrs. Mary Morgan, Mr. Alphonso Browning and Mrs. Sarah C. Browning, his wife, Mrs. Harriet K. Loring, wife of W<sup>m</sup>, Mrs. Jane Ayer, wife of Mr. Albert A., Mrs. Abby A. Browning wife of Sam P., Miss Abby Phillips, Miss Susan R. Prentice, Miss Marynette T. Rogers, Mr. Perry G. Hoxie, Mr. Rensalear C. Swan, Mr. James Browning, Mr. Thomas T. Browning, Mr. Wm. H. Prentice, 2<sup>nd</sup>.
May 3, Mrs. Sabrina Brown, Mrs. Eliza Latham, Mrs. Eliza Crary, Mr. Robert Y. Latham, Mrs. Happy L. Latham, wife of R. Y. L., Mr. Albert G. Ayer, Mr. William Loring, Mr. William Morse, Mr. Lucas H. Witter, Miss Abby Witter, Miss Margaret E. Crary, Miss Wealthy A. Reed, Mrs. Emily J. Davis, wife of Oliver D.
July 5, Miss Sally A. Crary, Miss Mary A. Witter, Miss Lucy L. Loring, Miss Emma D. Browning.

### ADMISSIONS BY LETTER.

1848. March 3, Mrs. Susan, wife of Ansel Brown, from the first Church in Lisbon.
1851. July 6, John Myers Jun. from the Church in Ledyard.
" 6, Minerva, wife of John Myers Jun. from the Queen's River Baptist Church South Kingston, R. I.
1854. July 2, Mrs. Elizabeth A., wife of Mr. Elisha Rude from the Church in North Stonington.
1855. July 1, Mrs. Sarah Haikes Andrews, wife of Gustavus D. Andrews from the first Congregational Church, Butternuts, N. Y.
1857. March 1, Miss Lucy W. Browning from the Thirteenth St. Pres. Church, New York City.
" May 1, Received from the second Congregational Church, Preston the following members.
Mr. Amos Standish, Mrs. Clarissa Standish, his wife.
Mr. Francis H. Averill, Mrs. Mary Averill, his wife.
Mr. H. B. Benjamin, Mrs. Elvira Harvey, wife of Henry H.
Mrs. Mary Ann Stetson, Miss Lydia M. Spicer, Miss Mary G. Standish.

### DISMISSIONS BY LETTER.

1848. Jan. 23, Mrs. Eunice G. Rogers formerly Miss Palmer to the first Church in Norwich.
" March 3, Mrs. Eunice Huntington, formerly Miss Avery, to the Church in Griswold.
" " 3, Mr. Samuel Prentice to the Church in Greenville.
1849. Aug. 26, Mr. George W. Phillips and Mrs. Mary C. his wife to the Church in Bozrah.

# STATISTICS OF THE CHURCH.

1850. Jan. 13, Mr Alexander S. Prentice to the second Church in Norwich.
" April 14, Mrs. Sally Ann Hewitt to the Church in North Stonington.
1851. June 22, Mrs. Catharine Prentice to the Church in Greenville.
1852. April 25, Mr. John Morgan to the S. Church in Hartford.
1856. Dec. 21, Mrs. Sarah H. Andrews to the Baptist Church, Preston.
1857. Feb. 14, Miss Sarah Meech to the third Church, Norwich.
1858. Jan. 1, Mrs. Cynthia B. Benjamin to the Church at Mystic Bridge, of which Rev. W. R. Long is pastor.
Mch. 4, Mr. DeWitt C. Prentice to the first Presbyterian Church, City of St Peter, Minnesota.

---

### BAPTISMS OF INFANTS.

1848. April 23, Thomas, son of William T. and Nancy C. Browning.
May 7, Helen Maria, Daughter of George W. and Mary C. Phillips.
1850. Dec. 1, Amos Avery, Son of Wm. T. and Nancy C. Browning.
1851. Sept. 21, Martha Amelia and Holis Hyde, children of Charles and Lucy Ann Palmer.
1856. Sept. 14, William, Son of William T. and Nancy C. Browning.

---

### BAPTISMS ON PROFESSION OF FAITH.

1847. July 4, Sarah Matilda Meech.
1848. July 2, Mrs Polly Meech.
1849. " 1, Mrs Lucy Rude.
1850. March 10, Mrs Julia Ann Swan.
July 7, DeWitt Clinton Prentice.
1853. Nov 6, Mrs. Esther Kimball, Mr Henry Brown Rude, Miss Louisa Walbridge Meech.
1854. March 12, Mr Ira Almon Judd.
Nov 5, Miss Esther Cordelia Cook.
1856. May 4, Mrs Cynthia Billings Benjamin.
1857. Jan 4, Mr Charles Palmer.
M'c'h 1, Mr Alphonso Browning, Mrs Sarah Cole Browning, Mrs Harriet Kinne Loring, Mrs Jane Ayer, Mrs Abby Ann Browning, Miss Abby Phillips, Miss Susan Russ Prentice, Miss Marynette Turner Rogers, Mr. Perry Green Hoxie, Mr Rensellear Courtland Swan, Mr James Browning, Mr Thomas Lathrop Browning.
" May 3, Mrs Sabrina Brown, Mrs Eliza Latham, Mrs Eliza Crary, Mr Robert Young Latham, Mrs Happy Lawton Latham, wife of R. Y. L., Mr Albert Gallatin Ayer, Mr William Morse, Mr Lucas Henry Witter, Miss Abby Witter, Miss Margaret Elizabeth Crary, Miss Wealthy Ann Reed.
July 5, Mrs Emily Jane Davis, Miss Sally Almira Crary, Miss Mary Ann Witter, Miss Lucy Lester Loring.

---

### DEATHS.

1847. Aug 13, Mrs Phebe Ames. Aged 72 years
Nov 13, Mr Roswell Park. " 89 "
15, Mrs Sally Marion. " 64 "

## STATISTICS OF THE CHURCH.

1848. Feb'y 4, Miss Frances A.
　　　　Browning. Aged 22 years
　　April 17, Col David Baldwin. " 49 "
　　May 8, Sarah M. Meech. " 19 "
　　June 25, Mrs Hannah D.
　　　　Witter. " 85 "
　　Aug 1, Mrs Anna Prentice. " 79 "
　　Dec 31, Mr Ansel Brown. " 59 "
1849. Feb. 16, Mrs. Eunice Spicer. " 80 "
　　Mch. 16, Miss Sarah Standish. " 82 "
　　Aug. 25, Mr. Elijah Bailey. " 84 "
　　Oct. 5, Mrs. Dimis S. Collins. " 43 "
　　　　Also at Willimantic, in Sept. her child of a few months age.
1850. Feb. 20, Mr. Appleton Woodward. Aged 64 years.
　　Mch. 1, Mrs. Susan Brown. " 58 "
　　July 5, Mr. Samuel Brackett
　　　　(Suicide). " 56 "
　　" 8, Mrs. Hannah Fitch. " 86 "
1851. Feb. 4, Mr. Charles Y. Palmer. " 24 "
　　July 7, Mrs. Elizabeth Fanning. " $86\frac{1}{2}$ "
　　Aug. 30, Mr. Jephthah Geer. " 77 "
　　" 30, Edmund Clarence, son
　　　　of Capt. C. L. Meech. " $1\frac{1}{8}$ "
　　Oct. 3, Mrs. Mary A. Meech,
　　　　wife of Capt. C. L.
　　　　Meech. " 42 "
　　" 6, Mrs. Polly Frink. " 71 "
　　Nov. 24, Mr. Aaron Gates. " 56 "
　　Dec. 4, Mr. Nathan Benjamin. " 49 "
1852. Feb. 18, Amos A. Standish.* " 1 "
　　" 28, Horace A. Standish.* " 7 "
　　May 17, Mrs. Lydia A.
　　　　Wheeler, wife of Oliver P. Wheeler. " 38 "
　　Aug. 14, Mrs. Fanny B. Witter,
　　　　wife of Capt. Iris
　　　　Witter. " 56 "
　　Nov. 22, Mrs. Eunice Hewitt,
　　　　relict of Mr. Charles
　　　　Hewitt. " 63 "
　　Dec. 10, Eugene, son of Robert
　　　　Williams. " $1\frac{1}{4}$ "
　　" 13, Dea. George Loring. " 66 "
1853. Feb. 12, Mr. Asher Prentice
　　　　(N. Stonington). " 84 "
　　April 15, Mrs. Ruth Gore, wife
　　　　of Asa A. Gore Esq. " 73 "
　　May 31, Mrs. Elizabeth Prentice, relict of Mr.
　　　　Asher Prentice. " 84 "
　　June 19, Elisha Ayer Esq. " 96 "
　　" 23, Emma Isadora Morgan, daughter of Daniel B. Morgan. " 2 " 4 mo. 20 das

---

* Children of Horace Standish.

| | | | |
|---|---|---|---|
| 1853. | July 31, Joseph Aldinger (German). | Aged 52 | years |
| | Aug. 20, Mr. John Davis. | " 66 | " |
| | Oct. 29, Henry Palmer Esq. | " 77 | " |
| 1854. | Mch. 3, Mrs. Susan Prentice. | " 59 | " |
| | " 30, Miss Clarissa Smith. | " 65 | " |
| | April 10, Mr. Samuel Morgan. | " 77 | " |
| | July 15, Dr. Avery Downer. | " 91⅔ | " |
| | " 22, Mrs. Julia Ayer, wife of Col. Geo. Ayer. (Drowned). | " 37 | " |
| | " 28, Mrs. Nabby Crary, wife of Elisha Crary, Esq. | " 77 | " |
| | Aug. 10, Mrs. Olivet Geer, wife of Mr. Jephthah Geer. | " 79 | " |
| | " 28, Miss Charlotte W. Baldwin. | " 19 | " |
| | Sept. 1, Mr. Dwight B. Stetson. | " 20 | " |
| | Oct. 22, Mr. Joseph H. Doane at Chicago, Mich., & interred here Oct. 27. | " 58 | " |
| 1855. | Jan. 17, Mrs. Hannah Park, wife of Mr. Franklin Park. | " 62 | " |
| | Feb. 6, Mrs. Lydia Barstow, wife of Joshua Barstow Esq. | " 79 | " |
| | Mch. 27, Mr. Elisha A. Crary. | " 53 | " |
| | June 12, Mr. Elias Brewster. | " 67 | " |
| | Sept. 22, Irving H. Standish, son of Moses Standish. (Long Society). | " 9 | " 1⅓ mo. |
| | " 30, Ida Maria Prentice, daughter of Wm H. Prentice. | " —— | " 3 mo—9 da. |
| | Oct. 6, Mrs. Levena Palmer, wife of Denison Palmer. | " 74 | " |
| | " 10, Joshua Barstow Esq. | " 79 | " |
| | Nov. 30, Mr. Erastus Morgan. | " 73 | " |
| 1856. | Feb. 10, Sarah, daughter of Wm Morse. | " —— | " 2 mo. 14 da |
| | April 24, Mrs. Lucy Maria Loring at St Louis Mo. interred here April 30. | " 26 | " |
| | July 21, Mr. Henry Brown. | " 77 | " |
| | " 23, Charlie Baldwin, son of Thomas S & Susan E. Wheeler. | — — | — 3 days. |
| | Nov. 28, Mrs. Cynthia Meech, wife of Dea. Charles Meech. | " 74 | " |
| 1857. | April 26, Mrs. Bailey, wife of Elijah B. | " 80 | " |
| | Aug. 26, Mr. Edwin F. Holden. | " 33 | " |
| | Oct. 29, Mrs. Lucy Ann Rude, wife of Daniel B. Morgan. | " 36$\frac{5}{12}$ | " |
| | Nov. 11, Mrs. Amy Williams. | " 83 | " |

1857. Dec. 9, Charles Franklin, son of Chester S. and Lucy Prentice. — — — 12 days.
" 28, Warren Cook Esq. Aged 49 years
1858. Jan. 4, Mrs. Emeline Browning. " 49 "
" 12, Mrs. Eunice Latham. " 76 "
" 26, Mrs. Abby A. Browning, wife of Sam. P. Browning. " 26 "

## THE MINISTRY OF THE REV. ELIJAH W. TUCKER.

January, 1859 — March 12, 1865.

### Admissions by Profession.

1859. July 3, Mrs. Harriet M. Marion.
" Nov. 6, Mrs. Mary L. Bliven.
1862. Jan. Mrs. Lucy E. Bailey.
" May 4, Miss Lydia A. Palmer.
July 6, Miss Joanna S. Crary.
1863. Nov. 2, Mrs. Samuel P. Browning.
1865. April 30, Mrs. Cornelia Meech, Miss Alla T. Boswell, Miss Sarah I. Bailey, Miss Nancy L. Bates, Mr. Perry L. Bailey and Mr. Thomas Browning.

### Admissions by Letter.

1859. June 26, Rev. E. W. Tucker and his wife from the church at Goshen in Lebanon.
" July 10, Mrs. Eliza Meech from the Congregational church in Norwich.
1861. Jan. 6, Gertrude Meech from Congregational church in Montville.
1863. July Mrs. Maria Crary from Congregational church in Stonington.

### Dismissions.

Mrs. Sabrina Brown and Mrs. Mary A. Stetson to the Congregational Church in Norwich.
1859. Nov. 4, Mrs. J. A. Swan to the Congregational church in Norwich.
1860. March 25, Mrs. Elizabeth A. Rude to the church at Milltown.
1862. April Mrs. Abby Sears to the First Congregational Church in Rockville.
1863. July Rosina A. Downer to the Congregational Church in Norwich.
1864. Jan. Miss Louisa W. Meech to the church in Vineland, N. J.
Miss Gertrude Meech to the church in Vineland, N. J.
1865. March 19, Rev. E. W. Tucker and his wife, Hannah W. Tucker, to Cong. Church in Northfield, Ct.

### Baptisms of Infants.

1861. July 5, Sarah Perry, Daughter of William T. and Nancy C. Browning.

## STATISTICS OF THE CHURCH.

### THE MINISTRY OF THE REV. ASHER H. WILCOX.

June 29, 1865 — September 2, 1869.
and
January 30, 1870 — 1872.

NAMES OF THOSE IN FULL COMMUNION AT THE TIME OF HIS INSTALLATION

Thomas Browning Esq.,
Dea. William T. Browning,
Dea. William Loring,
William Morse,
Chester S. Prentice,
Samuel P. Browning,
Albert Ayer,
Henry Prentice,
John Myers Jr.,
Chas Palmer,
Alphonso Browning,
James Browning,
Thomas L. Browning,
Thomas Browning,
William H. Prentice,
Robert Y. Latham,
Andrew Frink,
Lucas Witter Jr.,
Frank Averill,
Butler Benjamin,
Courtland Swan,
Perry Bailey,
Perry Hoxie,
Henry B. Rude,
Ira Judd,
Mrs. Amy Browning,
Wid. Amy Prentice,
Mrs. Louisa Downing,
Miss Catherine Browning,
Miss Elizabeth Browning,
Mrs. Dea. Loring,
Mrs. Albert Ayer,
Mrs. Sam. P. Browning,
Mrs. Noyes F. Meech,
Mrs. Martha Witter,
Mrs. Henry Prentice,
Mrs. Dea. Wm Browning,
Mrs. Charles Palmer,
Mrs. Minerva Myers,
Mrs. Robert Y. Latham,
Mrs. Mary Averill,
Mrs. James Bailey,
Mrs. Park Woodmansee,
Mrs. Alphonso Browning,
Mrs. Edwin Morgan,
Mrs. Oliver Davis,
Mrs. Maria Crary,
Wid. Caroline Swan,
Miss Fanny Witter,
Miss Sally Yarington,
Wid. Lucy Rude,
Wid. Esther Kimball,
Wid. Eliza Crary,
Wid. Clarissa Standish,
Miss Mary G. Standish,
Mrs. George Marion,
Lydia Mott,
Mary Woodward,
Mrs. Mary Bliven,
Miss Mary E. Prentice,
Miss Margaret E. Crary,
Miss Mary Witter,
Miss Emma Browning,
Miss Lucy Browning,
Miss Lydia A. Palmer,
Miss Joanna Crary,
Miss Nancy Bates,
Miss Alla Boswell,
Miss Sarah Bailey,
Wid. Elizabeth Browning,
Wid. Betsey Combs,
Mrs. Lydia Judd,
Mrs. Abby Beckwith,
Miss Lucy Loring,
Wid. Elvira Harvey,
Miss Marianette T. Rogers,
Mrs. Sabra Park,
Mrs. Louisa Williams,
Miss Esther Cordelia Cook.

### ADMISSIONS BY BAPTISM.

1865. July —, George Ayer, Wid. Lydia A Holden, Mrs. Francis Baldwin, Miss Mary E. Baldwin, Mrs. Sarah Ecclestone and Miss Abby Ayer.

1867. March 3, James H. Myers, Samuel O. Prentice, Miss Eliza H. Witter, Mrs. Mary R. Robbins, Miss Mary Loring, Miss Lydia Emma Davis, Miss Emily C. Woodmansee, Miss Juliette Witter, Mrs. Hariet A. Hewit, Mrs.

## STATISTICS OF THE CHURCH. 193

|      | |
|---|---|
| 1867. | Susan Bates, Miss Abby Myers, Miss Abby Benjamin, Mrs. Grandison Phillips, Miss Ellen Phillips, Miss Annette Holden and Miss Laura Phillips. May —, George W. Marion, Morison Robbins, William Mitchell, Christopher Morgan and Mrs. Emily J. Cook. |
| " | Sept. —, Stillman Fish. |

### Admissions by Profession

1865. July —, Amos A. Browning, Charles Palmer Jr. and Mrs. Harriette T. Wilcox.
1867. March 3, Erasmus Avery, William Miller, Hollis Palmer, Levi Ecclestone, Mrs Margaret Miller, Miss Mary E. Avery, Miss Eunice Avery, Miss Martha Palmer, and Miss Mary Hickey.
1868. July 5, Edward D. Swan and Miss Mary A. Avery.
1869. M'c'h 7, Austin White.
  May 2, Mrs Lydia White.
1871. Mch 5, Jonah Witter, Herbert Brown, Cha$^s$ Robbins, Frank S. Robbins, William E. Crary, Frederic W. Marion, Clarence W. Prentice, Mrs Mary A. Brown, Miss Lovina I. Marion, Miss Harriet M. Marion and Miss Harriet A. Hewitt.
  May 7, Hezekiah Robbins, Mrs Lucy Hopkins, and Mrs Mary Swan.
  July 2, Miss Augusta Brown.

### Admissions by Letter

1867. Mch 3, Mrs Eunice Avery, from the Congregational Church in Ledyard.
  May —, Mrs Sarah A. Bailey, from the Cong. Ch'h in Ledyard.
" July 7, Mrs Mary E. Morgan, from Cong. Church in North Stonington.
1868. July 5, John D. Lyman, from Cong. Church in Griswold.
  "  "  Mrs Elizabeth Campbell, Fr near Paisley, Scotland.
1869. March 7, Dwight E. Wheeler, from Cong. Church in North Stonington.
1870. May 1, Mrs Jane E. Avery, from Cong. Church, North Stonington.
" July 3, James Barnes and his wife, Mary Barnes from 2$^{nd}$ Presbyterian Church in Mobile.

### Infants Baptized

1867. July —, Robert C. Miller, and Margaret E. Miller.
1869. July —, Mary A. Miller, William G. Browning and Elizabeth K. Wilcox.
1872. Jan 7, Emma I. Brown.

### Dismissions

1870. March 4, Thomas L. Browning to the 1$^{st}$ Cong. Church, Hudson City, New Jersey.
  April 24, Thomas Browning to the Broadway Church in Norwich.
1871. Feb 19, Dwight E. Wheeler to the Cong. Church in Dunlap, Iowa.
  "  "  Alphonso Browning and his wife, Sarah C. Browning to Cong. Church in Goshen.

## MARRIAGES

1865. Oct 29, George J. Richmond & Mary J. West.
1866. Sept 30, Nathan Harrington & Amelia S. Bromley.
" Nov 27, Henry B. Latham & Eunice Hewitt.

## DEATHS

1865. Aug. 16, Wid. Maria Prentice.
" Dec. 22, Geo. Henry Marion. Age 13 years.
1866. Jan. 14, Miss Nancy Bates. " 15 "
" Feb. 13, Joseph M. Combs. " 72 "
" June 13, James E. Benjamin.
" Oct. 4, Olive Palmer.
" Dec. 29, Emily Jane Witter.
1867. Dec. 22, Mrs. Amy P. Browning. " 75 "
1868. April 25, Henry Prentice. " 65 "
" May 28, Dea. William T. Browning. " 54 "
" Sept. 24, Mrs. Louisa T. Downing. " 74 "
" Nov. 18, Mrs. Betsey G. Fanning. " 87 "
1869. Elizabeth Boswell. " 25 "
1870. Jan. 20, Doct. Eliazer B. Downing. " 83 "
" Feb. 15, Wid. Amy Prentice.

## THE MINISTRY OF REV. ANDREW J. HETRICK.

November 3, 1872 — December 27, 1874.

and the intervening period to the ministry of Rev. George A. Bryan.

### ADMISSIONS BY PROFESSION.

1873. May 4, Noyes W. Avery, Arthur U. Avery, Frank S. Goodwin, William R. Browning, Miss Lucy A. Avery, Miss Hariet L. Avery, Miss Fanny A. Avery, Miss Mary P. Woodmansee and Miss Sarah L. Cook.
1874. Jan. 4, Wm I. D. Bagley, William A. Myers, John Stanton, George F. Talbot, Mrs. Ellen A. Stanton and Mrs. Sarah E. Myers.
1875. Mch. 7, Mrs. Elizabeth H. James.
1876. Jan. 2, Jennie B. Campbell.

### ADMISSIONS BY LETTER.

1874. Jan. 4, Miss Hannah B. Witter from Central Methodist church in Norwich.

### INFANTS BAPTIZED.

1875. July 4, Jennie B. Miller, who was born Aug. 13 '74.

### DISMISSIONS.

1873. April 20, Mrs. Sarah A. Bailey to the Cong. church in North Stonington.
1875. April 11, Mrs. Lucy L. Greenman to the Broadway church in Norwich.
" June 27, Mrs. Mary E. Wheeler (Baldwin) to the Cong. Church in Milltown.
" May 2, Charles L. Palmer to the Presbyterian Church at the Irwin Station, Penn.

# STATISTICS OF THE CHURCH. 195

1875. Dec. Gave William Mitchel a letter to East Main Street, M. E. Church, in Norwich.
1876. Feb. 20, Butler H. Benjamin & Abby S Benjamin to Cong. church in Long Society.

## THE MINISTRY OF REV. GEORGE A. BRYAN.
### May 7, 1876 — April 27, 1884.

#### Admissions by Profession.

1878. May 5, Charles E. Ellis, and Abby S. Meech.
1879. Jan. 5, Josie E. Avery.
1883. Nov. 2, Miss Mary F. Snell.
1884. March 2, Fred E. Ellis & Amos Avery.
" Nov. 2, James Woodworth.

#### Admissions by Letter.

1877. Nov. 4, Rev. George A. Bryan from Cong. Church in Yale College New Haven and Mrs. Elizabeth H. Bryan from Cong. Church in North Stonington.
1882. May 7, Mrs. Mary L. Avery from the 1st Cong. Church in Griswold.

#### Infants Baptized.

1878. July 7, Peter William Miller.
1882. July 2, Clara May, Frank Hollis, & Mary Emma, children of Hollis H. & Lydia E. Palmer.

#### Dismissions.

1876. June 30, Catharine Browning & Elizabeth Browning to the Cong. Church in Milltown.
1878. Oct. 16, Mary Townsend (Hickey) to Howard Avenue Ch. New Haven.
" Nov. 24, Jennie B. Frankla (Campbell) to the 2d Cong. Church in Norwich.
Feb. 20, Ellen M. Phillips to Broadway Ch. in Norwich.
" 20, Gave John B. Lyman a letter to Central Baptist Church in Norwich.
, Mrs. Harriet T. Wilcox, the Cong. Church in Plainfield.
1881. Feb. 20, Ira A. Judd to Cong. Church in Canterbury.
1882. May 7, Levi Ecclestone & Sarah J. Ecclestone, his wife, to the 2d Cong. Church in New London.
1883. May 6, Mrs. Laura A. Cook, to the Broadway Church in Norwich.
" " 20, Frank S. Robbins to the Methodist Church in Jewett City.
" June 24, Lovina Marion, to the Methodist Church in Norwich N. Y.
" Nov. 2, Mrs. Emma D. Goffe to the Cong. Church in East Hampton.
1884. May 4, Rev. George A. Bryan and his wife Mrs. Elizabeth H. Bryan to the Cong. Church in Wapping, Ct.
" June 22, Mrs. Juliette D. Ackley to the second Cong. Church in Norwich.
" " 29, Amos A. Browning to the Broadway Cong. Church in Norwich.

## STATISTICS OF THE CHURCH.

### DEATHS.
———, Mrs. Lucy D. Rude.
———, Miss Sarah L. Cook.

### THE MINISTRY OF REV. RICHARD H. GIDMAN
October 5, 1884 —

LIST OF MEMBERS JAN. 1, 1884.

Ackley Juliette D.,
Averill Francis H.,
Averill Mary P.,
Avery Erasmus,
Avery Eunice S.,
Avery Eunice H.,
Avery Noyes W.,
Avery Harriet L.,
Avery Josie E.,
Avery Mary L.,
Ayer Albert G.,
Ayer Abby,
Bailey Lucy E.,
Bailey Perry L.,
Barnes Mary R.,
Bates Susan,
Bliven Mary L.,
Boswell Alla,
Brown Mary A.,
Brown Herbert,
Browning Amos A.,
Browning Samuel P.,
Browning Desire W.,
Browning James,
Browning William R.,
Bagley William D.,
Bagley Frances,
Bryan George A.,
Bryan Elizabeth H.,
Combs Betsey,
Cook Cordelia E.,
Cook Emily J.,
Cook Sarah L.,
Crary Joanna S.,
Crary Maria S.,
Crary William E.,
Campbell Elizabeth,
Davis Emily J.,
Ellis Charles E.,
Frink Andrew S.,
Foote Fannie A.,
Fish Stillman A.,
Goodwin Frank S.,
Hewitt Harriet A.,
Hewitt Lucy A.,
Hopkins Lucy L.,
Hoxie Perry G.,
James Elizabeth,
Latham Robert Y.,
Latham Happy L.,
Loring William,
Loring Harriet K.,
Loring Mary F.,
Marion George W.,
Marion Sarah M.,
Marion Harriet,
Marion Fred W.,
Meech Eliza A.,
Meech Abby S.,
Miller Margaret,
Morgan Mary E.,
Morgan Wealthy A.,
Morgan Christopher,
Morse William,
Myers John,
Myers Minerva,
Myers Abby,
Myers James H.,
Myers William A.,
Palmer Hollis H.,
Palmer Lydia E.,
Palmer Charles,
Palmer Lucy A.,
Palmer Martha A.,
Prentice Chester S.,
Prentice S. Oscar,
Prentice Mary E.,
Prentice Clarence W.,
Prentice William H.,
Robbins Morrison,
Robbins Mary R.,
Robbins Charles,
Robbins Hezekiah,
Rude Lucy D.,
Rude Henry B.,
Standish Mary G.,
Swan Caroline,
Swan R. Courtland,
Swan, Edwin D.,
Swan Mary J.,
Stanton John,
Stanton Ellen M.,
Schattle Sarah I.,
Snell Mary F.,
Thompson Augusta,
Talbot George F.,
White Lydia A.,
Witter Jonah,
Witter Fanny,
Witter Eliza H.,
Witter Lucas H.,
Witter Mary A.,
Witter Hannah R.,
Woodmansee Eunice C.,
Woodmansee Mary P.,

## STATISTICS OF THE CHURCH. 197

### ADMISSIONS.

1885. Jan. 4, Rev. Richard H. Gidman by letter from the Broadway Tabernacle Church, New York and his wife, Mary H. Gidman by letter from the Cong. Church in Bethlehem, Conn.
" March 1, Oliver P. Avery, Anna Browning and Emma Geisthardt by profession.
" Sept. 4, Mrs. Sarah A. Bailey and Miss Freelove Bailey by letter from Cong. Church in North Stonington.
1886. Jan. 3, Gertrude Churchill by profession.
1888. Nov. 4, Mrs. Kate O'Brien by profession.
1890. Jan. 5, Mrs. Harriet Frances Cheesebro and Miss Cora Frances Cheesebro united with the church and were baptized.
" ————, Mr. George V. Shedd and Mrs. Abby Shedd by letter from the 2$^d$ Cong. church in Norwich.
" Sept. 7, Thusa L. Gidman by profession.
1891. Jan. 4, Chester E. Wood baptized and admitted.
1892. March 6, Mr. Charles K. Crary & Mrs. Ida J. Crary & Mrs. Lydia Crary baptized and admitted.
1894. Sept. —, Mrs. Jennie Emily Malloy, Etta Frances Malloy, Adelcia Frances Baldwin, Etta May Baldwin and Margaret Phillips Meech baptized & admitted.
" " Clara May Palmer by profession.
1898. July —, Misses Ida Swan and Sophia Cheesebro baptized and admitted.
" " —, Mary E. Palmer by profession.

### DISMISSIONS.

1886. March 5, Miss Joanna Crary to the second Cong. church in Norwich.
" June 20, Perry L. Bailey to the Broadway Cong. church in Norwich.
1887. April 29, John Stanton and his wife, Ellen M. Stanton to the Cong. church in Bozrahville.
" May 29, James H. Myers to the Central Baptist Church in Norwich.
1888. Aug. 31, Mrs. Mary A. Brown to the Baptist church in Preston.
" Dec. 5, Mrs. Desire W. Browning and Miss Anna Browning to second Cong. church in Norwich.
1889. April 19, Eunice H. Fish (Avery) to the Congregational church in Mystic.
" June 23, Mrs. Mary J. Swan to the Cong. church at Westerly.
1890. Dec. 21, Gertrude Griswold (Churchill) to the Cong. church, at North Woodbury, Conn.
1891. Feb. 1, Mrs. Sarah M. Marion to the 7$^{th}$ day Adventist church in Norwich.
1892. April 17, Mrs. Fannie A Foote (Avery) to the first Cong. church in Colchester.
" Oct. 23, Mrs. Eliza H. Davis (Witter) to the Broadway church at Norwich.
1893. Mch. 26, Mrs. Lucy A. Hewitt and Mr. Charles E. Ellis to the M. E. church at Norwichtown.
1895. ————, Mr. James Woodruth to the Second Adventist church of Westerly, R. I.

1896. Feb. 26, Mr. Charles S. Robbins to the Second Cong. church in Norwich.
" May 17, Mr. Noyes W. Avery to the first Cong. church of Stonington.
Miss Cora Cheesebro to Cong. church of Greenville.
1897. ———, Mrs. Harriet L. Loring to the Park Cong. church of Norwich.
1898. ———, Mrs. Mary L. Bliven to the Cong. Church in Daytona Florida.
" ———, Miss Margaret Phillips Meech to the church in ———

### DEATHS.

1885. ———, Hezekiah Robbins.
" ———, Samuel P. Browning.
1886. Jan. 25, Mrs. Eliza Meech age 69.
" Feb. 16, Mrs. Betsy Combs age 91 yrs. and 6 mo.
1888. ———, Mrs. Elizabeth Campbell.
" ———, Mary G. Standish.
1889. ———, Mr. Charles Palmer.
" ———, Mr. Robert Y. Latham.
1892. ———, Mrs. Caroline Allen. (Swan).
" ———, Mrs. Lucy E. Bailey.
" ———, Mr. William Morse.
1894. ———, Mrs. Abby Ayer.
" ———, Mrs. Harriet K. Loring.
1895. ———, Mr. Albert G. Ayer.
" ———, Mrs. Mary T. Averill.
" ———, Mr. Francis H. Averill.
" ———, Miss Abby S. Meech.
1896. ———, Mr. Jonah Witter.
" ———, Miss Fannie Witter.
" ———, Dea. William Loring.
1897. ———, Mr. Chester S. Prentice.
" ———, Mrs. Abbie P. Shedd.
" ———, Mrs. Maria S. Crary.

### LIST OF MEMBERS NOV. 16, 1898.

Avery Erasmus,
Avery Eunice S.,
Avery Mary L.,
Avery Amos,
Avery O. Perry,
Bailey Sarah A.,
Barnes Mary R.,
Bates Susan,
Boswell Alla,
Brown Herbert,
Browning James,
Bagley William D.,
Bagley Frances,
Baldwin Etta May,
Cheesebro Harriet F.,
Cheesebro Sophia,
Cook Cordelia E.,
Cook Emily J.,
Crary William E.,
Crary Lydia,
Crary Charles K.,
Crary Ida J.,
Cheesebro Emily Malloy,
Davis Emily J.,
Ecclestone Harriett A.,
Frink Andrew S.,
Fish Stillman N.,
Gidman Richard H.,
Gidman Mary H.,
Gidman Thusa,
Geisthardt Emma,
Goodwin Frank S.,
Hopkins Lucy L.,
Hoxie Perry G.,
Haskell Adelia Baldwin,
James Elizabeth,

## STATISTICS OF THE CHURCH.

Latham Happy L.,
Loring Mary F.,
Marion George W.,
Marion Harriet,
Marion Fred W.,
Miller Margaret,
Morgan Mary E.,
Morgan Wealthy A.,
Morgan Christopher,
Myers John,
Myers Abby,
Myers William A.,
O'Brien Kate,
Palmer Lucy A.,
Palmer Martha A.,
Palmer Hollis H.,
Palmer Lydia E.,
Palmer Clara M.,
Palmer Mary E.,
Prentice Mary E.,
Prentice S. Oscar,
Prentice Clarence W.,
Prentice William H.,
Robbins Morrison,
Robbins Mary R.,
Rude Henry B.,
Shedd George V.,
Swan Edwin D.,
Swan R. Courtland,
Swan Ida,
Shattel Sarah Bailey,
Snell Mary T.,
Talbot George T.,
Thompson Augusta,
Wheeler Josie E.,
Witter Lucas H.,
Witter Mary A.,
Witter Hannah B.,
Woodmansee Eunice C.,
Woodmansee Mary P.

# APPENDIX

### THE ORIGINAL CONFESSION OF FAITH & COVENANT.

"We believe that there is one only God, being from himself, & for himself, of whom, & for whom, are all things, who is infinite, eternal, & unchangable in power, wisdom, goodness, justice, holiness & truth. There are three sacred persons of the God-head, God the father, God the son, & God the holy-ghost, equally God, & yet but one God. God hath from all eternity, foreordained what shall come to pass, & did not only foresee, but foredetermine, the eternal state of men & angels; together with God's general providence, which is expressed about all things, & his special government over the rational creature. — God made the Angels, & Men in holiness, but some of the angels abode not in the truth, which are called devils. — God gave to man when he made him, a rule of obedience for life, & threatened death in case of disobedience which rule of obedience, our first Parents transgressed, by eating the forbidden fruit, & we in them, & so death passed upon all men. — The sin of our first parents became the sin of all mankind by imputation; & such as are adult, do imitate them, by an approbation of sin, naturally, & choosing sin. — God the father, having eternally elected some of mankind unto life, did in the fulness of time, send his son to redeem them & God the father, & God the son, sent, & do send the spirit to sanctify them.

We believe, that Jesus Christ, taking our nature upon him, as mediator between God & Man, hath made full satisfaction to God, for the sins of all the elect, & purchased life for them, by the merit of his active & passive righteousness, & having received all power from the father, doth in execution of his prophetical, priestly & kingly office reveal unto, & work in all his elect, whatsoever is necessary for salvation, by his holy spirit.

In the new Covenant, God hath promised life, to all that believe in his name, through Christ Jesus; and the mediate object of justifying faith, is Christ, in his person & office as he is revealed in the gospel, & by union with Christ, by faith, believers are made partakers of his benefits, so that through free grace, they are justified adopted & sanctified, & shall enjoy eternal life. — — We believe the scriptures of the old testament, & new, to be the word of God; by the dispencing of which, the spirit convincing of sin & misery, & giving knowledge of Christ, doth beget faith, repentance & new obedience in the elect. — — We believe that the moral law, in the hands of Christ, is a rule of obedience to believers; & that the sum of this law, is to love God with all our hearts, & our neighbor as ourselves. — — We believe that there are two seals of the Covenant of grace, baptism, & the Lords supper; baptism is a sign of our entrance into grace, & the Lords supper, is a sign of our growth in grace. — — We believe the communion of Saints, the resurrection of the body, & life everlasting, Amen."

" We believe, Lord help our unbelief."

"God having graciously received us into the Covenant of his grace, which he hath sealed to us in baptism; We acknowledge ourselves, indispensably bound, to hold fast the doctrine of faith & good manners, contained in the scriptures of truth, & to attend all those duties, therein prescribed, for the increase of our faith, growth in holiness, & maintaining a good conscience. — — And knowing, that confession of the name of Christ, is not to be separated from faith in the heart, Rom. 10. 9. and he that is united to Christ, & hath communion with him, ought to maintain communion regularly, with all his members; we whose hearts God hath moved in this place, to join together in the worship of God, & partake of the Lords table, & therein desire to have the prayers, & approbation of the churches of Christ, who may take knowledge of us: "

" We for the satisfaction of all men declare as followeth."

"That we unfeignedly resign ourselves, & our seed unto the Lord, receiving Jesus Christ, the son of the living God, very God & very man, & the only mediator, between God & man, as our Lord & Saviour, relying upon the free grace of God, for salvation, & blessedness, & heartily submitting ourselves, to be ruled by his word & spirit.— And as he is the author of order, unity & peace, we solemnly promise, that by the assistance of God's grace, we will labour, mutually to watch over one the other, which Christ hath enjoined, according to our respective place, in this chh. to submit to the discipline of Christ, which we desire may take place amongst us, & the worship of God to be upheld in the power & spirituality thereof; as also to oppose error, & teach all under our care, as far as in us lies, to know & fear the Lord."

NOTE.— The above is copied from the record of the installation of the Rev. Mr. Rosseter, March 14, 1744. The record is: "Mr. Rosseter & the church mutually made profession of their faith according to the articles which the church had adopted & improved from its first foundation & renewed covenant with each other before the Council." &c.

# INDEX

AARON, 185
ABELL, 172
ACKLEY, 195-196
ADAMS, 81 83 131-132 135
  139 143 145-149 167
AERY, 153
AIRES, 133
ALDEN, 172
ALDINGER, 190
ALLEN, 4 94 112 182 198
ALLYN, 15 80 82
AMES, 44 131 137-142 154
  156-157 159-160 163
  168-170 172 174 176-
  177 180 183-184 188
AMOS, 152-153 160 164
  168
ANDERSON, 166
ANDREWS, 112 187-188
ANDROS, 157
ANDROSS, 143 143-144
  146
ANDRUSS, 167
ANSLAY, 156
ARNOLD, 4 111
ATWELL, 85
AUGUSTUS, Roman
  Emperor 9
AVERIL, 181

AVERILL, 22-23 130 132
  138-139 141 143-144
  181 187 192 196 198
AVERY, 1 4 15 25 30 34-35
  50 53-55 57 63 66 75 80
  84 86 103 112 133-134
  149-152 154-155 157-
  160 163 166-168 173
  175-176 178-180 182-
  186 188 193-198
AYER, 85 152-153 169 180-
  181 183 185 187-190
  192 196 198
AYERS, 175
AYRES, 156 172
AYRS, 133
BABCOCK, 158 173 181
BAGGS, 184
BAGLEY, 1 5 194 196 198
BAGS, 183
BAILEY, 168 178-180 184
  186 189-194 196-198
BAILY, 167
BALDWIN, 145 157 169
  172-174 177 179 181
  184 186 189-190 192
  194 197-198
BARKER, 71 170
BARNES, 4 156 162 168

BARNES (Cont.)
183 185 193 196 198
BARNS, 155 166 182
BARSTOW, 35 39 157 165
169 173-174 176 178
180 186 190
BATES, 191-194 196 198
BECKLEY, 182
BECKWITH, 192
BEEBE, 182
BEEMAN, 142 144-145 145 151
BEJAMENS, 182
BELCHER, 34 Capt 33
BELLAMY, 21
BELLOWS, 134 152-153 166
BEMIS, 184
BENJAMIN, 130 137-143
156-157 166-167 170
172-173 176 180 187-189 192-195
BENJAMINS, 173 178 184
BENNET, 166
BENNETT, 136 184
BENNIT, 142 144 146-148 157
BENTS, 167
BESSEX, 130
BILLINGS, 34 44-45 132
136 138-142 144 146
158 167-168
BILLINS, 132
BINGHAM, 173
BISHOP, 72 85 131 140-143 173
BLAKE, 79 156
BLASON, 157
BLINMAN, 79
BLISS, 155 157
BLIVEN, 191-192 196 198
BLODGET, 154 161 164
BLOT, 82
BOARDMAN, 157 172 177 179
BOGLE, 15
BOOTH, 71
BOSWELL, 191-192 194 196 198
BOWDISH, 154 157 162-163
BRACKETS, 172
BRACKETT, 189
BRAMAN, 166-167
BRANCH, 17 30 53 102 105
130-133 137-139 147-159 163-164 176
BREWESTER, 105
BREWSTER, 14 20-21 25
30 57 85-86 102-103
129 131-132 132-134
136-138 140-144 146-163 167-169 172-173
175 180-181 183 190
BRISTOL, 166
BROMLEY, 182 194
BROWN, 22 29 44 132 138
140 155 157-158 166-169 172-173 180 183-185 187-191 193 196-198
BROWNING, 1 4 49 58 79
112 170-171 175-182
184 186-189 191-198
BRUMLEY, 166-168 181
BRUMLY, 173
BRYAN, 4 41 63 74 120 122 194-196
BUCKINGHAM, 4 70 75
BUDDINGTON, 172 181
BUEL, 174
BULL, 181

BUNDEY, 156-157
BUNDY, 155-156 162
BURDICK, 1
BURTON, 23 131 137 142 144
BUSHNEL, 185
BUSSWELL, 82
BUSWELL, 130 138 140
BUTLER, 156 167
BUTTOFF, 185
BUTTON, 167-169 171 173 175 183
CADY, 144
CALHOUN, 181
CALKINS, 155
CAMPBELL, 193-196 198
CANFIELD, 167
CAPRON, 32 169-170 174-175
CARY, 133 148 156 181
CAULKINS, 18 24 31 81 91
CAZWELL, 185
CHAMBERLAIN, 143
CHAMPLAIN, 180
CHAMPLIN, 80
CHAPMAN, 167 172
CHEESEBRO, 197-198
CHESEBRO, 1
CHITTENDEN, 71 179
CHOAT, 40 178
CHOATE, 185
CHURCHILL, 197
CLARK, 53 83 135-136 138-142 145-151 155 157-158 166-168 170 172 176 181
CLEFT, 23
CLEVELAND, 35 69 137-138 184
COGSDELL, 141
COGSWELL, 142-144

COIL, 34
COLLINS, 40 63-64 71-72 176-179 182 186 189
COMBS, 177 179 184-186 192 194 196 198
CONGDON, 167
COOK, 54 59 132 143-144 157 159 166-167 170-176 178 180-182 185 187-188 191-196 198
COOMBS, 166
CORBIN, 172
CORNING, 172-174 181-182
COSSUMP, 157
COY, 130
COZZENS, 181
CRAIG, 174
CRAIRY, 177-180 182-183
CRANDAL, 133
CRAPO, 181
CRARY, 1-2 35 70 101 150 154 156-158 167-169 173 182 186-188 190-193 196-198
CRARYS, 169
CROCKER, 181 183
CULVER, 175
CUMMINGHAM, 174
CUNNINGHAM, 157
DABOLL, 157
DAGGET, 68
DANE, 135 141-142 145-146
DANIELS, 166
DARBY, 166
DAVENPORT, 51
DAVI----, 138
DAVIS, 138 155 173 182-183 185 187-188 190 192 196-198

DAVISON, 15 22 102 130 137-140 142 155
DEMING, 167
DEMMINGS, 172
DENISON, 56 103 181 183
DENNIS, 182
DENNISON, 132 147-148 155-159 161-164
DEWEY, 185
DOANE, 172 190
DORRANCE, 167 182
DOUGLASS, 19 129 137-138 157
DOWNER, 30 34 36 68 156 164-165 169 176 180 183 186 190-191
DOWNES, 170
DOWNING, 39 70 75 170-172 176-177 179 182 186 192 194
DUNNING, 31
DUNWELL, 168
ECCLESTONE, 192-193 195 198
EDDY, 136 147-150 156
EDWARDS, 27 50
EELLS, 167
ELDREDGE, 4 96
ELLICE, 139
ELLIOT, 143-144
ELLIOTT, 131
ELLIS, 145 157 174 195-197
EMERSON, 98
EMES, 157
EVELLE, 15
FAGINS, 167
FANNING, 39 167 169-173 175-176 183-184 186 189 194
FARNHAM, 157

FARNUM, 82
FELLOWS, 138
FFOBES, 44
FISH, 193 196-198
FISHER, 132 153 159
FITCH, 15 18 22 57 71 82 131-132 136-137 142-146 157 159 166-167 173 175 183 189
FLINT, 15
FOBES, 19 30 45 129 131 134 136 142-150 152-165 167
FOOTE, 196-197
FORBES, 79 83-85 102
FORD, 131 142-144 146 182
FORSEITH, 175
FORSIDES, 165
FORSYTH, 169 176
FORTHINGHAM, 56
FOWLER, 70 166 182
FOX, 134 146 148
FRANKLA, 195
FREEMAN, 30 131-134 140-156 158-161 164 166 168
FRINK, 80 136 146 148-150 152 156 158-159 168 174 176 178-182 184-186 189 192 196 198
FULLER, 28-29 36 56 63-64 68-69 133 164 182
GAGER, 84
GALLUP, 103 181-182
GARDNER, 173
GATES, 53 82 85 131-132 134 136-137 139-143 143-145 147-148 151-153 155-156 158 161 172-173 183-185 189

GAVITT, 181
GEARS, 44
GEER, 22 68 80 82 156-157 170-171 176-181 181 184-185 189-190
GEERS, 45 131 135 137-139 141-143 155
GEISTHARDT, 1 197-198
GEORGE, 167 The 3d King 33
GERE, 172 174
GIBS, 149
GIDDINGS, 173-174
GIDDINS, 146 172
GIDMAN, 1-4 13 34 63 74 196-198
GILE, 130 135 137 140-142
GILES, 167
GOFFE, 195
GOODWIN, 194 196 198
GORDON, 132
GORE, 144-145 167 169-171 174 176 189
GORTON, 172
GOSMER, 157
GOSS, 86
GRANT, 175 177
GRAY, 167
GREEN, 166
GREENMAN, 182 194
GREENSLIT, 136 141
GRIFFIN, 181
GRINALDS, 183
GRINALS, 177 179
GRISWOLD, 69 82 197
GUILE, 45 184
GULLIVER, 182
GUYANT, 172
HAINES, 15 135 137
HAKES, 180 182 184
HALE, 15

HALKIN, 138
HALKINS, 139 141 143
HALL, 1 166 173
HALSEY, 32 54 58 172 174 180
HAMLIN, 131
HAMLINTON, 155
HANKS, 138-140
HARKNESS, 180
HARRINGTON, 194
HARRIS, 132 143 145 169
HARRISON, 185
HARVEY, 183 187 192
HASKEL, 167
HASKELL, 23 198
HAZEN, 173
HENDLEY, 166
HERBERT, 85
HERRICK, 68 130-131 135 137-142 144 156-157 172 174-175
HERSKELL, 180-182
HERVEY, 172
HETRICK, 4 41 63 74 119 194
HEWETT, 181-182
HEWIT, 172 192
HEWITT, 1 3-4 9 66 75 186 188-189 193-194 196-197
HIBBARD, 143
HICKEY, 193 195
HIDE, 170
HILL, 22 85 131 134 144-147 150-153 155 158
HILLIARD, 170-173 175-176 185
HILLYAR, 157
HILLYARD, 169
HINCKLEY, 166
HINKLEY, 173 182

HODGE, 140-143 145
HODGES, 134 150-153
HOLDEN, 173 180-182 190 192-193
HOLMES, 177-179 181
HOMES, 178
HOPKINS, 1 193 196 198
HOUGH, 172
HOXIE, 187-188 192 196 198
HULL, 181
HUNT, 40 63-64 72-73 186
HUNTINGTON, 19 65 80 129 132 145 180-182 187
HUTCHINSON, 137 158 172
HYDE, 38-40 63-64 70-71 169-171 173 176
INGREHAM, 177 179 182-183 185
JACKSON, 159
JAMES, 154 162-164 194 196 198
JEFFERS, 156
JENCKS, 86
JENNINGS, 158
JEWETT, 182
JOHNSON, 23 130 137 155-156 158 161 172
JOHNSTON, 173
JONES, 50 133-134 149-153 157 166 168 184
JOSEPH, 45
JUDD, 187-188 192 195
JUEL, 82
KANFIELD, 181
KEENE, 153-154
KEENEY, 135
KENEDY, 156 182
KIGHT, 158
KILLAM, 156 180
KILLUM, 131-133 143-149 153 173
KIMBAL, 133-134 148 155 157-158 161 187
KIMBALL, 30 37 133 148-153 167 169-176 180-184 187-188 192
KINGSLEY, 41-42
KINNE, 131 138-145 156-158 160-162 167
KINNEY, 34 180 185
KNITE, 22 130 135
KYNION, 172
LAMB, 132 137 145 149 151 154-155 158 167
LAMBERT, 173-174
LAMBS, 161
LAMPHERE, 168
LANE, 156
LARI, 155
LARIBEE, 131 131 137-138 140 146 157-158
LARRABEE, 80
LARRIBBEE, 130
LARRIBE, 148
LARRIBEE, 102 105 149
LATHAM, 1 173-175 181 187-188 191-192 194 196 198-199
LATHROP, 157 167
LAWRENCE, 167
LEET, 156 166
LEFFINGWELL, 80 84
LENARDSON, 45
LEONARD, 79 83 112 155-156 158 161 168-169 181
LEONARDSON, 19 83 102 129 131 135 138-141 143
LESTER, 34 157

LEWIS, 166
LINCOLN, 95
LINSLEY, 165
LITTLE, 134 150-153 158
LONG, 188
LONGFELLOW, 20
LONGWOOD, 173
LORD, 67 136 155
LORING, 30 176-179 181-182 184 186-190 192 196 198-199
LOVETT, 82
LYMAN, 193 195
MACFARLIN, 154 157 164
MACFARLING, 154
MACKQUITHY, 141
MACLAIN, 158
MACNIELL, 146
MADISON, 182
MAIN, 70 157 172
MAINE, 167
MAINOR, 133
MALLOY, 197
MALTBY, 165
MARIAN, 172
MARION, 188 191-197 199
MASON, 15 73 80
MATHIEU, 5
MAY, 69
MCCOOMBS, 172
MCDOWELL, 132
MEACHAM, 68
MECH, 183
MEECH, 32 35 39 132-134 137 139 146-153 155-159 165-169 171-173 175-176 178-189 191-192 195-198
MILE, 157
MILLER, 193-196 199
MINER, 172 178-179 181
MINOR, 16 132
MITCHEL, 195
MITCHELL, 84 193
MIX, 137 143 163 166 176 178 186
MOOR, 134
MOORE, 174
MORGAN, 1 17 19 30 34-35 37 79-80 85-86 102 104 129 131 133-135 138-144 148-158 160-164 166-170 172 174-190 192-193 196 199
MORROW, 4
MORSE, 1-2 53 57 156-157 187-188 190 192 196 198
MORTIMORE, 183
MOTT, 29 32 34-36 42 156 167 169-170 173-177 179 186 192
MOTTS, 168
MYERS, 187 192-194 196-197 199
NEWTON, 83 169 172 176 185
NORTHROP, 4 91 111
NORTHRUP, 157
NOTT, 21 39 69 71
NOYES, 19 65-66 129
O'BRIEN, 197 199
OLDEN, 167
OSOOD, 182
OSYER, 166
PACKER, 167
PAINE, 53 56
PALMER, 1-2 4 19 37 53 57 68 129-130 146-147 158 166 172-173 178 180-183 185-199
PARISH, 130 135 138-144

210

PARISH (Cont.)
146-147 173
PARK, 19 50 52-54 56-57
66 79-80 83-85 102 104
129-139 141-161 167-
168 171 174-175 178
180 185-186 188 190
192
PARKE, 17 29-30 44
PARKES, 183
PARKS, 173 177 179 182
PARMENTER, 177
PARTRIDGE, 131 134 142-
144 151 156 174
PAYNE, 167
PECK, 19 113 129
PELLET, 181
PENDLETON, 166 185
PENFIELD, 66
PERKINS, 85 156 158 183
PETERS, 32 157 167 172
175
PETTIS, 53
PHILIPS, 173
PHILLIPS, 160 172-173
176 178-181 184-188
193 195
PIERCE, 130 134 137-138
156
PITCHER, 166
PLIMTON, 80
PLUMER, 154
PLUMMER, 138 140-141
151-153 156-160
POLLARD, 175
POLLY, 132 136 144
POPPLE, 172
PORTER, 156 164
POTTER, 157
POWEL, 165
POWERS, 161

PRENTICE, 1 4 72 101 130
135 137-146 148 156-
157 168-179 182-183
185-194 196 198-199
PRIDDE, 170-171 176
PRIDE, 174 184
PUNDERSON, 166
PUTNAM, 156-157
QUINCE, 166
QUOMINE, 158
RANDAL, 157
RANDALL, 144
RATH, 166
RAWSON, 157
RAY, 158
READE, 4 112 114
REED, 83 143 187-188
RENALDS, 131 148-149
RENNOLDS, 174
RENOLDS, 130-131 142
144 148 153 155-156
184-185
REYNOLDS, 19
RICHARDS, 19 30 44 79 81
83 102 112 129-131
133-135 140-147 151-
153 156 158
RICHARDSON, 132 147
RICHMOND, 181 185 194
RIX, 130 141-142 155-156
158 166 170-171 176
ROATH, 167
ROBBINS, 66 157 166 172
174 180 192-193 195-
196 198-199
ROBES, 132
ROBINSON, 73 132 136
143 147 156 173
ROCKWELL, 156-157 167
ROGERS, 170 176 182 186-
188 192

ROGGERS, 179 184
ROOD, 140 169 171 174-175 178-179 183-185
ROSE, 84 131 141 143-148 167-168
ROSETER, 159
ROSSETER, 27-31 37 156 158-160 164 167 201
ROSSITER, 63-64 66-68 152-153
ROUSE, 157 167 177 179
RUDD, 87
RUDE, 130 155-158 160 166 168 173 182 186-188 190-192 196 199
RUID, 134 137-138 142 144-145 154
SAFFORD, 29 35 53 82 133 137-139 154-157 161-163 165-166 168 174 178-180 183
SALTONSTALL, 19 65 129
SANDERS, 166
SAUNDERS, 166 185
SCHATTLE, 196
SEARL, 154
SEARLE, 162 166
SEARS, 191
SEERS, 167
SHAPLAY, 182
SHARP, 155 183
SHATTEL, 199
SHEDD, 1 38 197-199
SHEPPARD, 165
SHERMAN, 66
SHIPMAN, 112 172
SISSON, 156
SLOCUM, 181
SMITH, 39 68 130 132-133 136 138 145-155 157-162 164-166 168-172

SMITH (Cont.) 174 176 178-180 182-183 186 190
SNELL, 195-196 199
SPALDIN, 130
SPALDING, 137 156
SPICER, 155 166 168-170 172-174 176 178-181 185-187 189
STALLIN, 136 142-143
STALSON, 182
STANDISH, 20-21 57 70 83 102 104 129-133 138-146 152 172-173 175 178-181 183 186-187 189-190 192 196 198
STANTON, 15 17 66 103 133 135-142 144 147 149-152 154 157-158 166-168 180 194 196-197
STAPLES, 134
STARK, 68
STARKWEATHER, 37 131-132 134-135 139-150 152-164 166 170-173 175 180 183-185
STARKWER, 155
STAUNTON, 23
STEPHENS, 156
STERRIE, 135
STERRY, 34 44-45 139-141 154 156-157 160-164 166-168 173
STETSON, 180 187 190-191
STEVENS, 56 137
STEWART, 167
STODDARD, 167
STOREY, 157
STORRS, 68

STORY, 146-147 155-156 174
STRONG, 72
STUART, 167
SWAN, 132 136 145 148 175 177-181 183 185-188 191-193 196-199
SWANEY, 166
SWEET, 157
TALBOT, 194 196 199
TALCOTT, 180 182
TALLMAGE, 166
TAYLOR, 178
TEFFT, 86
THOMAS, 157 167 185
THOMPSON, 79 83 196 199
THOMSON, 169
THURSTON, 181
TOBES, 17
TODD, 165
TOWNSEND, 69 195
TRACY, 4 16-17 19-20 30 39 79-82 86 102 104 129-134 136 138-177 181 183-185
TRATE, 16
TREAT, 16-18 20-21 24-27 51 63-67 74-75 84 102 105 122 129 134 137-142 151-153 172 184
TROWBRIDGE, 35
TRUMBULL, 52 63 69
TUCKER, 23 40 63-64 73 111 191
TURNER, 180
TUTTLE, 177 179
TYLER, 15 17 19 27 32 34-35 37-39 57 63-64 69-70 75 79 81-82 102 104 129-135 138 142-144 146-147 153 155

TYLER (Cont.) 157-158 164-166 168-169 172-174
UNCAS, 14
UTLEY, 155 173 178 181
VINCENT, 167
WADE, 173
WALBRIDGE, 130 137-138 140
WARREN, 34 137
WASHINGTON, 35-36
WATSON, 175
WEAKLY, 156
WEBSTER, 54 73 101
WEDGE, 130 133 138-147 149
WEEKS, 173 180
WELCH, 19 79 86-87 102 129 132 137-139
WELDS, 15
WELLS, 154 161 167
WENTWORTH, 155
WEST, 102 130 137 194
WHALEY, 181
WHEELER, 5 80 86 172 180 183 189-190 193-194 199
WHIPPLE, 53 173
WHITE, 134 163 193 196
WHITEFIELD, 49
WHITFIELD, 27 43-44
WHITNEY, 102 130 130 134 151 156-158
WIBOURN, 156
WICKES, 166
WIGHT, 154 184
WILBUR, 157-158 163
WILCOX, 40 63 74 120 176 182 184 186 192-193 195
WILKESON, 131 142

WILKINSON, 157 167
WILKISON, 153
WILLIAM, 157
WILLIAMS, 102 129-131
  137-139 142 145-146
  154-155 157 160-161
  163 172-173 178 180
  182 185-186 189-190
  192
WILLOUGHBY, 56
WILSON, 1
WINTHROP, 80
WINTWORTH, 146
WITHERELL, 19 129
WITTER, 19 30 34-35 53 68
  79 85-86 102 129 132-
  134 137-140 146-166
  168-169 171-176 178-
  181 183 186-189 192-
  194 196-199
WOOD, 83 167 197
WOODARD, 131 177 182-
  183
WOODBRIDGE, 15
WOODBURN, 132 145 147
  153
WOODMANCY, 180
WOODMANSEE, 1 73 192
  194 196 199
WOODRUTH, 197
WOODWARD, 50 81 133
  136 138-139 141-144
  147-151 153 155-156
  167 181-182 186 189
  192
WOODWORTH, 166 195
WORDSWORTH, 10
WRIGHT, 181
YARINGTON, 179 192
YARRINGTON, 146 151 155
  167 170-172 176 179-
  181 186
YARRINTON, 132 139 148-
  150 153 157 159
YERRINTON, 140
YORK, 158 167
YOUNG, 173

# Program

## Centennial Exercises

# Preston Baptist Church

Preston City, Conn.

---

**1815-1915**

# Centennial Hymn.

### Tune "WARE."

Now to the Lord a grateful song,
To Him eternal thanks belong;
A Hundred years, His love and power
   Have conquests made, in this dear bower.

Our fathers worshipped in this place,
And God sustained them by His grace;
Their faces we behold no more,
   They walk upon the golden shore.

We thank Thee for the men of God,
Who have proclaimed the Living Word,
Who prayed, and toiled through all the years,
   In faith, and love, and hope, and tears.

They did not sow the seed in vain,
Our eyes have seen the ripening grain;
The garnered sheaves do now appear
   In this, our anniversary year.

Eternal Father, hear our cry,
Bend over us a pitying eye,
And lead us through the years to come,
   Till we shall reach our heavenly home.

*—Rev. L. W. Frink.*

# Preston City Baptist Church

## History in Brief

1698. Nov. 12. Congregational Church of Preston organized.
1700–1740. Dark cloud of formalism over New England established churches.
1740. Great awakening under Whitfield, Edwards, etc.
1747. Separatists' Church of Preston organized.
1798. Elder Wm. Northrop from R. I. baptized Widow Anna Yerrington in Lake Amos.
1799. Eight more baptized.
1809. Mrs. James Treat of this village joined Second Groton Church, which opened the way for Pastor Burrows to preach here.
1810. Serious impressions made on the community.
1811. Elder John Sterry preached in March and baptized Miss Poly Tyler and Miss Lucy Rockwell. Deep conviction. Mr. James Treat opened his house for permanent meetings a month later. He and M. T. Richards baptized; 42 baptized during revival.
1812. Meeting house raised and built.
1814. Made branch church of Groton Second, with 78 members.
1815. April 1st. Mr. Gustavus F. Davis began ministry to church. Oct. 10th. Council called to recognize as independent Baptist Church.
1816. Mr. Davis ordained first pastor. Served 3 years. Received 25.
1820. Elder Levi Walker became pastor. Stonington Union Association met here.
1821. Brother Levi Meech licensed to preach. Assisted pastor.
1822. An interesting work of grace. Levi Meech ordained.

1824. Closed their pastorate. Twenty-five members received.
1819-28. Church passed through trial.
1826-28. Irregular preaching; discouragements.
1828. Elder Luther Goddard became minister for 3 years. Added 37. May 18th. S. S. organized. Had great influence on community.
1830. Association met with church.
1831. April 8th. First Deacons appointed. Elder Alfred Gates accepted call of church.
1832. Meeting house repaired. Bell supplied by James Treat and Joseph Doane.
1833. Mr. Bela Hicks ordained as missionary to Poquetanoc.
1834. Elder N. E. Shailer and Elder Ira Steward assisted in large revival.
1835. Elder Gates resigned; 75 received during ministry. Elder Shailer called.
1837. Twenty three baptized.
1840. Association met here.
1842. Elder Jn. Greene, a Seventh Day Baptist, held revival services; 43 baptized. October. Elder Amos Watrous began a revival; 15 more baptized. Close of Elder Shailer's pastorate of 8 years; 118 received to church.
1843. Elder H. R. Knapp began labors; remained 2 years; 14 baptized.
1845. Elder Nicholas V. Steadman took up the work.
1846. Elder Steadman ordained. A spiritual revival led to his baptizing 38.
1847. Elder Cyrus Miner took up duties of pastor. Owing to poor health resigned in 1851.
1851. Elder Nicholas H. Mattison accepted call to the church.
1852. Mr. James Treat, a leading benefactor of the church, died, leaving $1000 as a permanent ministerial fund in the church.
1856. A deep work of grace began in Palmer School House; 38 baptized.

1859. Brother Mattison closed labors, 66 having been received in church. July. Elder Miles G. Smith began his ministry with the church. Revival at Haskell School House; many saved; 9 baptized.

1860. July 22. Meeting house reopened after extensive renovation.

1864. By a gift of $1500 Dr. Tyler made it possible for church to secure a splendid parsonage.

1865. A revival of marked interest from which 16 baptized. Oct. 10. Celebration of jubilee and reviewing the 50 years these interesting facts observed. Large proportion of all families of constituent members converted. Church remained essentially same in doctrine. No schisms nor parties; always a praying and revival church. Well attended covenant meetings. Seven licensed to preach. Four pastors ordained. To date had 11 pastors.

1866. Bro. Wm. H. Kliny licensed to preach. Mr. Wm. H. Doane presented S. S. with a fine cabinet organ and 50 singing books. A strip of land north of the church presented by Stephen Tyler, Warren A. Andrews, Joseph A. Doane to the church.

1867. Church sheds erected and grounds improved

1868. Received $140 from Deacon Cyrus Gates for ministerial fund.

1869. July 11. Pastor Smith's resignation on account of ill health read. Not accepted, but voted 3 months absolute rest with salary.

1870. April 16. Brother Smith's 2nd resignation accepted, and a resolution of gratitude and esteem voted by the church for his life and work among them. July 24. Rev. E. B. Joy commenced labors as pastor. Nov. 25. Vestry of church dedicated to Almighty God.

1873. Brother Lemuel Frink licensed to preach the Gospel.

1874. January. Rev. Joy's resignation accepted, and he closed work in May. Supplies till November. Rev. E. S. Hill accepted pastoral charge.
1875. Nov. 18. Funeral services of Rev. Miles G. Smith.
1876. Union week of prayer with Congregational Church. Good spirit. Church repaired. One sermon Sundays during winter till Easter.
1877. Dec. 23. Voted to have two sermons Sundays for winter.
1879. Association met with church. No conversions recorded. No evening service in winter. Three weeks' special meetings.
1881. Parsonage repaired.
1882. Rev. Hill closed pastorate March. In April a letter sent to Rev. F. H. Cooper of Hamilton Theological School to supply with view to settlement. Call extended and accepted. June. Voted to read Church Covenant at each Covenant meeting.
1883. Voted to exchange Psalmist for the Baptist Hymnal, edited by Mr. W. H. Doane and Rev. E. H. Johnson, D. D. Bro. Doane donated 25 copies. Nov. 12 and 13. Church entertained Ministers' Conference, and revival commenced, continuing 5 weeks; 30 conversions.
1885. Association church letter records the church in mourning and sadness through the death of many members, and an accident resulting in broken arm of Pastor Cooper. Church well united.
Oct. Revision of articles of faith.
Resignation of Brother Cooper accepted.
1886. Mr. Chas. Brown made gift of $500 to church to supply ministry in memory of his father. March. Congregational Meeting House burned. Resolution of sympathy voted, and an offer of the free use of the audience room by this church for afternoon service

was accepted. A hearty call extended to Bro. Joseph McKean, student at Newton, to supply till graduation in June, then become regular pastor. July 31. Council called and Bro. McKean ordained.

1888. Jan. 1. Dea. J. W. Gallup died. Records read " A good man beloved by all." Jan. 8. Franklin P. Kinney elected deacon. April. Resignation of Rev. McLean read, unanimously rejected, so deferred. Nov. Rev. McLean at Niantic candidating and accepted.

1889. Licentiate Geo. W. Swan supplied pulpit. Feb. 19. Fourteen rose for prayer. Feb. 21. Twenty-five rose for prayer. March. Twelve baptized ; others converted. October. Rev. John F. Temple accepted call. Pulpit was vacant 10 months.

1890. Joseph A. Doane and wife presented a basket for carrying communion articles. W. H. Doane presented S. S. with 50 copies " Bright Array " singing books. S. F. Meech presented 25 copies " Select Gems " song book for conference meeting use.

1891. Entertained Association.

1892. Change of pastor. Bro. Temple resigned and Rev. James S. Cranston unanimously chosen. S. R. Meech gave 25 copies Gospel Hymns 5 and 6 to the church.

1893. Records read : " Our pastor returned from Association very much warmed up in spirit and had some extra meetings with good results."

1894. Question of free pews discussed, and have weekly collection, but decided to still rent pews.

1895. October. Rev. Wm. H. Johnson held 3-weeks' evangelistic meetings ; 10 rose for prayer.

1896. Rev. J. S. Cranston severed relationship with church. Mr. C. Leavens Eldredge supplied pulpit, March to October, then unanimously called as pastor.

1897. March. Bro. Eldredge ordained. Oct. 13. First church roll call. Rev. L. W. Frink gave historical address and Rev. G. W. Kinney spoke on "Vantages and Disadvantages." Roll call address by Rev. J. H. McKean.

1899. Pastor Eldredge resigned.

1900. January. Rev. N. B. Prindle called. Meeting house painted inside and out, and parsonage repaired.

1901. Pew renting abolished; envelope system with weekly offering adopted; proved more satisfactory.

1902. Church letter reads: Baptistry built; 20 baptized. Death of D. T. Richards.

1903. Church letter states: "Extra meetings following week of prayer both in church and adjoining districts in homes; 11 baptized." Lucius Brown gave land north of the church. Nov. Bro. Prindle given liberty to work at Ledyard.

1904. Records show 4 baptized, and efforts made to reach those destitute of Gospel.

1905. Church received gifts of individual Communion set from Bro. W. H. Doane and a legacy of $500 from Bro. Seth Main's estate, and $26 from Bro. S. T. Meech. Association met here. Eleven baptized. State Secretary Rev. F. H. Divine began a 3-weeks' series of evangelistic meetings Dec. 31st.

1906. As result of meetings 58 baptized up to May.

1908. Received a valuable collection of books as library nucleus for the parsonage from Mrs. Eunice Edson.

1911. Church roll call, and manual prepared. Morning roll call service. Welcome address and historical abstract by pastor. Sermon by Dr. A. B. Coates. Lunch. Afternoon: Devotions. Consecration address, Rev. P. C. Wright. Roll call and Communion. Mr. W. H. Allen made gift of front stone steps, Mrs. Edson 150 copies of her late husband's semi-centennial historical discourse. Woman's Home and Foreign Missionary Societies organized. Cottage prayer meetings in out-lying districts. Baptisms 4. Union Thanksgiving service. Rev. L. M. Keneston preached.

1912. Bro. Prindle resigned in October to become state evangelist in Vermont. Resolution of gratitude and esteem of his life. Gift to retiring pastor of $25 by Young People's Societies.

1913. Pulpit supplied nearly a year, when Rev. L. L. Holmes accepted call for one year, ending October. Pulpit supplied.

1915. Feb. Rev. A. L. Tedford began pastoral work. Centennial celebration Oct. 10-11.

### Constituent Members

The constituent members were:

James Treat
Mary Treat
Mundator T. Richards
Polly Tyler Richards
John Starkweather, Jr.
Lydia Starkweather
Daniel Meech
Lucy Meech
Cyrus Gates
Patty Gates
Hezekiah Haskell
Sally Haskell
William T. Browning
Catherine Browning
John Starkweather, Sen.
Hannah Starkweather
Walter Brown, Jr.
Daniel M. Tyler
Levi Meech
Joseph Tyler
Stephen Tyler
Jabez Avery
Asa Barnes
Joseph Wilbur
Cyrus P. Barnes

Martha Browning
Susan Freeman
Betsy Bill
Lucy Bill
Homer Andrews
Abigail Davis
Elizabeth Barnes
Mahald Hewitt
Prudence Taylor
Sally Clark
Adah Tyler
Polly Woodward
Fanny Slocum
Clarissa Woodward
Polly Holloway
Zipporah Rockwell
Polly Boardman
Anna Bushnell
Anis Brown
Wealthy Gates
Sally Starkweather
Betsy Rockwell
Sabrina Killam
Zerviah Coates
Polly Standish

Michael Daniels
William G. Cory
Simeon B. Burdick
Thomas Hall
Frances Doane
Mary Lester
Margaret Ayer

Nancy Ayer
Eunice Dewey
Eunice Fanning
Anna Yerrington
Nabby B. Parks
Avis Brown
Betsy Wheeler

## SUMMARY OF MEMBERSHIP

Total number of persons who have been members of the church up to Oct. 10, 1915:

| | |
|---|---:|
| Constituent members | 64 |
| Added since by letter or baptism | 823 |
| Total | 887 |
| Present number of members | 178 |
| Dismissed to other churches | 334 |
| Died in fellowship | 284 |
| Dropped, unknown, etc. | 27 |
| Constituent members | 64 |
| Total | 887 |

# List of Pastors and Officers of the Church Since its Organization

## PASTORS

GUSTAVUS F. DAVIS,  
LEVI WALKER, SR., .............. 1815 to 1828 inclusive  
LEVI MEECH,  
LUTHER GODDARD.................................1828 to 1831  
ALFRED GATES .................May 27, 1831, to April, 1835  
NATHAN E. SHAILER..............April, 1835, to April, 1843  
HENRY R. KNAPP................April, 1843, to March, 1845  
N. V. STEADMAN....  .............April, 1845, to April, 1847  
CYRUS MINER.................April 18, 1847, to April 1, 1851  
E. LUMIS....................April 1, 1851, to October 1, 1851  
N. H. MATTISON........ October 19, 1851, to January 1, 1859  
MILES G. SMITH .............July 31, 1859, to May 15, 1870  
F. B. JOY....................July 24, 1870, to April 26, 1874  
E. S. HILL.......... .... November 8, 1874, to March 26, 1882  
F. H. COOPER..  ........ May 21, 1882, to November 1, 1885  
JOSEPH MCKEAN.........March 7, 1886, to December 2, 1888  
JOHN F. TEMPLE .......November 15, 1889, to May 22, 1892  
JAMES S. CRANSTON.............July 17, 1892, to April, 1896  
C. LEAVENS ELDREDGE........Nov. 1, 1896, to Nov. 15, 1899  
N. B. PRINDLE.................May 6, 1900, to Nov. 10, 1912  
L. L. HOLMES.............October, 1913, to October, 1914  
A. L. TEDFORD......................February, 1915, ——

10

## DEACONS

Joseph Wilbur............April 8, 1831, to September 3, 1847
Warren Andrews, Sen......April 8, 1831, to August 13, 1848
Cyrus Gates................April 8, 1831, to February, 1868
Warren Andrews, Jr......November 25, 1848, to May 18, 1884
John W. Gallup.......November 25, 1848, to January 1, 1888
Gustavus D. Andrews.......October 24, 1885, to July 30, 1895
Franklin P. Kinney.................February, 1888 ———
Charles S. Woodmansee............November 20, 1897 ———

## CLERKS

M. T. Richards...........October 14, 1815, to March 30, 1816
Cyrus Gates...................March 30, 1816, to June, 1838
M. T. Richards.......January 14, 1840, to December 22, 1854
D. T. Richards..... December 22, 1854, to December 27, 1860
A. A. Haskell ........... December 27, 1860, to April 8, 1874
P. M. Wheeler............. April 8, 1874, to December, 1883
D. T. Richards......... .....December, 1883, to May 6, 1902
F. P. Kinney............... May 18, 1902, to January 5, 1910
H. J. Fitch............................January 5, 1910 ———

## CHURCH TREASURERS

W. T. Browning............ ................March 30, 1816
M. T. Richards........January 14, 1840, to December 15, 1846
Stephen Tyler......................December, 1846, to 1847
Warren Andrews......December, 1847, to December 28, 1848
M. T. Richards......December 28, 1848, to December 12, 1850
Charles B. Ayer.....December 12, 1850, to December 31, 1852
D. T. Richards......December 31, 1852, to December 22, 1853
M. T. Richards.....December 22, 1853, to December 29, 1857
D. T. Richards.....December 29, 1857, to December 27, 1858
M. T. Richards....December 27, 1858, to December 28, 1859
D. T. Richards.....December 29, 1859, to December 27, 1860
John W. Gallup.......December 27, 1860, to December, 1862
D. T. Richards...........December, 1862, to December, 1865
John W. Gallup..........December, 1865, to December, 1869
P. M. Wheeler........ December, 1866, to December 27, 1882
F. P. Kinney.....December 27, 1882, to December 22, 1886
D. T. Richards.....December 24, 1886, to December 24, 1887
J. O. Peckham, Jr.. December 24, 1887, to December 19, 1888
Dea. G. D. Andrews. December 19, 1888, to December 20, 1893
C. C. Pendleton..... December 20, 1893, to December 19, 1894
Charles S. Woodmansee...........December 19, 1894, ———

## TREASURERS OF CHURCH MINISTERIAL FUND

M. T. Richards... .December 31, 1852, to December 20, 1866
Charles Buttolph...December 20, 1866, to December 16, 1875
John W. Gallup.......December 16, 1875, to January 1, 1888
Charles Buttolph.....January 14, 1888, to December 18, 1889
D. T. Richards............December 18, 1889, to May 6, 1902
C. S. Woodmansee................December 31, 1902 ———

## Summary Views of Duty.

In consideration of our solemn doctrines and obligations, we believe it our duty to stand fast in one spirit, with one mind striving together for the faith of the gospel, having our manner of life, both in the world and in the church, as "becometh the Gospel," to "walk in wisdom toward them that are without," to exercise ourselves to have "always a conscience void of offence toward God and toward men," "living soberly, righteously and godly in the present world," and holding forth the word of life to its sorrowing and perishing souls.

### TOWARD EACH OTHER.

We esteem it our duty to walk in humilty and brotherly love, to watch over each other's conversation, to stir up one another to love and good works, "not forsaking the assembly of ourselves together," to worship God according to His revealed will, and when the case requires to warn, rebuke, and admonish one another, according to the rules of the Word of God; to sympathize with each other in joy or sorrow, to bear with one another's weakness and infirmities, to "make straight paths" for our feet, "lest that which is lame be turned out of the way, but rather let it be healed;" and particularly to pray for one another and those who preach the gospel that the word and ordinances may be blessed to the edification and comfort of each other's souls and for the ingathering of the impenitent to Christ.

All of which duties we desire through the gracious assistance of the Holy Spirit to perform that we may grow in grace and in the knowledge of our Lord Jesus Christ, looking for that blessed hope and the glorious appearing of the great God and our Saviour Jesus Christ. Who gave Himself for us, that he might redeem us from all iniquity, and purify unto Himself a peculiar people zealous of good works.

## THE COVENANT.

You being humbly sensible that it is a solemn thing to transact thus with the living God, do now in the presence of God and this assembly avouch the Lord Jehovah, Father, Son, and Holy Ghost to be your God, in and through Jesus Christ the only Mediator between God and man.

And in humble dependence on his grace you engage to walk in all the commands and ordinances of Christ. Subjecting yourself to the discipline of Christ and this church, as God in His word directs and requires. Having your conversation as becomes the Gospel, with truth, meekness, gentleness and peace.

And now may the God of all grace enable us to maintain our covenant vows, in such a manner as shall tend to the promotion of His glory, the prosperity of His church, and for our own salvation, for Christ's sake. Amen.

# Centenary Program

## SUNDAY MORNING, OCT. 10th, 10.45

Organ Voluntary
Call to Worship, (congregation standing) Pastor Tedford
Doxology
Invocation, Rev. F. S. Cooper
Anthem, "Sing unto the Lord"
Responsive Reading, Selection 4, Rev. L. L. Holmes
Hymn, "Holy, Holy, Holy" No. 209
Scripture, Rev. J. H. McKean
Prayer, Rev. N. B. Prindle
Announcement and Welcome
Special Thank Offering, and Blessing
Anthem, "Praise the God of our Salvation"
Hymn, "O God our help in ages past" No. 66,
Sermon, "The Heritage of the Church," Rev. J. H. McKean
Prayer, Rev. Lemuel Frink
Hymn, "Lead Kindly Light" No. 317
Benediction, Rev. L. M. Keneston
Communion, Pastors officiating
Hymn, "Jesus still lead on" No. 313

## SUNDAY EVENING, OCT. 10th

Praise Service,
Scripture, Rev. L. W. Frink
Anthem, "The Heavens declare the Glory of God"
Prayer, Rev L. M. Keneston
Announcement,
Evangelistic Hour, led by Rev. J. H. McKean
Hymn

Short Addresses, { Rev. F. S. Cooper
　　　　　　　　　 Rev. N. B. Prindle
　　　　　　　　　 Rev. L. L. Holmes

Male Quartette
Closing Moments, Rev. J. H. McKean
Benediction, Rev. F. S. Robbins

## MONDAY MORNING, OCT. 11th, 10.30

Mass Meeting under the auspices of the Baptist Ministers' Conference of New London and vicinity.
Devotions.
Address, "Our Topmost Note,"
    Rev. J. F. Vichert, D. D., Dean of Colgate Sem.
Discussion.
Benediction.
Centenary Collation, 12.30 in Vestry.

> "The art of feeding, as you understand,
> Is but a fraction of the work in hand;
> The nobler half is that ethereal meat
> The papers call 'the intellectual treat'."
> —*O. W. Holmes.*

Welcome. Free to All.

## AFTERNOON ASSEMBLY, 2.30

Devotional Service,     Rev. F. S. Robbins
Historical Address,     Rev. A. Lawrence Tedford
Reminiscences by Former Pastors and Others,
    Rev. F. S. Cooper, Rev. J. H. McKean
    Rev. N. B. Pindle, Rev. L. L. Holmes
Male Quartette.
Address,     Rev. A. B. Coats, D. D.
Prayer.

## MONDAY EVENING, OCT. 11th, 7.45

Hymn, "The Son of God goes forth to War"
Anthem, "Magnify the Lord"
Prayer,     Rev. J. H. McKean
    Silver Offering
Male Quartette,
Address, "The biggest thing in life,"
    Rev. J. F. Vichert, D. D.
Hymn, "God Be With You Till We Meet Again."
Prayer,     Rev. A. B. Coats, D. D.
"Praise God, From Whom All Blessings Flow."
Benediction,     Rev. F. S. Cooper

www.ingramcontent.com/pod-product-compliance
Lightning Source LLC
Chambersburg PA
CBHW051046160426
43193CB00010B/1082